X-O MANOWAR

SUCCESSION AND OTHER TALES

ROBERT VENDITTI | AMY CHU | JODY HOUSER | CLAYTON HENRY | PERE PÉREZ

CONTENTS

5 HERITAGE
X-O MANOWAR ANNUAL 2016 #1

Writer: Robert Venditti
Artist: Pere Pérez
Colorist: David Baron
Letterer: Dave Sharpe
Cover Artists: Phil Jimenez with Ulises Arreola

29 THE PRISONER
X-O MANOWAR ANNUAL 2016 #1

Writer: Amy Chu
Artist: Mike McKone
Colorist: Jeromy Cox
Letterer: Dave Sharpe

37 TAKING A MEETING
X-O MANOWAR ANNUAL 2016 #1

Writer: Jody Houser
Artist: Adam Gorham
Colorist: Andrew Dalhouse
Letterer: Dave Sharpe

Collection Cover Art: Phil Jimenez
with Ulises Arreola

45 FLIGHT OF THE X-OS

4001 A.D.: X-O MANOWAR #1

Writer: Robert Venditti
Artist: Clayton Henry
Color Artists: Brian Reber with Andrew Dalhouse
Letterer: Dave Sharpe
Cover Artists: CAFU with Michael Garland

69 SUCCESSION

BOOK OF DEATH: THE FALL OF X-O MANOWAR #1

Writer: Robert Venditti
Artist: Clayton Henry
Colorist: Andrew Dalhouse
Letterer: Dave Sharpe
Cover Artist: Cary Nord

97 GALLERY

David Baron
Carmen Carnero
Jeff Dekal
Clayton Henry
Brian Level
Pere Pérez
Omi Remalante Jr.

Editor: Tom Brennan (Associate Editor,
BOOK OF DEATH...)
Editor-in-Chief: Warren Simons

VALIANT.

Peter Cuneo
Chairman

Dinesh Shamdasani
CEO & Chief Creative Officer

Gavin Cuneo
Chief Operating Officer & CFO

Fred Pierce
Publisher

Warren Simons
Editor-in-Chief

Walter Black
VP Operations

Hunter Gorinson
VP Marketing & Communications

Atom! Freeman
Director of Sales

Matthew Klein
Andy Liegl
John Petrie
Sales Managers

Josh Johns
Director of Digital Media and Development

Travis Escarfullery
Jeff Walker
Production & Design Managers

Kyle Andrukiewicz
Editor and Creative Executive

Robert Meyers
Managing Editor

Peter Stern
Publishing & Operations Manager

Andrew Steinbeiser
Marketing & Communications Manager

Danny Khazem
Associate Editor

Lauren Hitzhusen
Assistant Editor

Ivan Cohen
Collection Editor

Steve Blackwell
Collection Designer

Rian Hughes/Device
Trade Dress & Book Design

Russell Brown
President, Consumer Products,
Promotions and Ad Sales

Caritza Berlioz
Licensing Coodinator

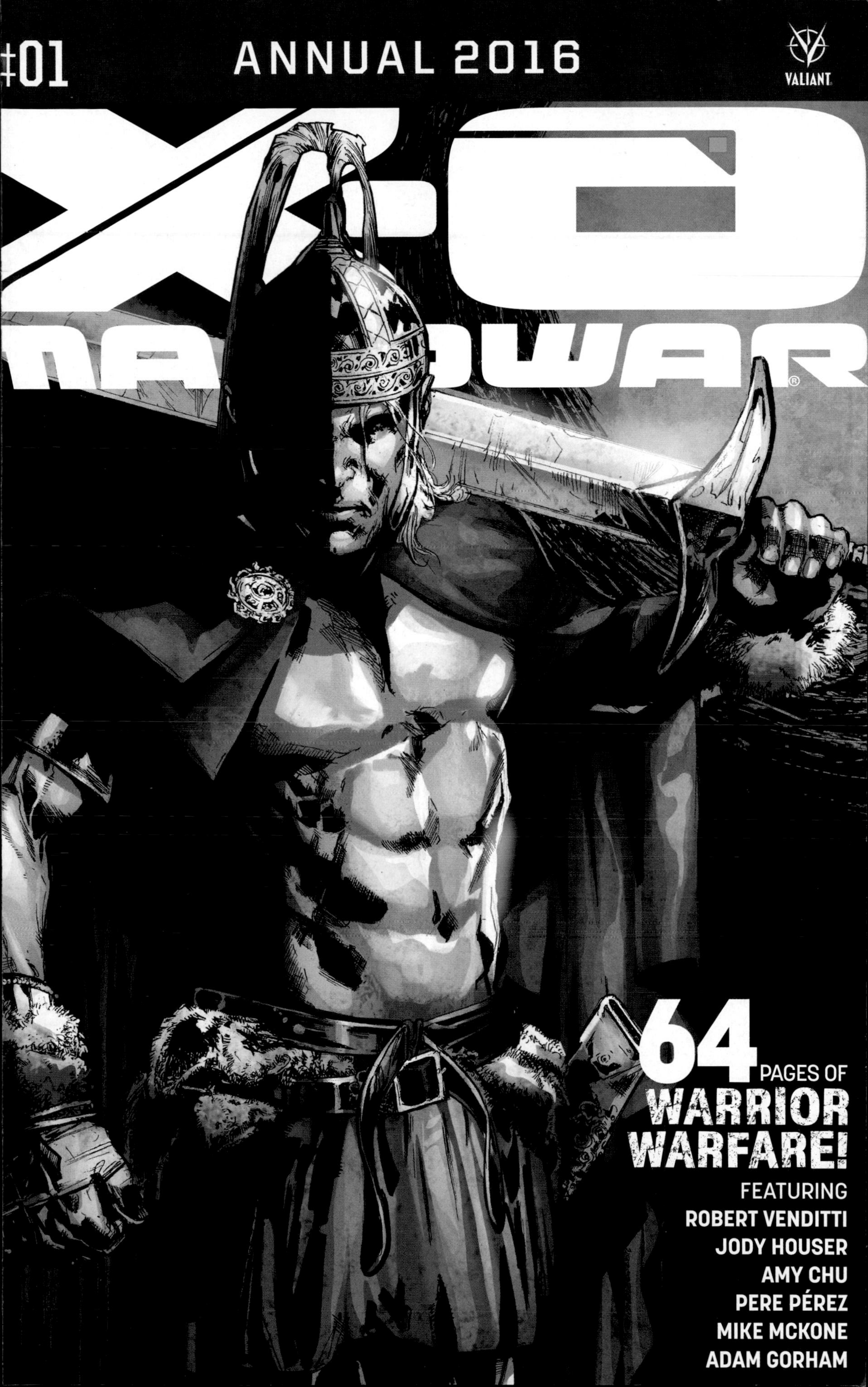
#01
ANNUAL 2016
VALIANT
64 PAGES OF
WARRIOR
WARFARE!
FEATURING
ROBERT VENDITTI
JODY HOUSER
AMY CHU
PERE PÉREZ
MIKE MCKONE
ADAM GORHAM

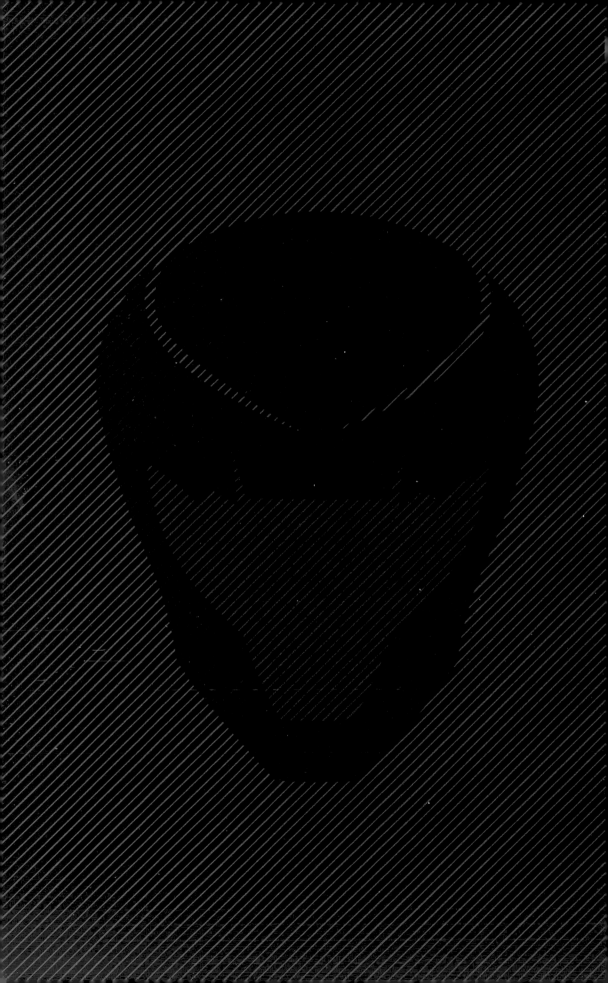

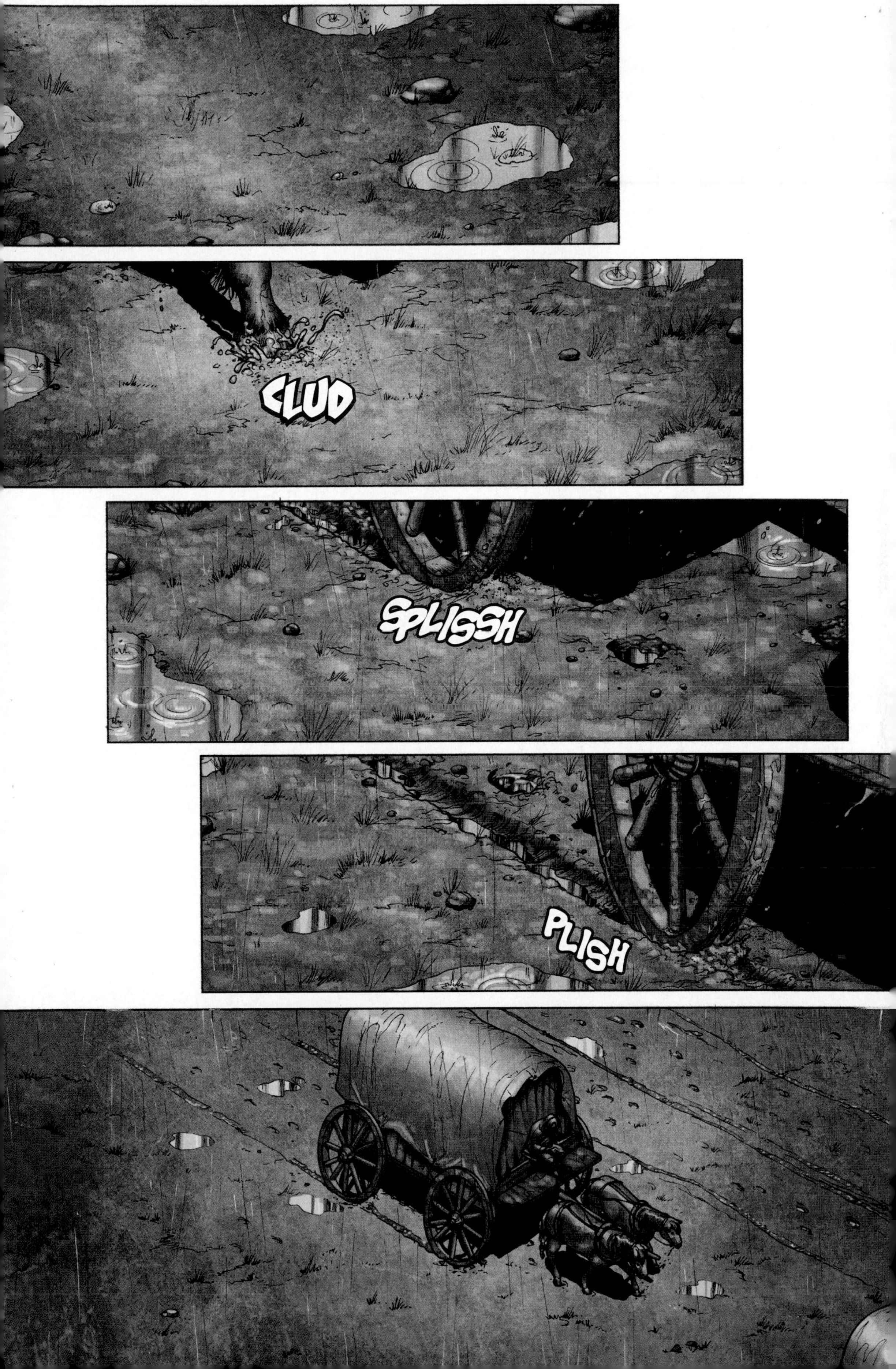
CLUD
SPLISSH
PLISH

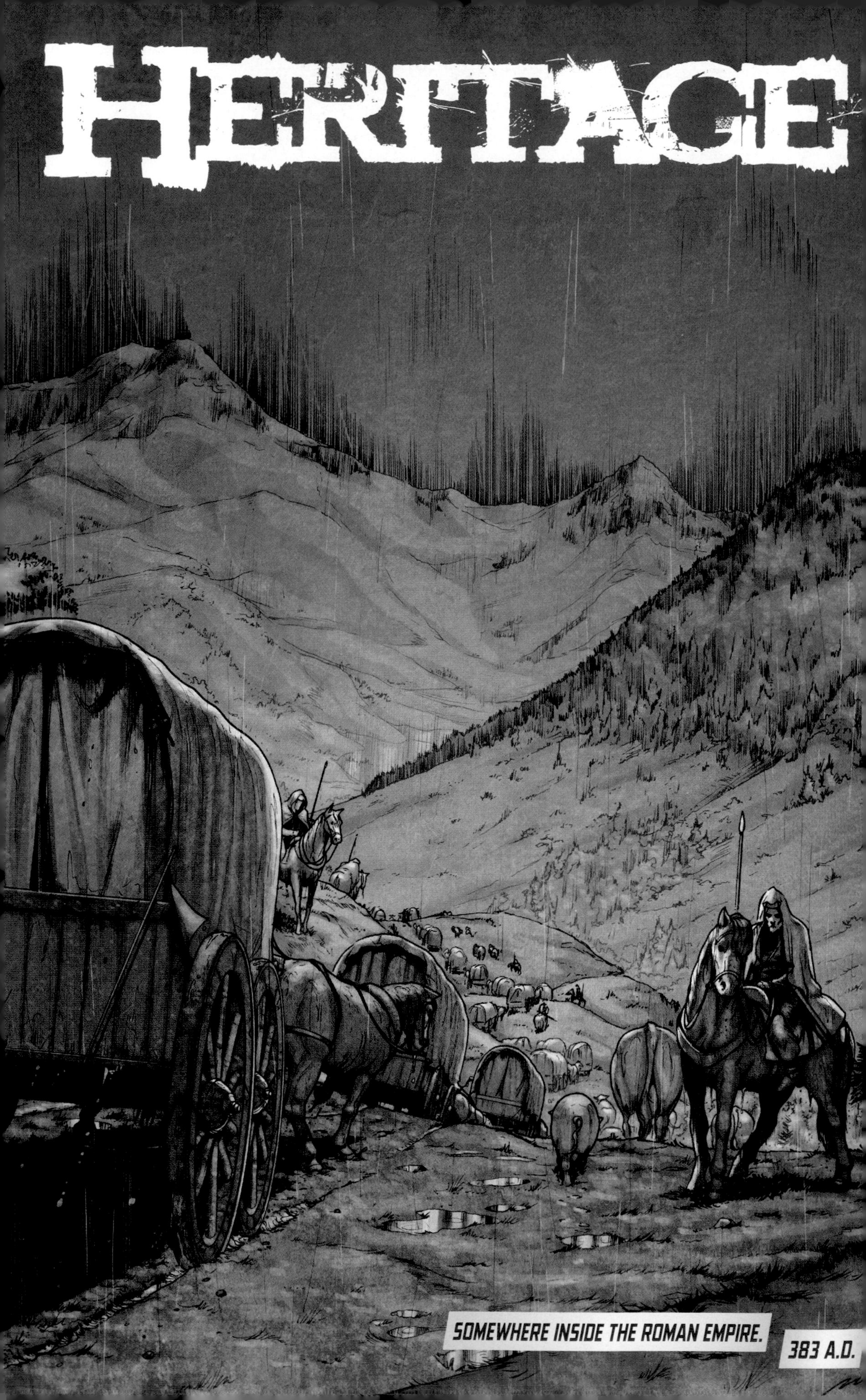
HERITAGE
SOMEWHERE INSIDE THE ROMAN EMPIRE.
383 A.D.

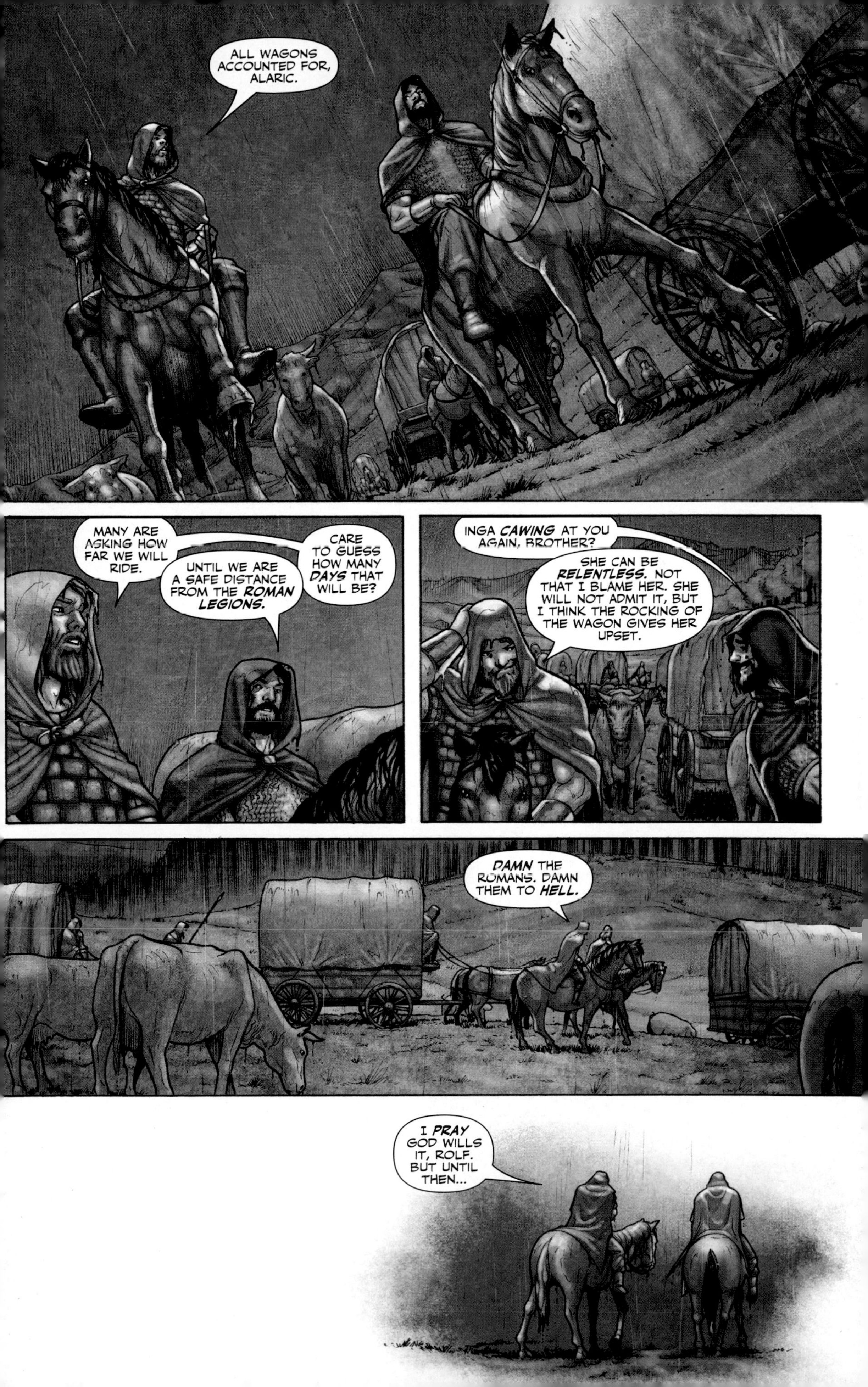
ALL WAGONS ACCOUNTED FOR, ALARIC.
MANY ARE ASKING HOW FAR WE WILL RIDE.
UNTIL WE ARE A SAFE DISTANCE FROM THE ROMAN LEGIONS.
CARE TO GUESS HOW MANY DAYS THAT WILL BE?
INGA CAWING AT YOU AGAIN, BROTHER?
SHE CAN BE RELENTLESS. NOT THAT I BLAME HER. SHE WILL NOT ADMIT IT, BUT I THINK THE ROCKING OF THE WAGON GIVES HER UPSET.
DAMN THE ROMANS. DAMN THEM TO HELL.
I PRAY GOD WILLS IT, ROLF. BUT UNTIL THEN...

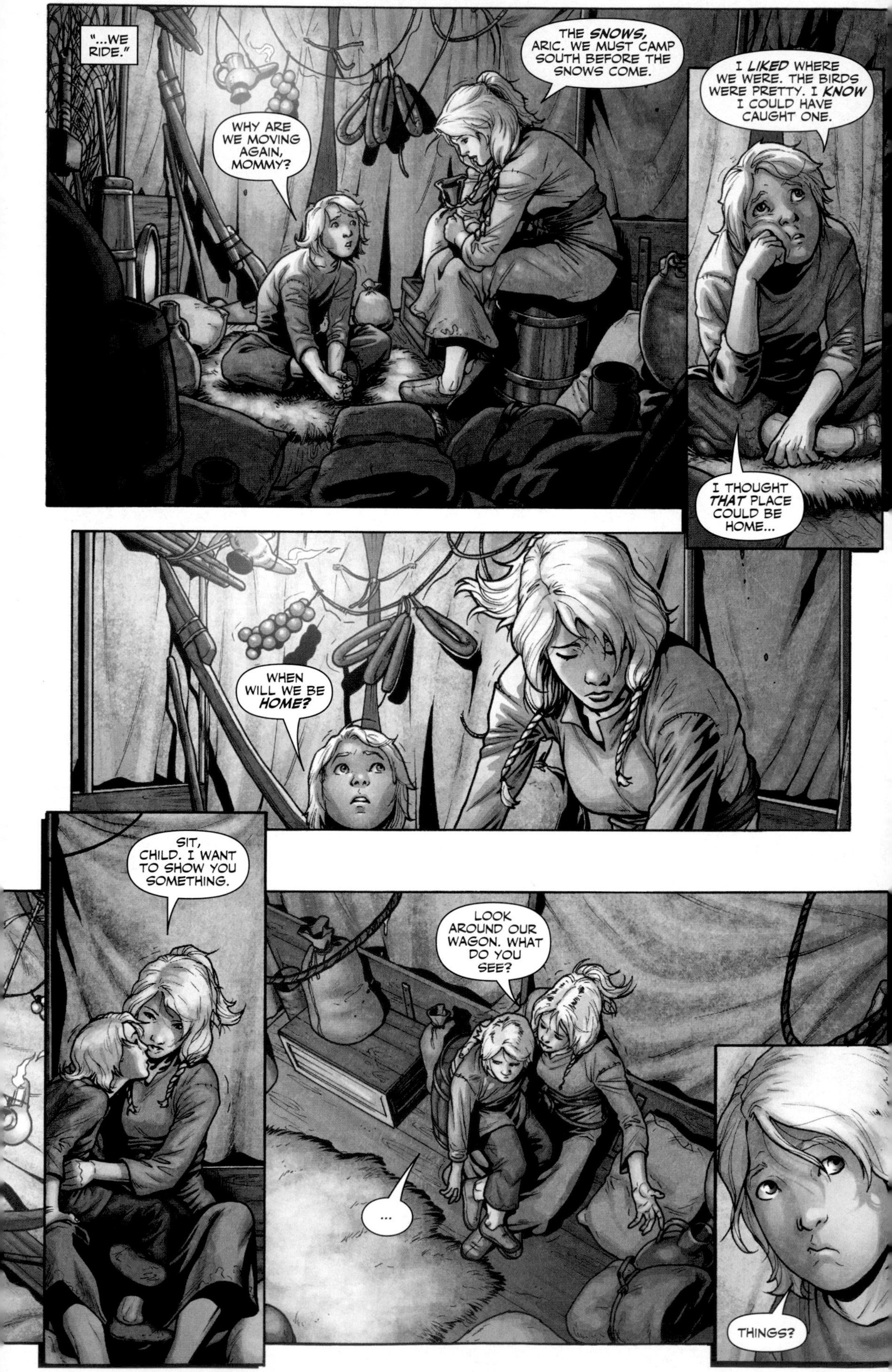
"...WE RIDE."
WHY ARE WE MOVING AGAIN, MOMMY?
THE SNOWS, ARIC. WE MUST CAMP SOUTH BEFORE THE SNOWS COME.
I LIKED WHERE WE WERE. THE BIRDS WERE PRETTY. I KNOW I COULD HAVE CAUGHT ONE.
I THOUGHT THAT PLACE COULD BE HOME...
WHEN WILL WE BE HOME?
SIT, CHILD. I WANT TO SHOW YOU SOMETHING.
LOOK AROUND OUR WAGON. WHAT DO YOU SEE?
...
THINGS?

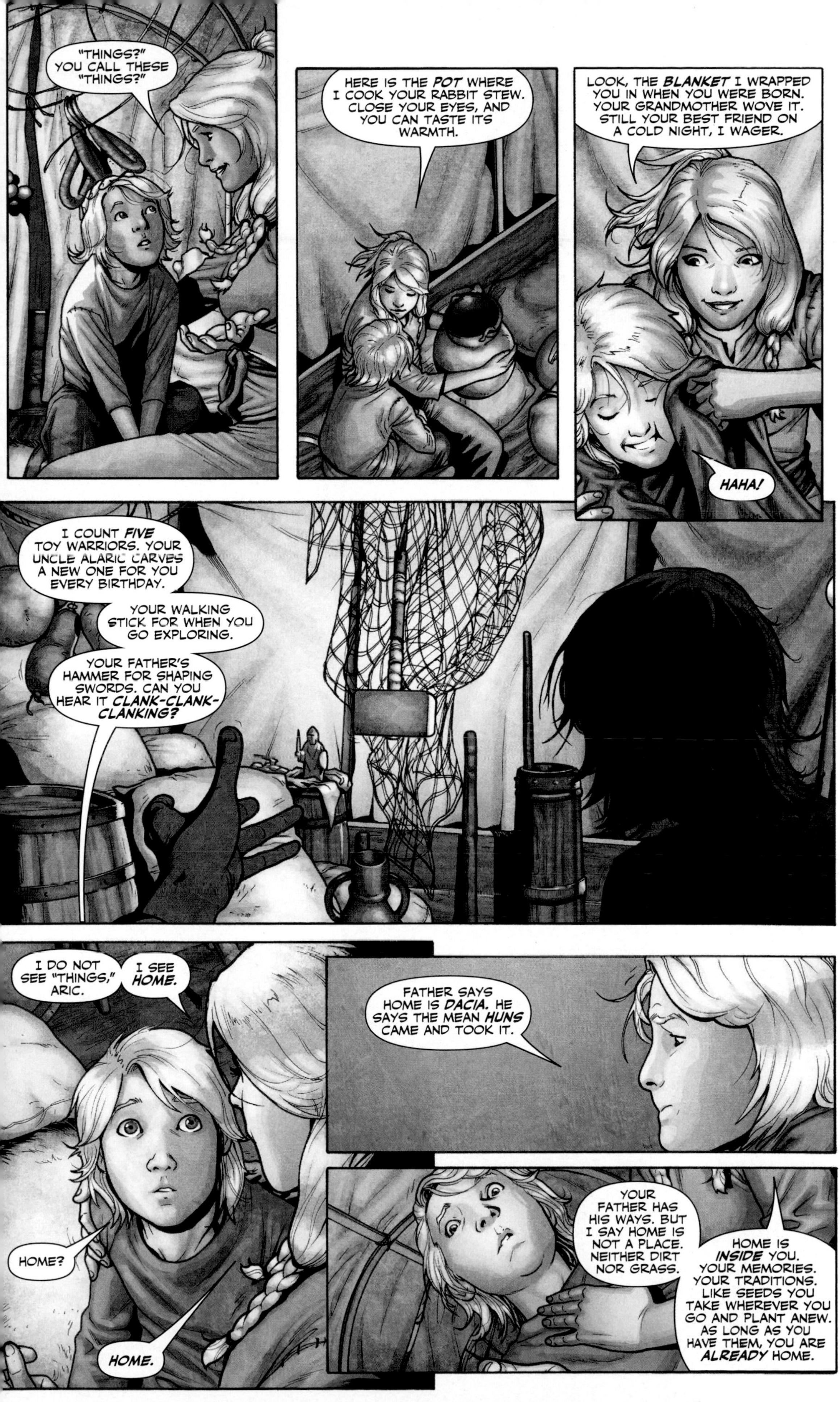
"THINGS?" YOU CALL THESE "THINGS?"
HERE IS THE POT WHERE I COOK YOUR RABBIT STEW. CLOSE YOUR EYES, AND YOU CAN TASTE ITS WARMTH.
LOOK, THE BLANKET I WRAPPED YOU IN WHEN YOU WERE BORN. YOUR GRANDMOTHER WOVE IT. STILL YOUR BEST FRIEND ON A COLD NIGHT, I WAGER.
HAHA!
I COUNT FIVE TOY WARRIORS. YOUR UNCLE ALARIC CARVES A NEW ONE FOR YOU EVERY BIRTHDAY.
YOUR WALKING STICK FOR WHEN YOU GO EXPLORING.
YOUR FATHER'S HAMMER FOR SHAPING SWORDS. CAN YOU HEAR IT CLANK-CLANK-CLANKING?
I DO NOT SEE "THINGS," ARIC.
I SEE HOME.
HOME?
HOME.
FATHER SAYS HOME IS DACIA. HE SAYS THE MEAN HUNS CAME AND TOOK IT.
YOUR FATHER HAS HIS WAYS. BUT I SAY HOME IS NOT A PLACE. NEITHER DIRT NOR GRASS.
HOME IS INSIDE YOU. YOUR MEMORIES. YOUR TRADITIONS. LIKE SEEDS YOU TAKE WHEREVER YOU GO AND PLANT ANEW. AS LONG AS YOU HAVE THEM, YOU ARE ALREADY HOME.

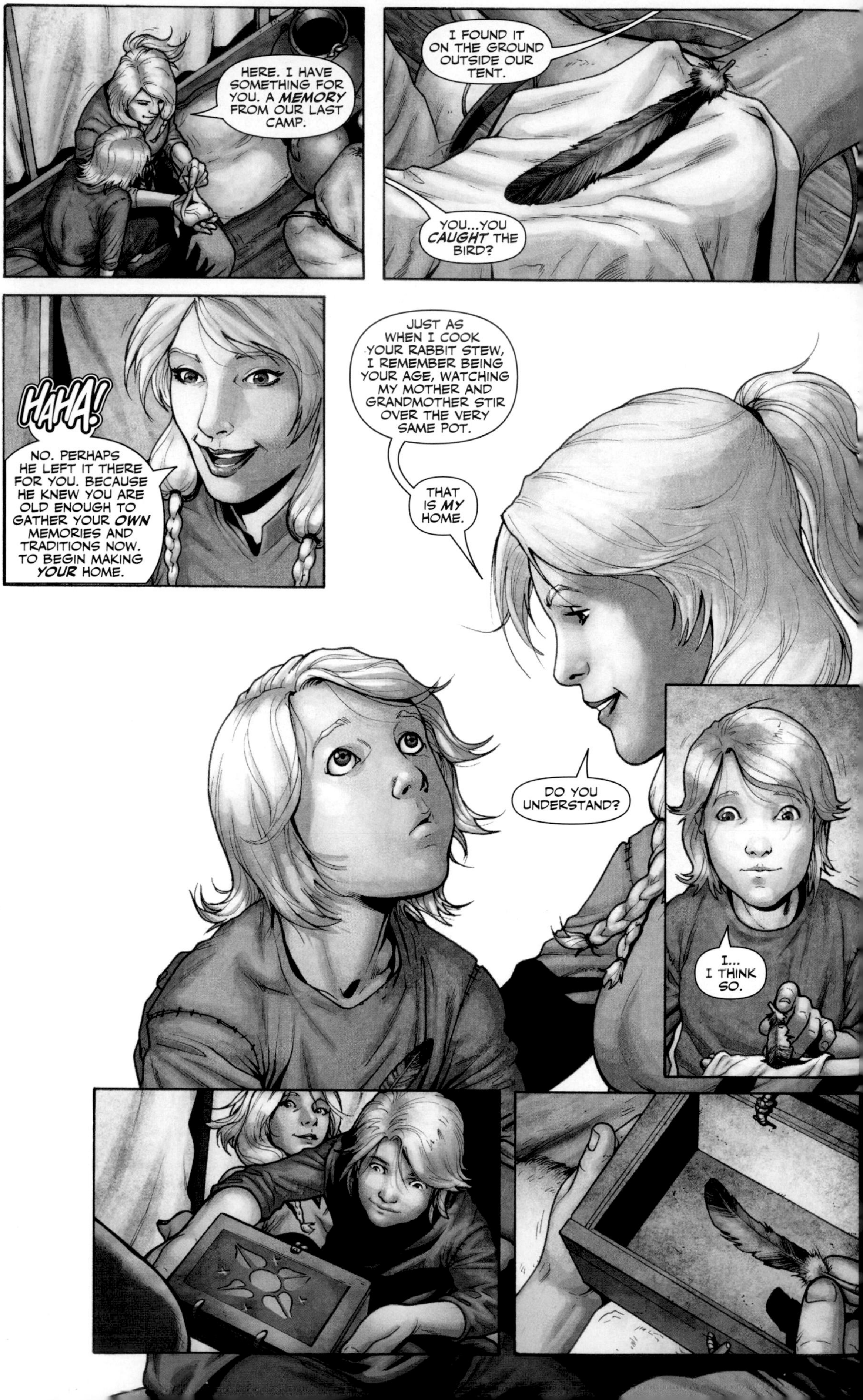
HERE. I HAVE SOMETHING FOR YOU. A MEMORY FROM OUR LAST CAMP.
I FOUND IT ON THE GROUND OUTSIDE OUR TENT.
YOU...YOU CAUGHT THE BIRD?
HAHA!
NO. PERHAPS HE LEFT IT THERE FOR YOU. BECAUSE HE KNEW YOU ARE OLD ENOUGH TO GATHER YOUR OWN MEMORIES AND TRADITIONS NOW. TO BEGIN MAKING YOUR HOME.
JUST AS WHEN I COOK YOUR RABBIT STEW, I REMEMBER BEING YOUR AGE, WATCHING MY MOTHER AND GRANDMOTHER STIR OVER THE VERY SAME POT.
THAT IS MY HOME.
DO YOU UNDERSTAND?
I... I THINK SO.

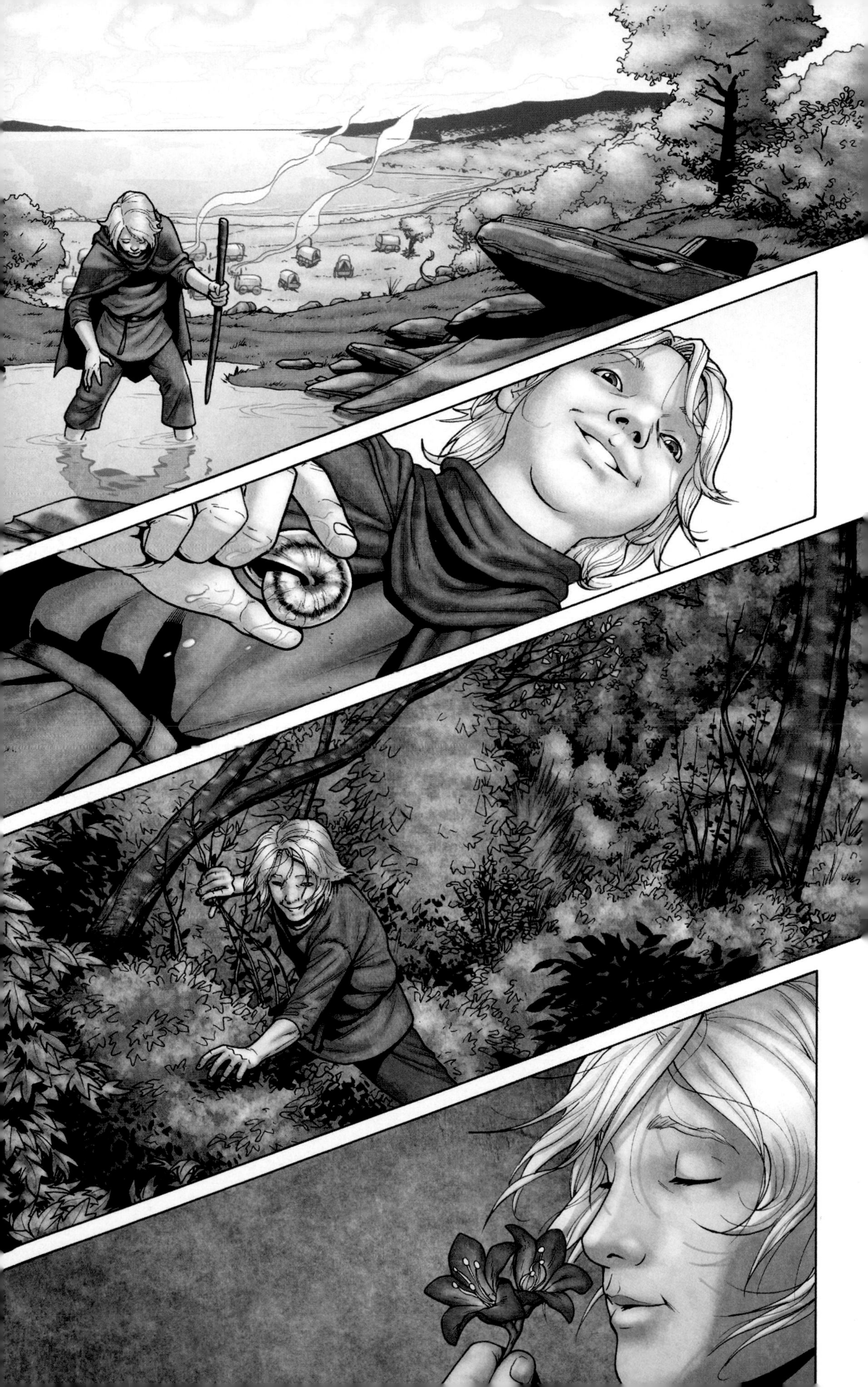

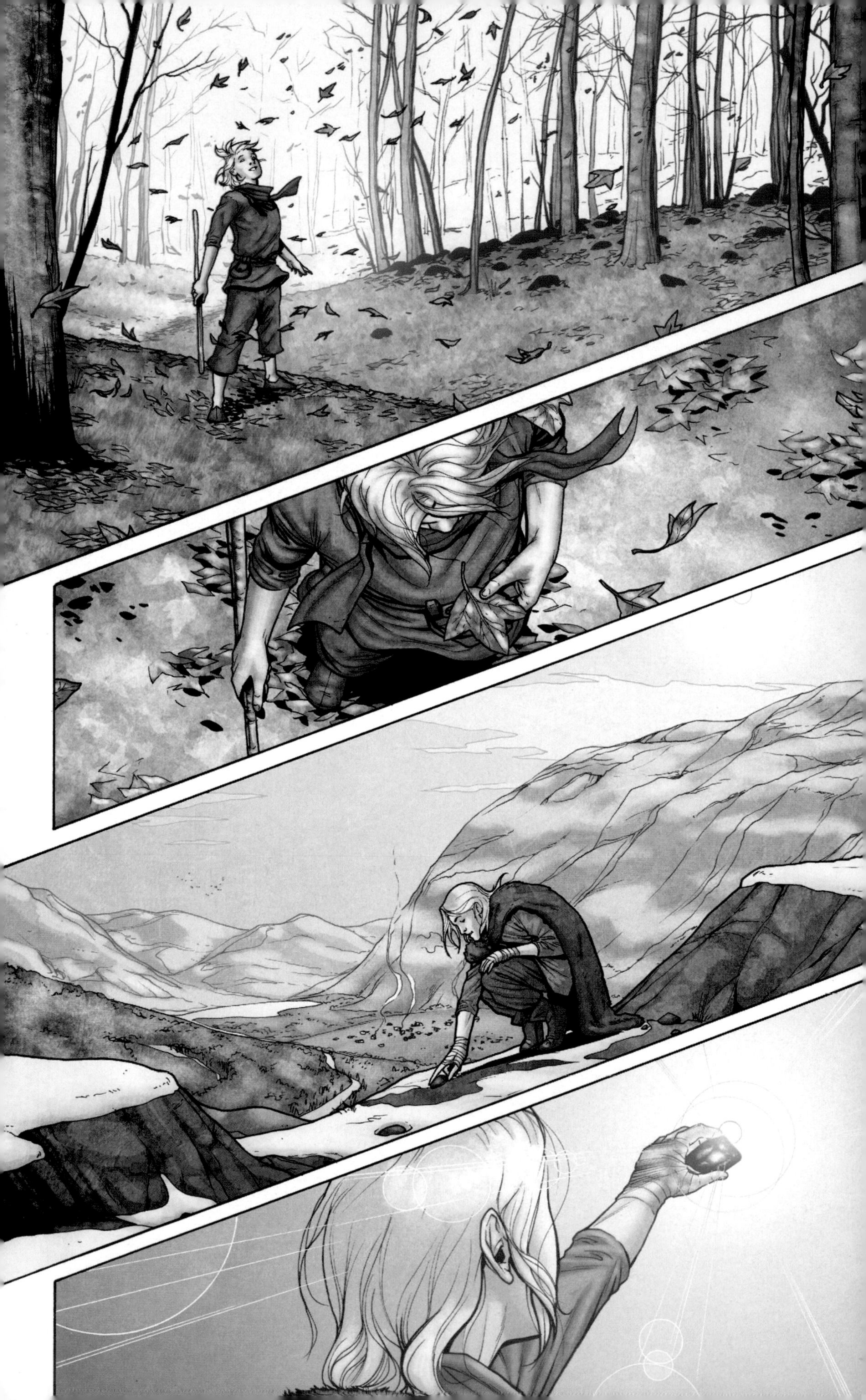

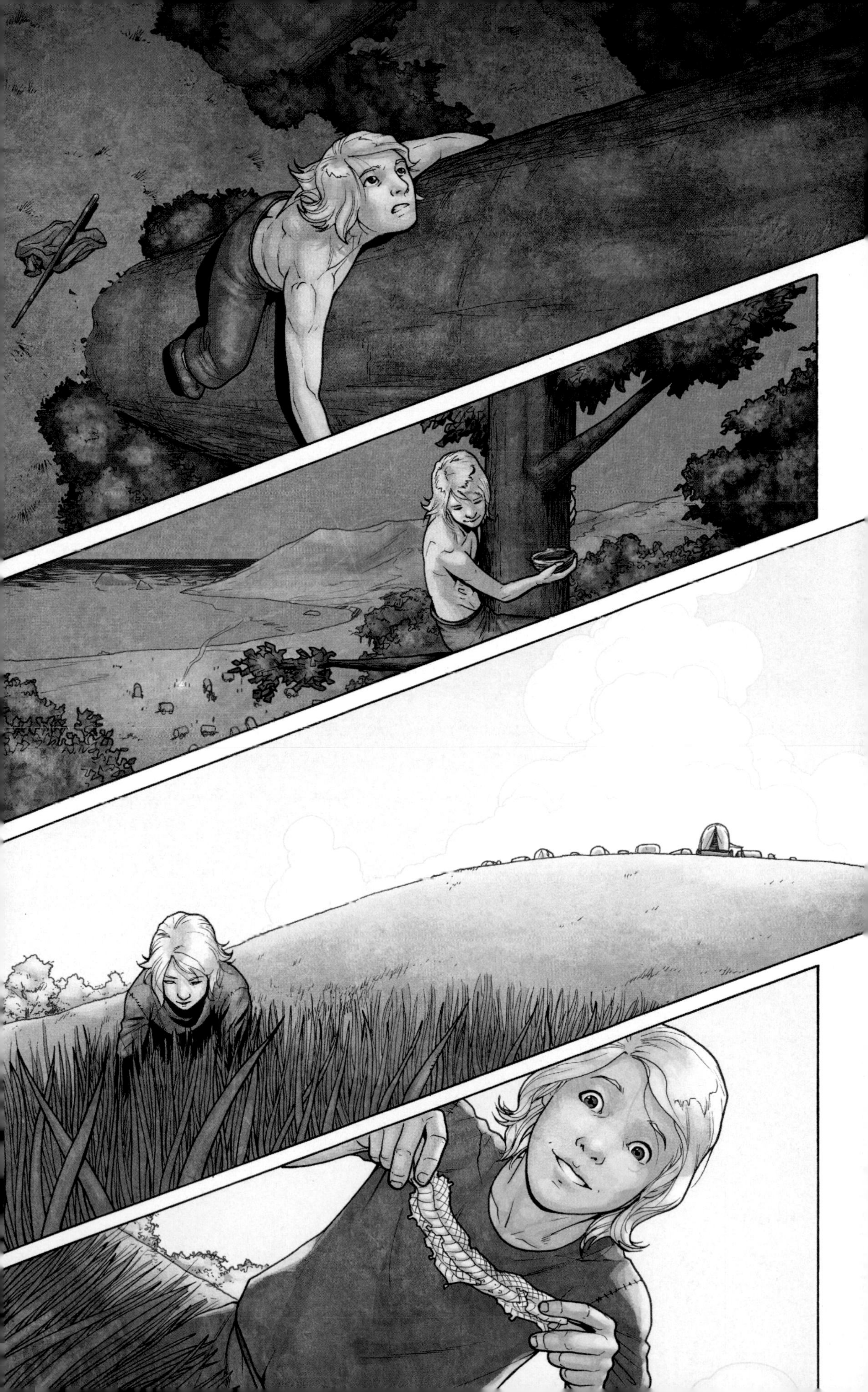

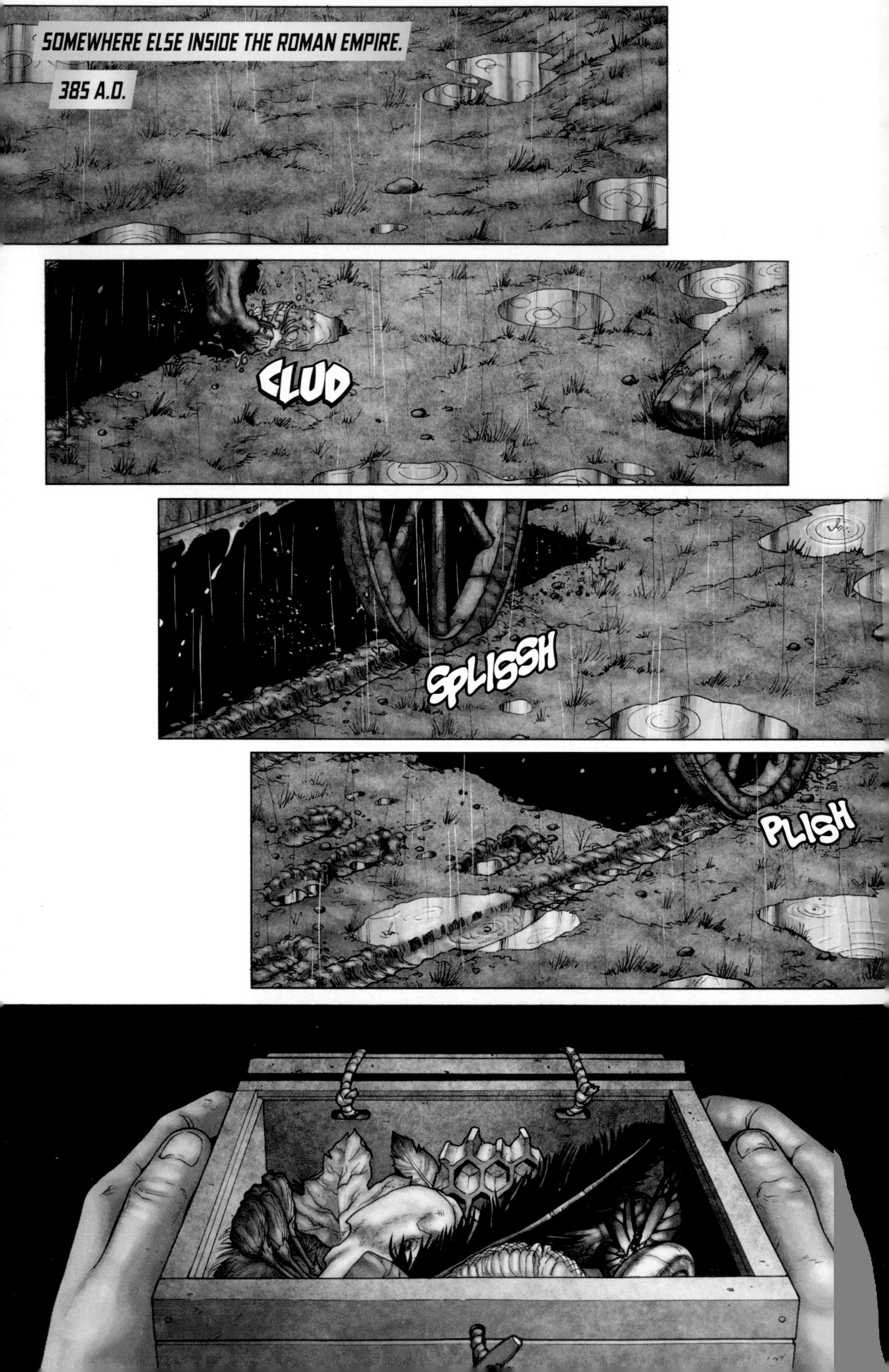
SOMEWHERE ELSE INSIDE THE ROMAN EMPIRE.
385 A.D.
CLUD
SPLISSH
PLISH

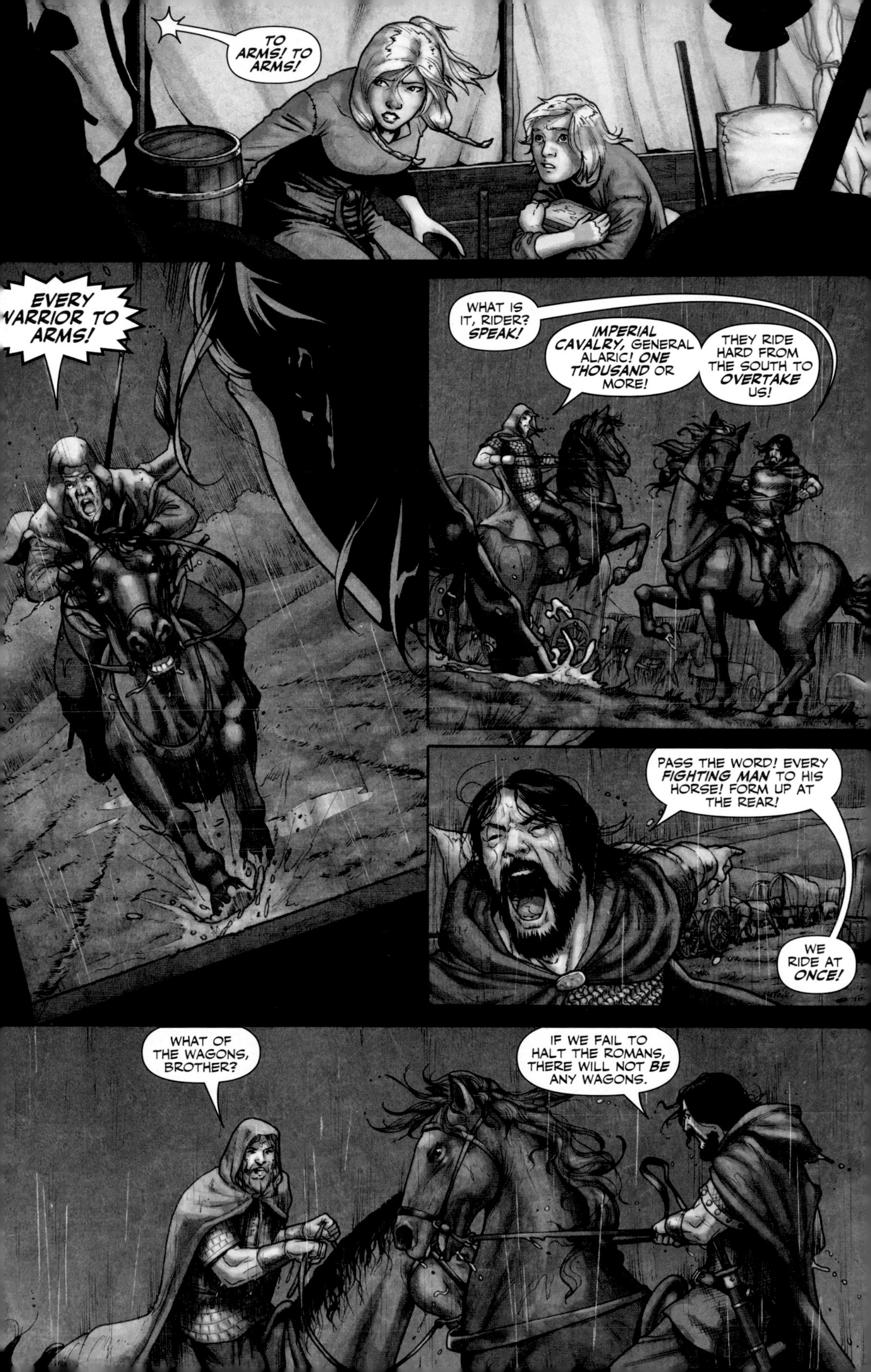
TO ARMS! TO ARMS!
EVERY WARRIOR TO ARMS!
WHAT IS IT, RIDER? SPEAK!
IMPERIAL CAVALRY, GENERAL ALARIC! ONE THOUSAND OR MORE!
THEY RIDE HARD FROM THE SOUTH TO OVERTAKE US!
PASS THE WORD! EVERY FIGHTING MAN TO HIS HORSE! FORM UP AT THE REAR!
WE RIDE AT ONCE!
WHAT OF THE WAGONS, BROTHER?
IF WE FAIL TO HALT THE ROMANS, THERE WILL NOT BE ANY WAGONS.

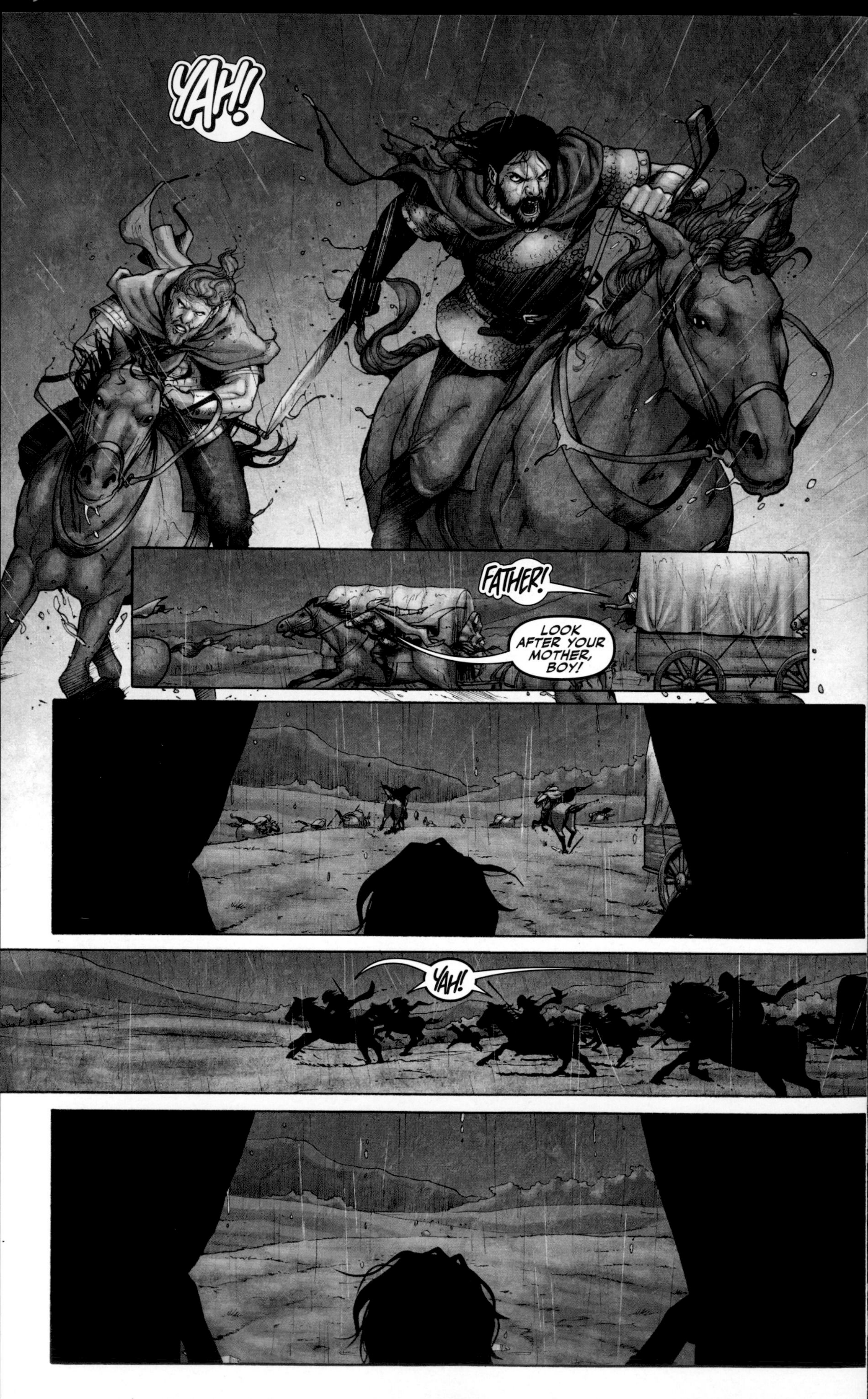
YAH!
FATHER!
LOOK AFTER YOUR MOTHER, BOY!
YAH!

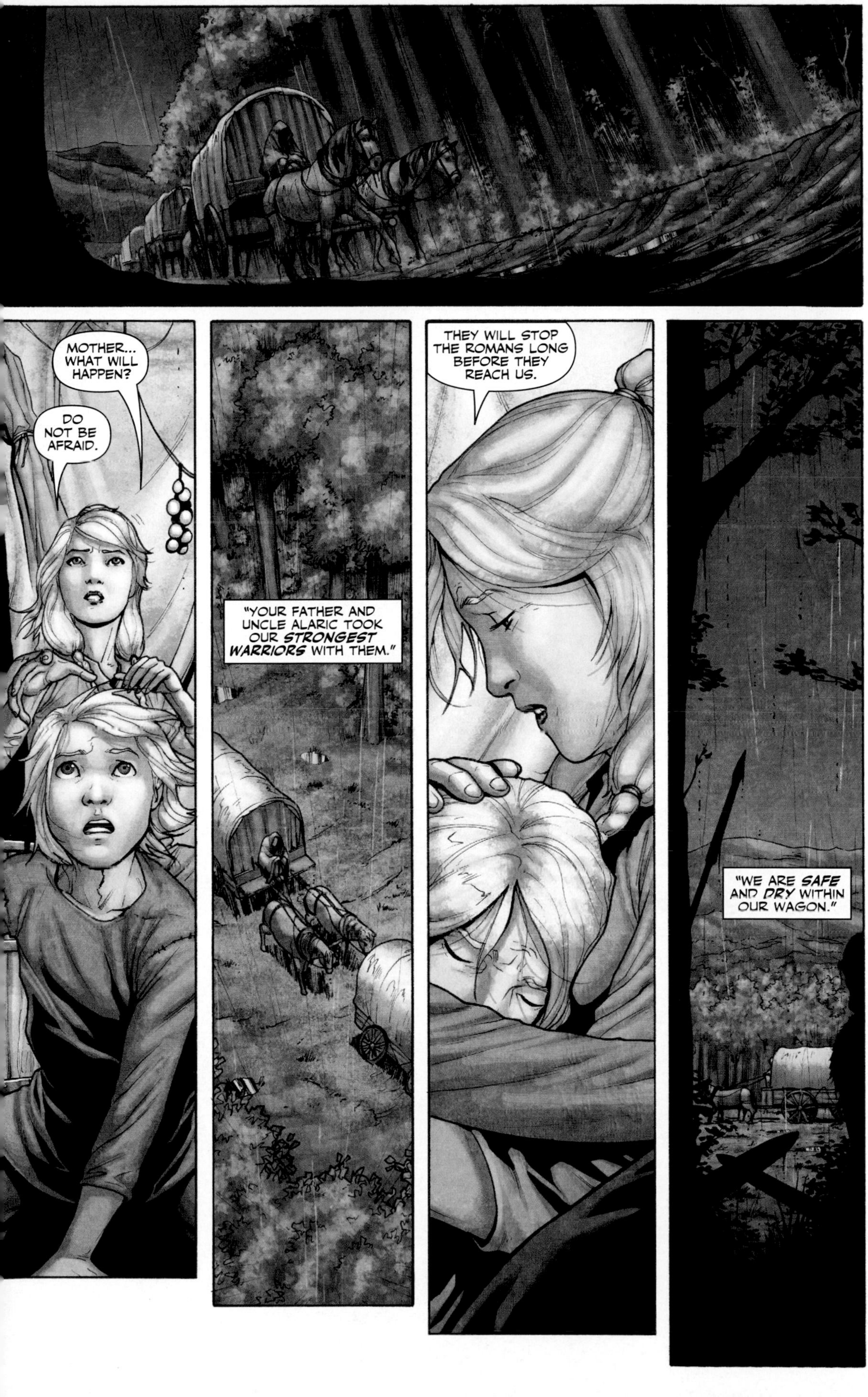
MOTHER... WHAT WILL HAPPEN?
DO NOT BE AFRAID.
"YOUR FATHER AND UNCLE ALARIC TOOK OUR STRONGEST WARRIORS WITH THEM."
THEY WILL STOP THE ROMANS LONG BEFORE THEY REACH US.
"WE ARE SAFE AND DRY WITHIN OUR WAGON."

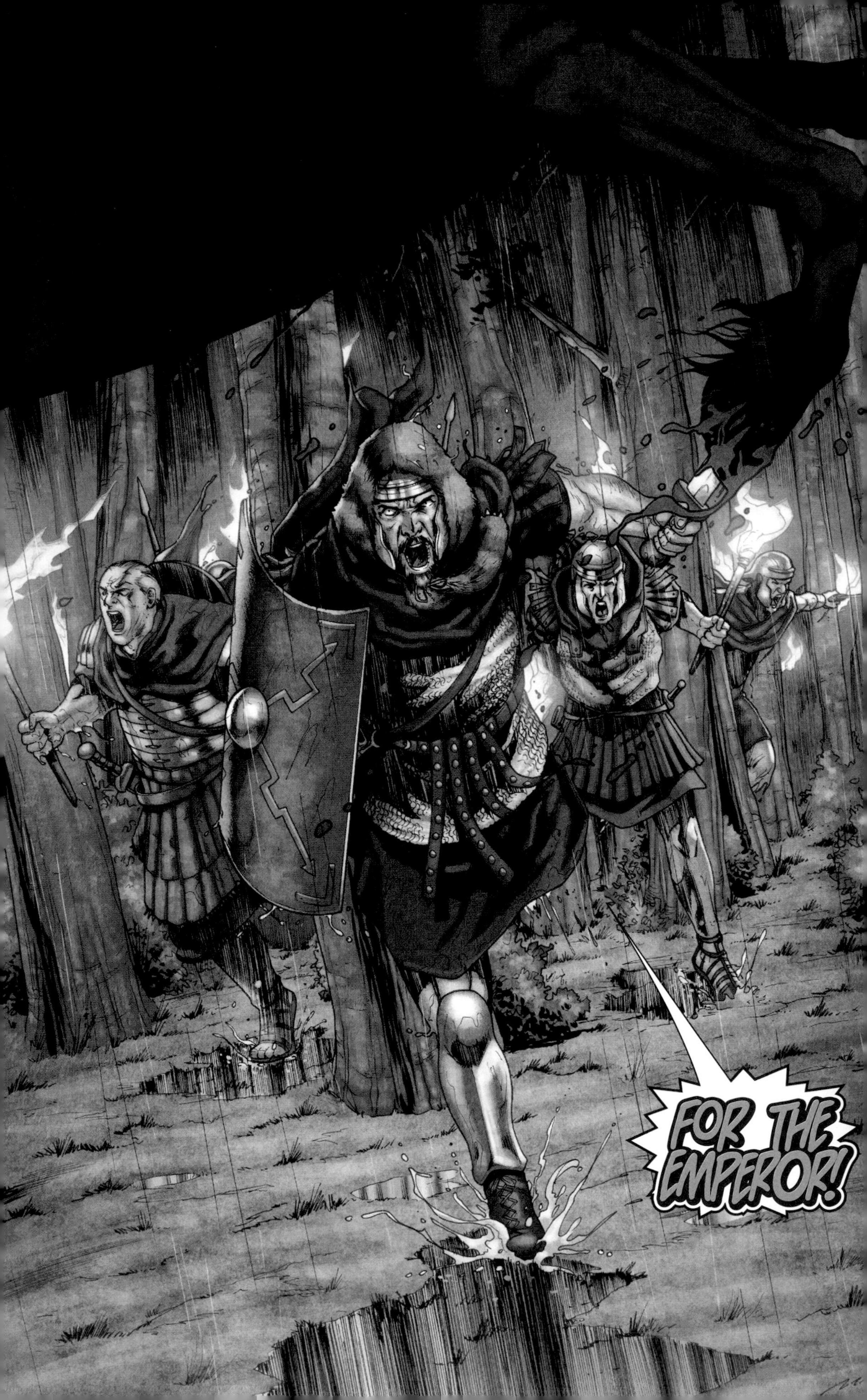
FOR THE EMPEROR!

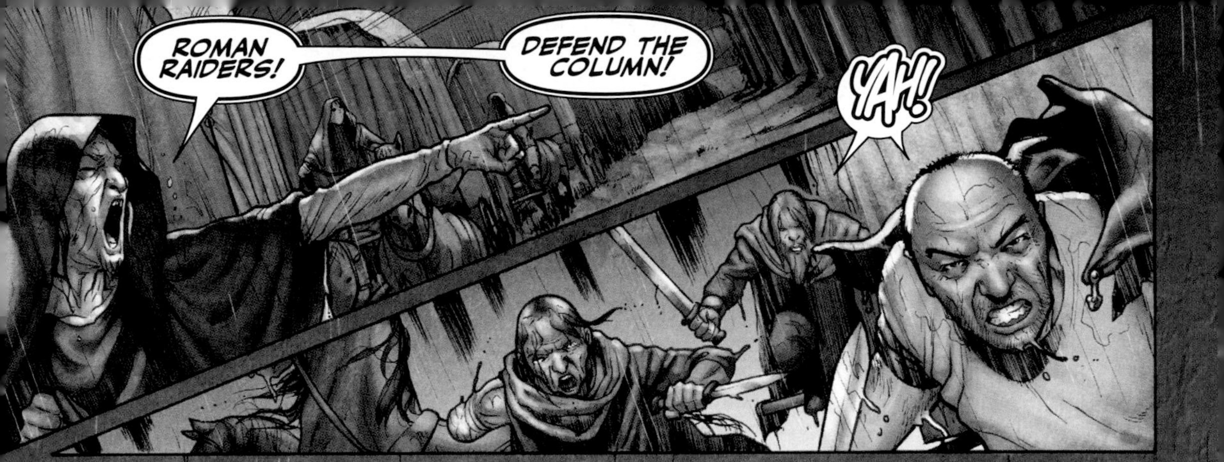
ROMAN RAIDERS!
DEFEND THE COLUMN!
YAH!
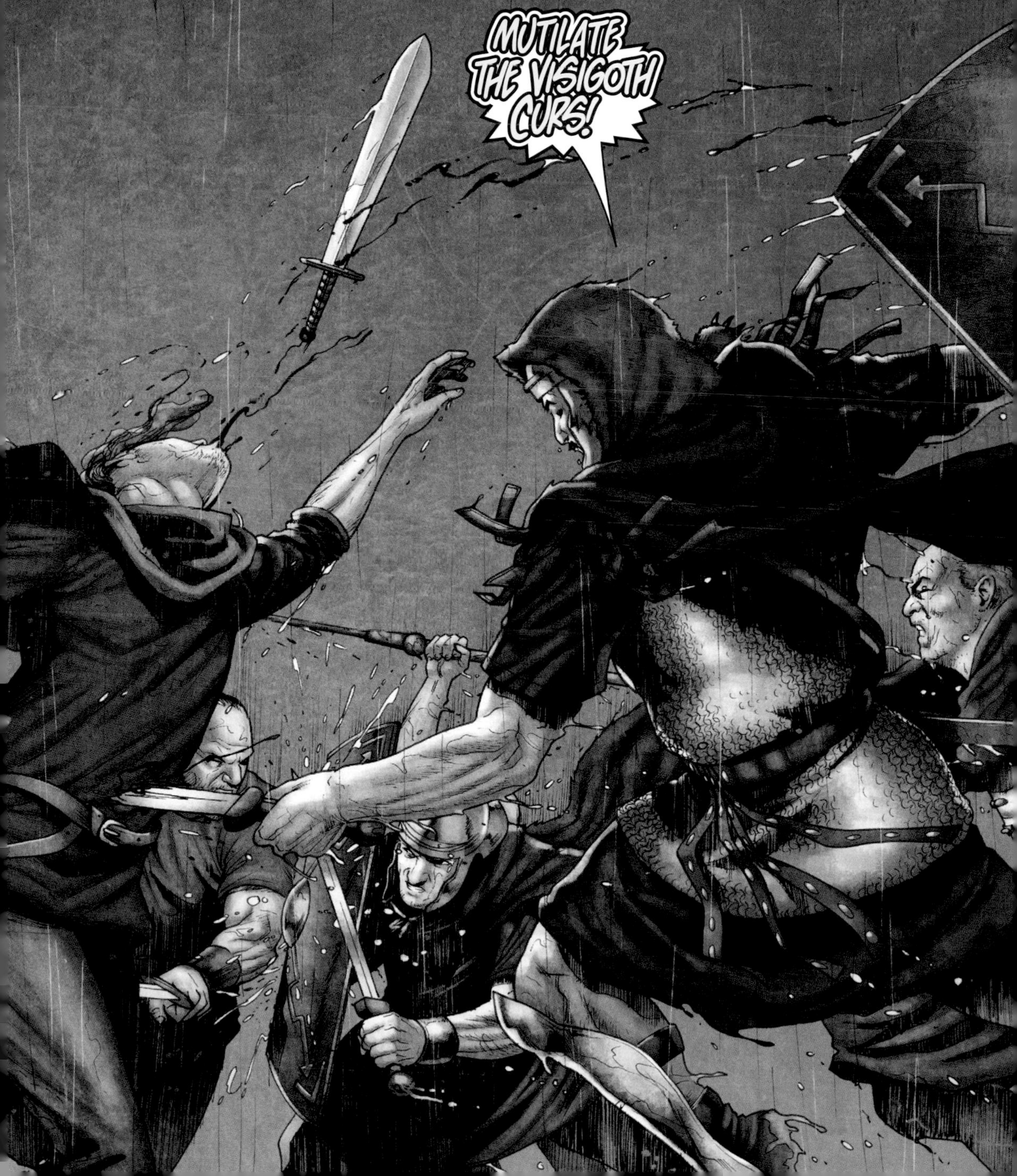
MUTILATE THE VISIGOTH CURS!

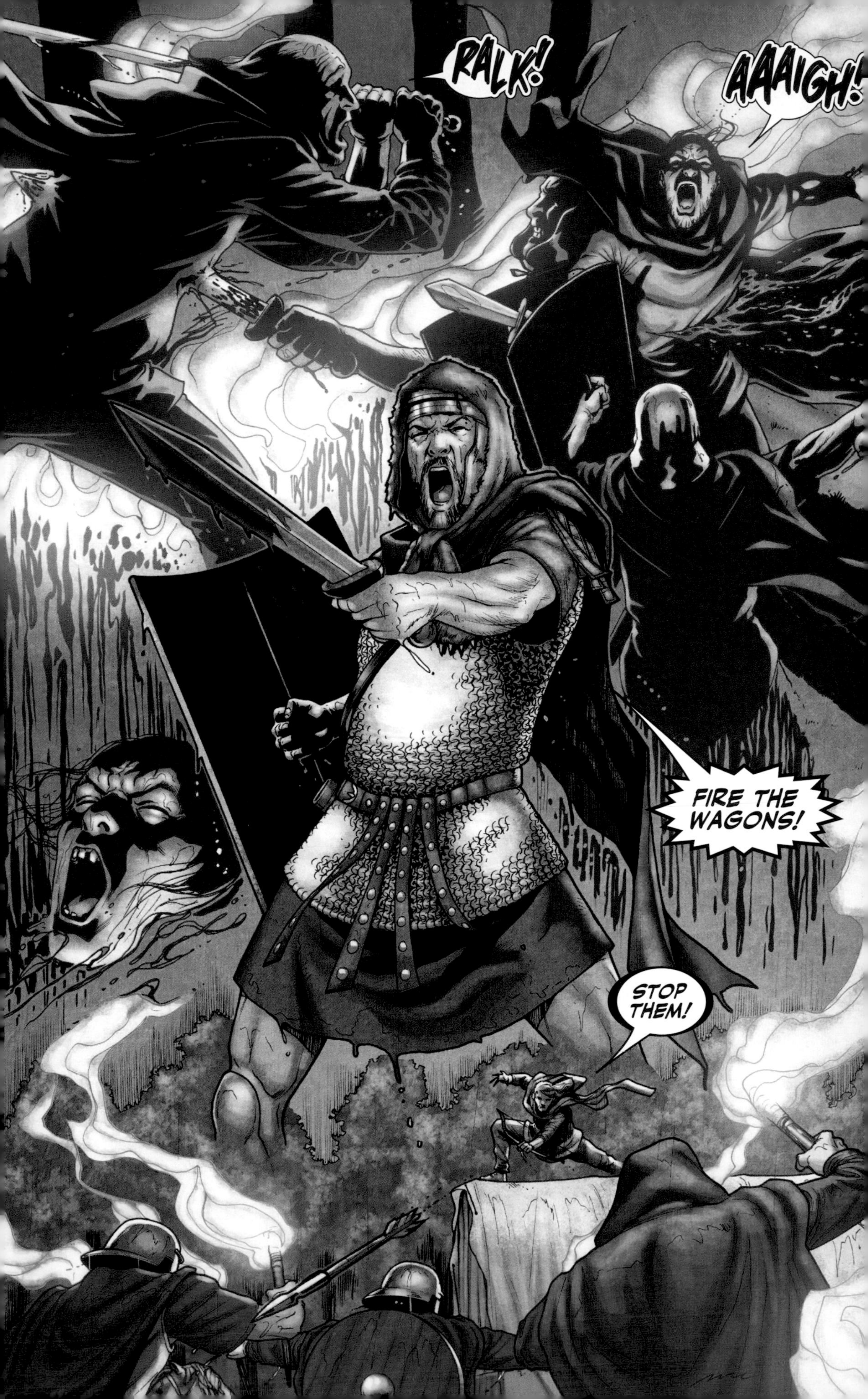
RALK!
AAAIGH!
FIRE THE WAGONS!
STOP THEM!

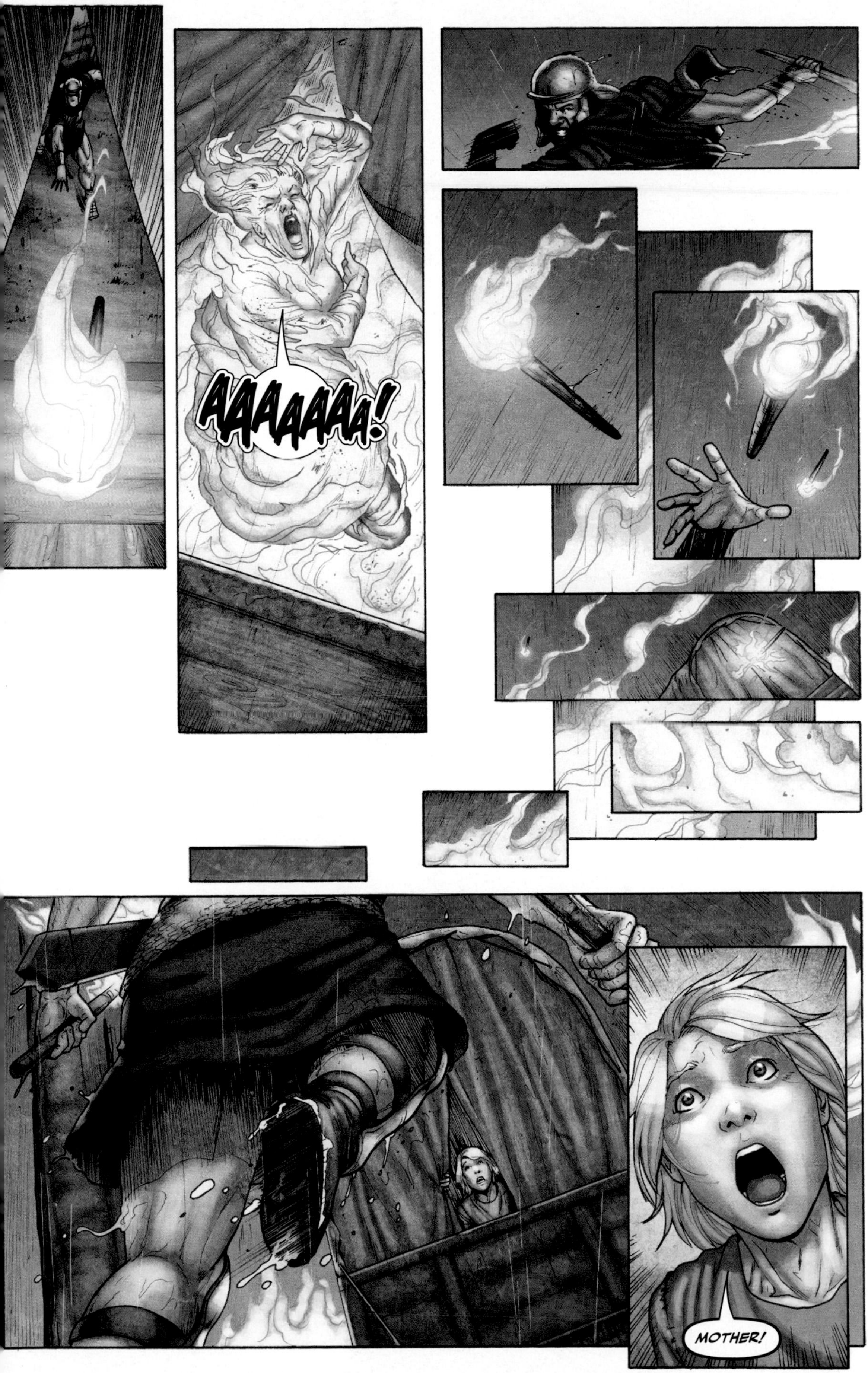
AAAAAAA!
MOTHER!

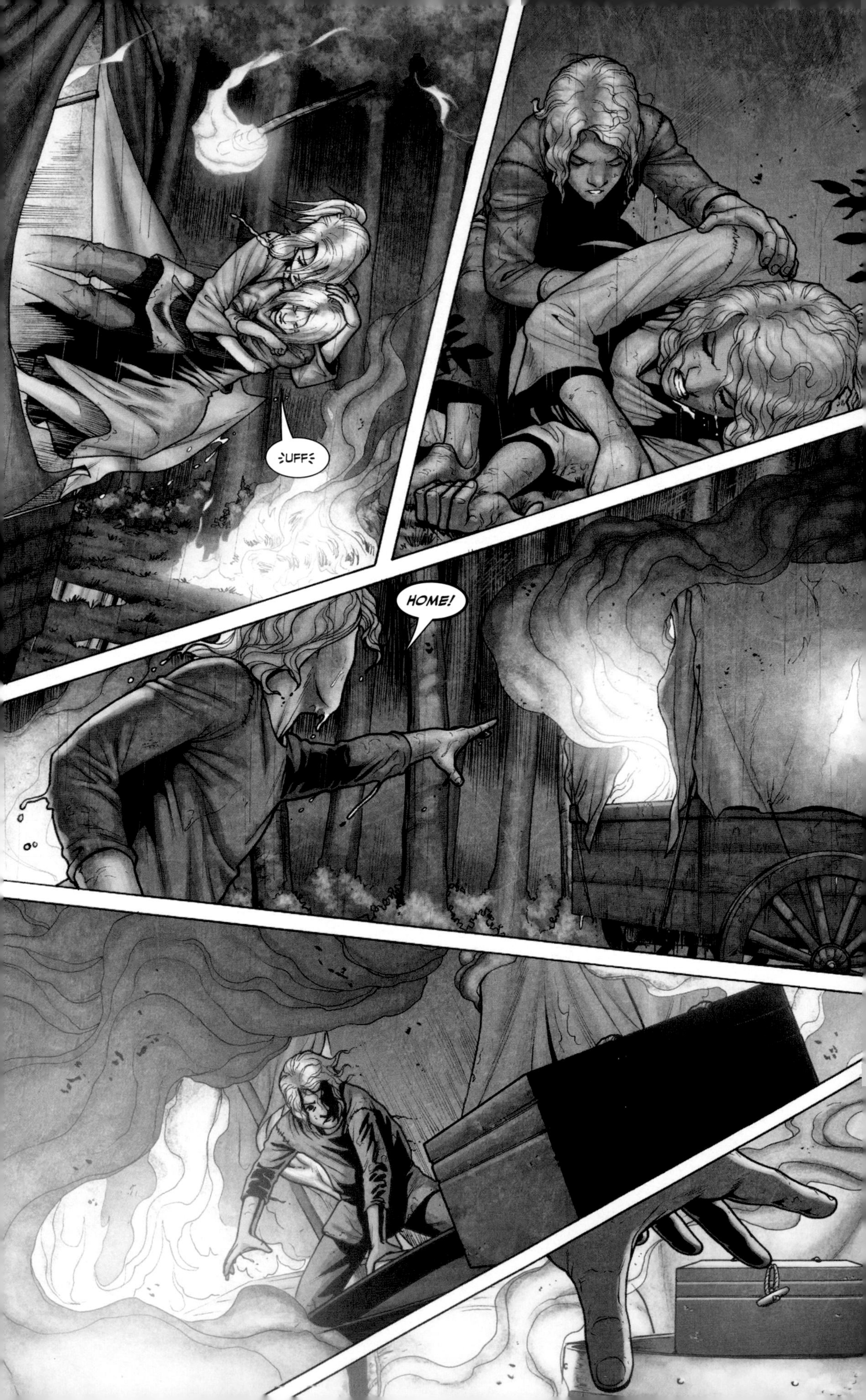
UFF
HOME!

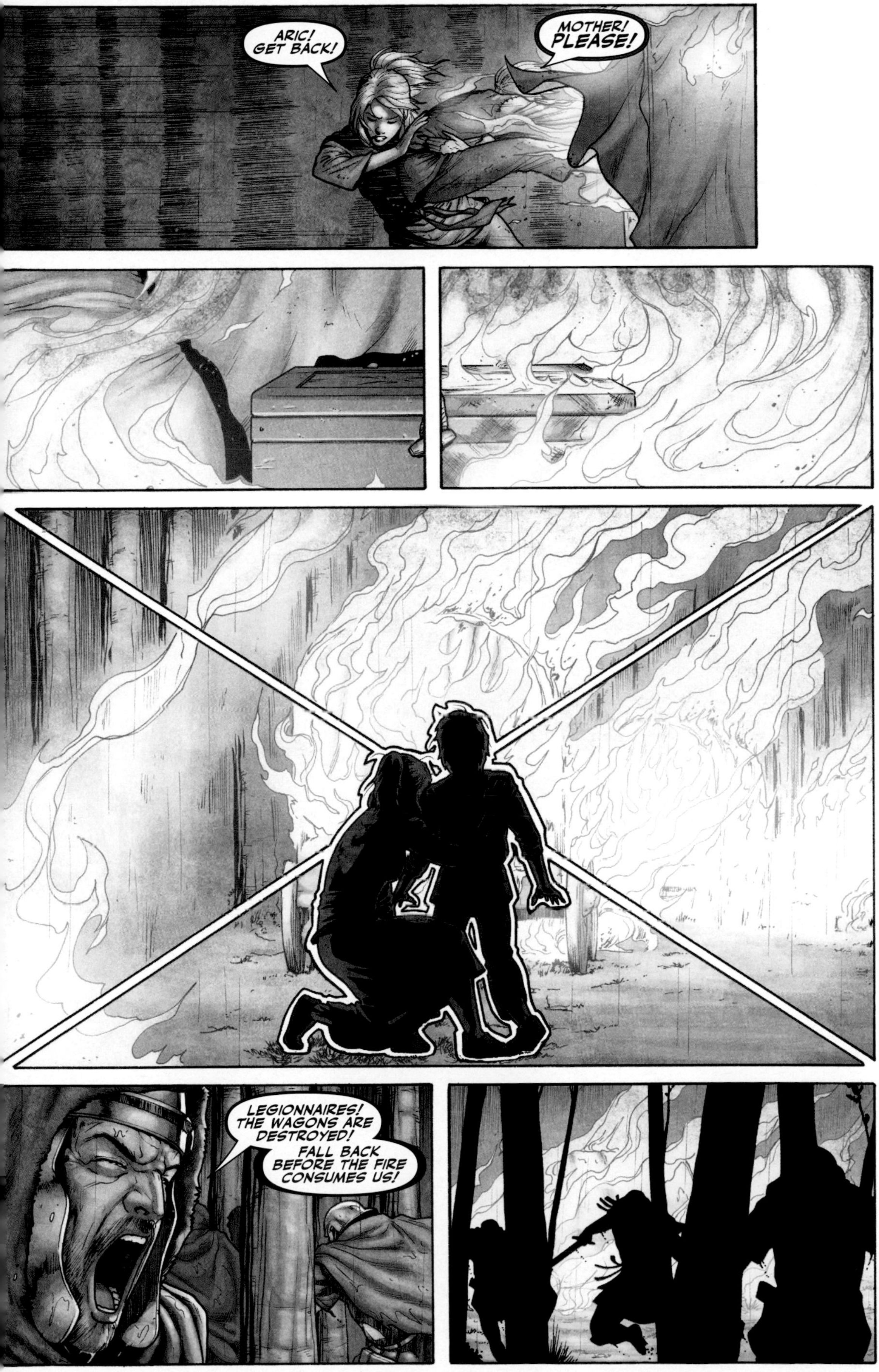
ARIC! GET BACK!
MOTHER! PLEASE!
LEGIONNAIRES! THE WAGONS ARE DESTROYED!
FALL BACK BEFORE THE FIRE CONSUMES US!

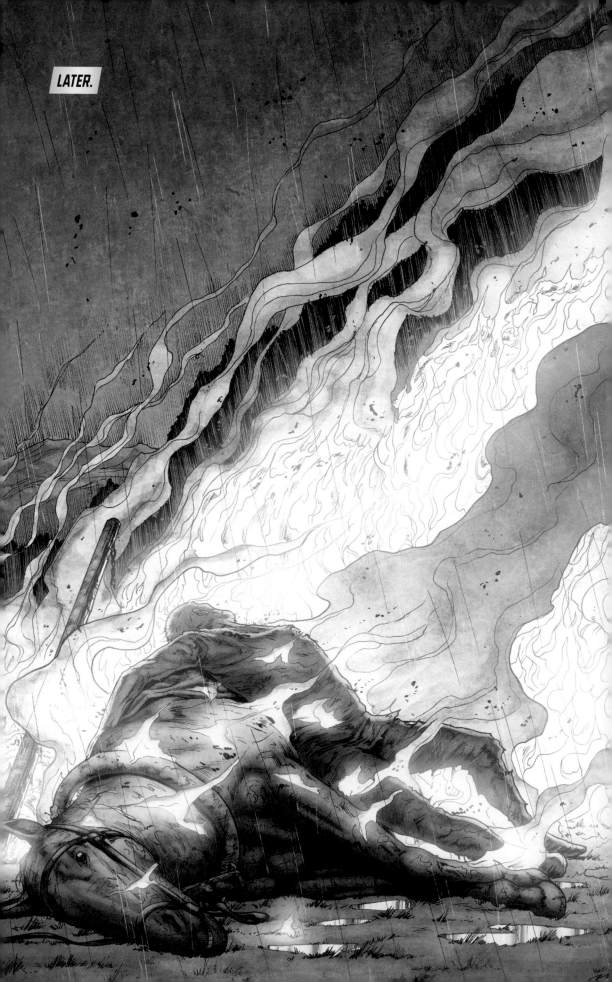

LATER.

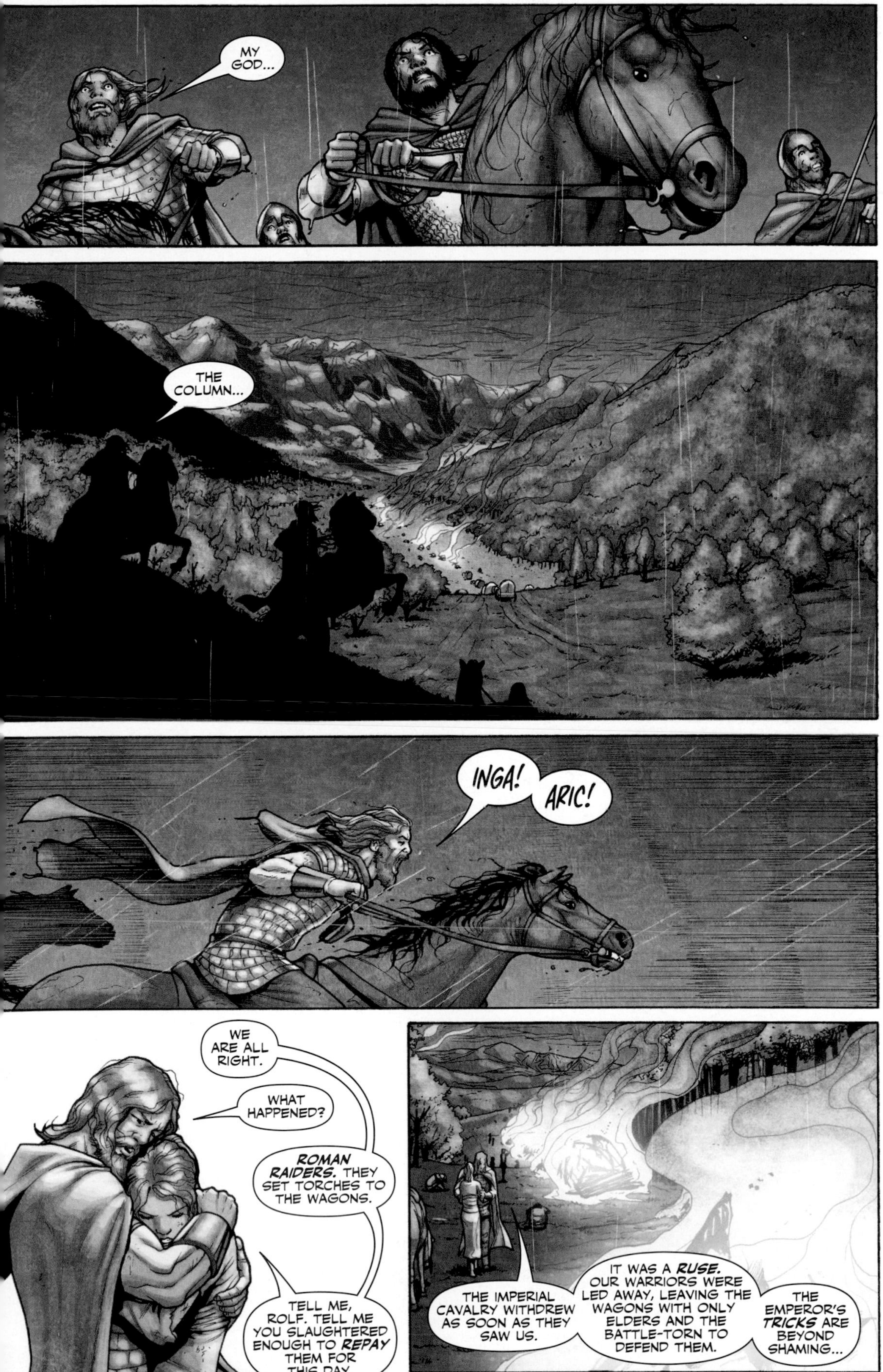
MY GOD...
THE COLUMN...
INGA!
ARIC!
WE ARE ALL RIGHT.
WHAT HAPPENED?
ROMAN RAIDERS. THEY SET TORCHES TO THE WAGONS.
TELL ME, ROLF. TELL ME YOU SLAUGHTERED ENOUGH TO REPAY THEM FOR THIS DAY.
THE IMPERIAL CAVALRY WITHDREW AS SOON AS THEY SAW US.
IT WAS A RUSE. OUR WARRIORS WERE LED AWAY, LEAVING THE WAGONS WITH ONLY ELDERS AND THE BATTLE-TORN TO DEFEND THEM.
THE EMPEROR'S TRICKS ARE BEYOND SHAMING...

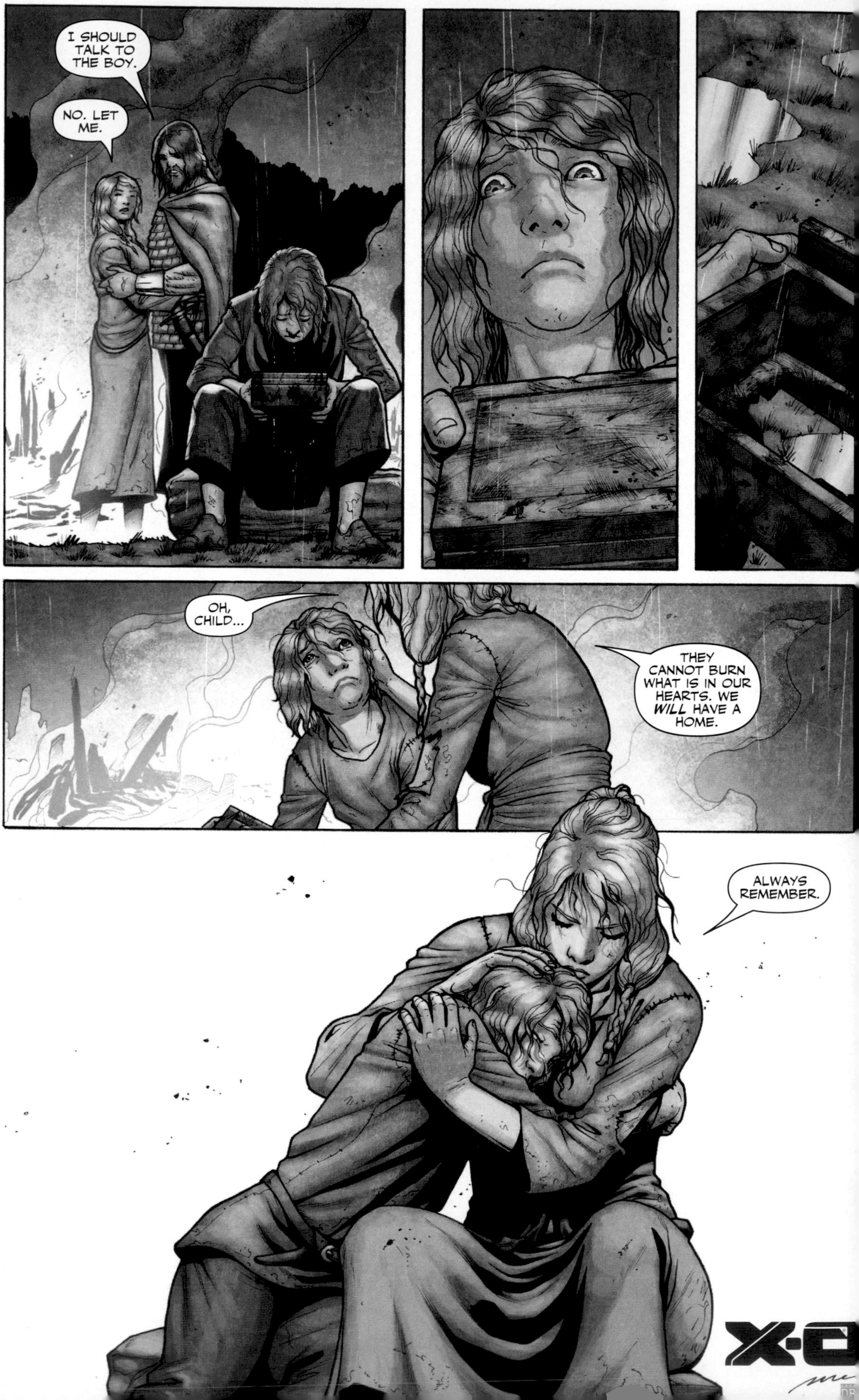
I SHOULD TALK TO THE BOY.
NO. LET ME.
OH, CHILD...
THEY CANNOT BURN WHAT IS IN OUR HEARTS. WE *WILL* HAVE A HOME.
ALWAYS REMEMBER.

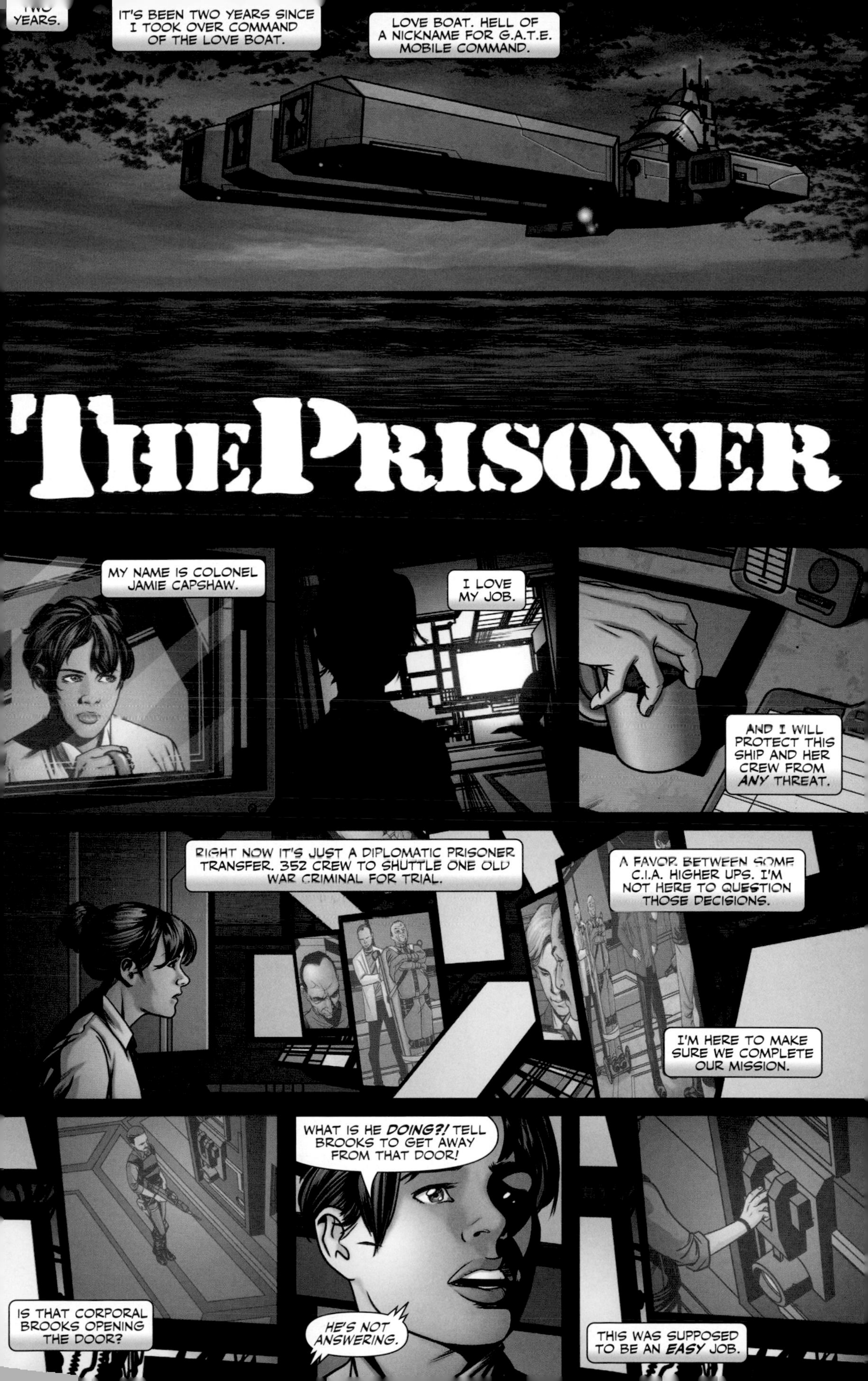

YEARS.
IT'S BEEN TWO YEARS SINCE I TOOK OVER COMMAND OF THE LOVE BOAT.
LOVE BOAT. HELL OF A NICKNAME FOR G.A.T.E. MOBILE COMMAND.
THE PRISONER
MY NAME IS COLONEL JAMIE CAPSHAW.
I LOVE MY JOB.
AND I WILL PROTECT THIS SHIP AND HER CREW FROM *ANY* THREAT.
RIGHT NOW IT'S JUST A DIPLOMATIC PRISONER TRANSFER. 352 CREW TO SHUTTLE ONE OLD WAR CRIMINAL FOR TRIAL.
A FAVOR BETWEEN SOME C.I.A. HIGHER UPS. I'M NOT HERE TO QUESTION THOSE DECISIONS.
I'M HERE TO MAKE SURE WE COMPLETE OUR MISSION.
IS THAT CORPORAL BROOKS OPENING THE DOOR?
WHAT IS HE *DOING?!* TELL BROOKS TO GET AWAY FROM THAT DOOR!
HE'S NOT ANSWERING.
THIS WAS SUPPOSED TO BE AN *EASY* JOB.

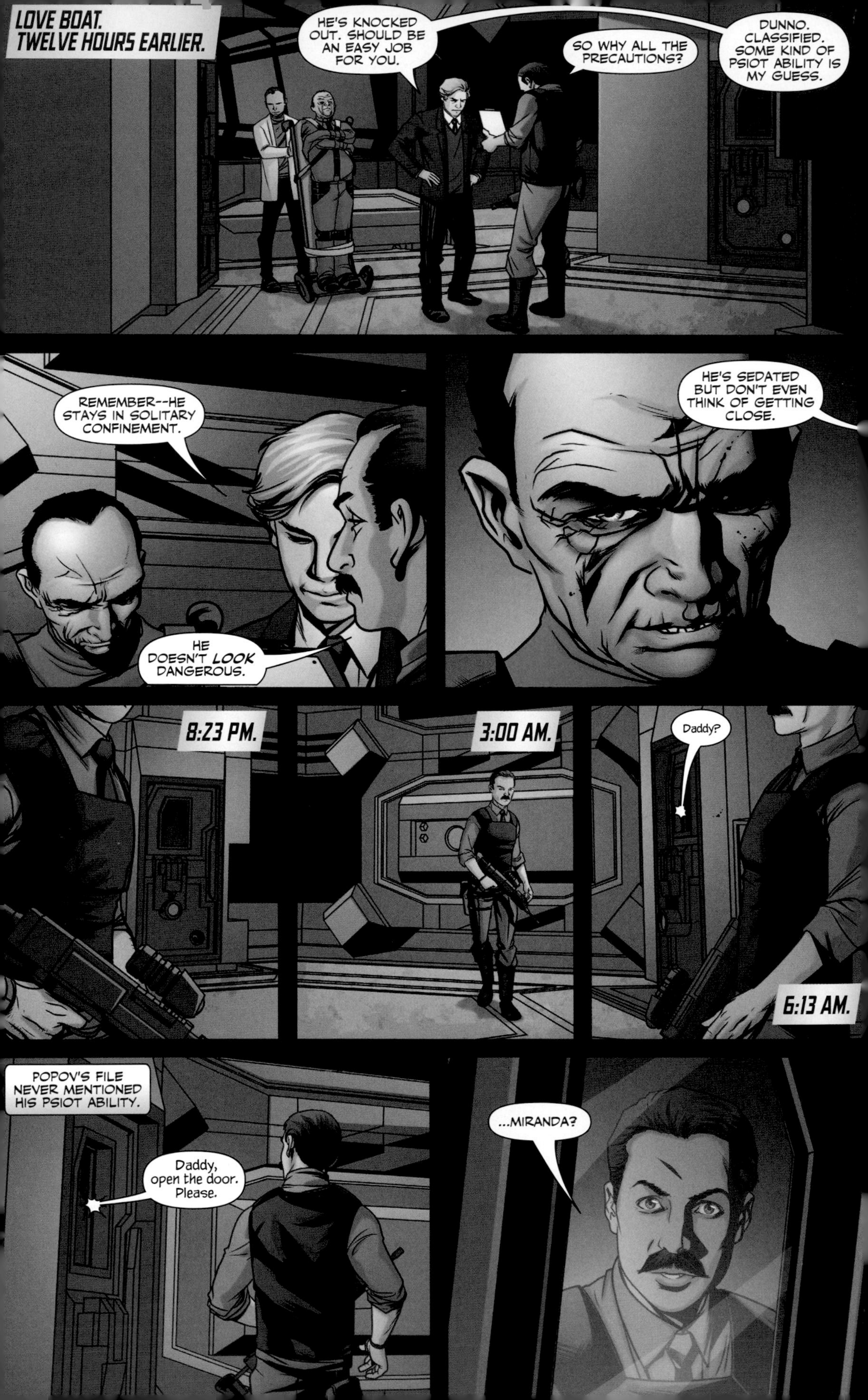
LOVE BOAT.
TWELVE HOURS EARLIER.
HE'S KNOCKED OUT. SHOULD BE AN EASY JOB FOR YOU.
SO WHY ALL THE PRECAUTIONS?
DUNNO. CLASSIFIED. SOME KIND OF PSIOT ABILITY IS MY GUESS.
REMEMBER--HE STAYS IN SOLITARY CONFINEMENT.
HE DOESN'T LOOK DANGEROUS.
HE'S SEDATED BUT DON'T EVEN THINK OF GETTING CLOSE.
8:23 PM.
3:00 AM.
Daddy?
6:13 AM.
POPOV'S FILE NEVER MENTIONED HIS PSIOT ABILITY.
Daddy, open the door. Please.
...MIRANDA?

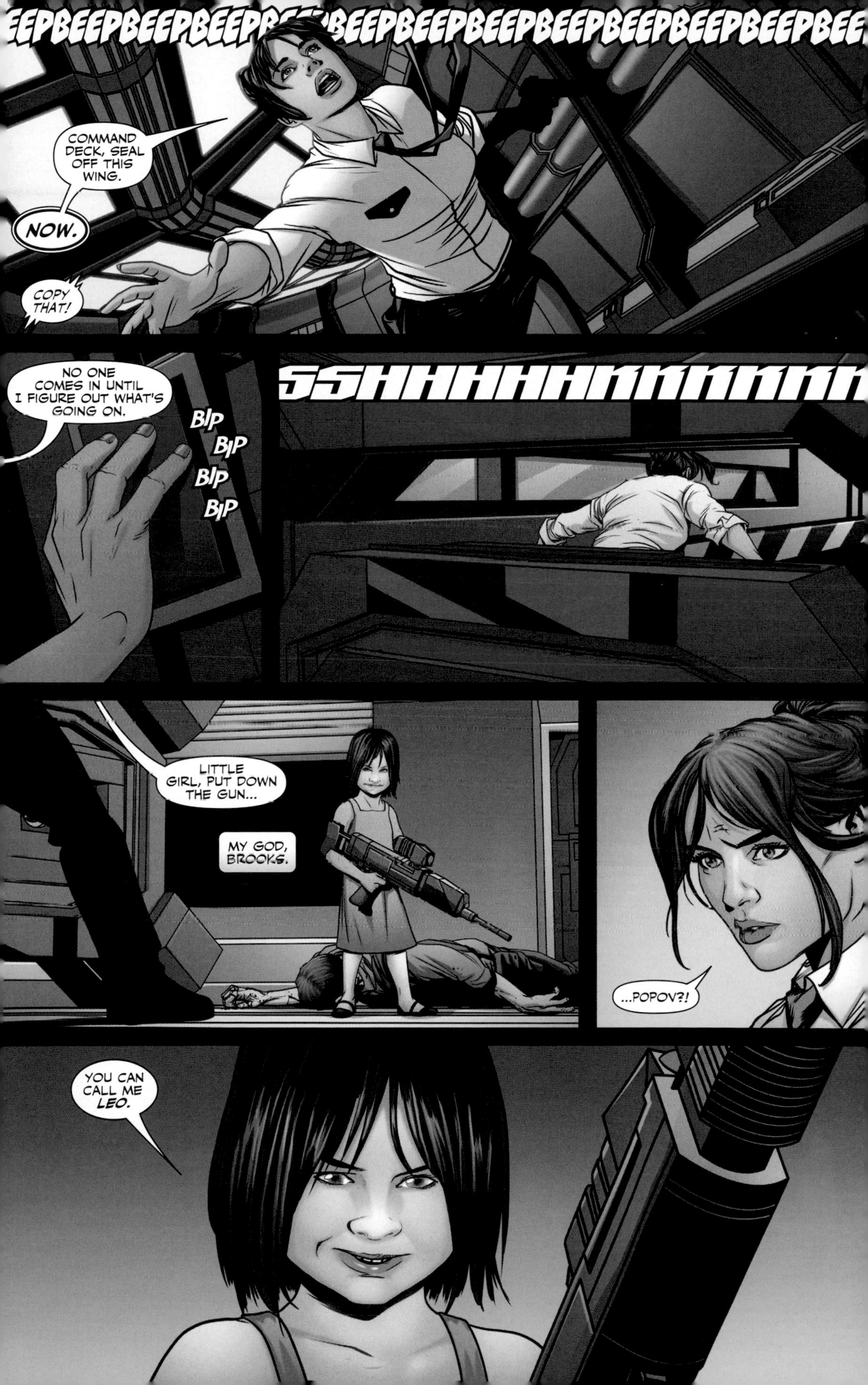
BEEPBEEPBEEPBEEPBEEPBEEPBEEPBEEPBEEPBEE
COMMAND DECK, SEAL OFF THIS WING.
NOW.
COPY THAT!
NO ONE COMES IN UNTIL I FIGURE OUT WHAT'S GOING ON.
BIP BIP BIP BIP
SSHHHHHHHHHHHH
LITTLE GIRL, PUT DOWN THE GUN...
MY GOD, BROOKS.
...POPOV?!
YOU CAN CALL ME LEO.

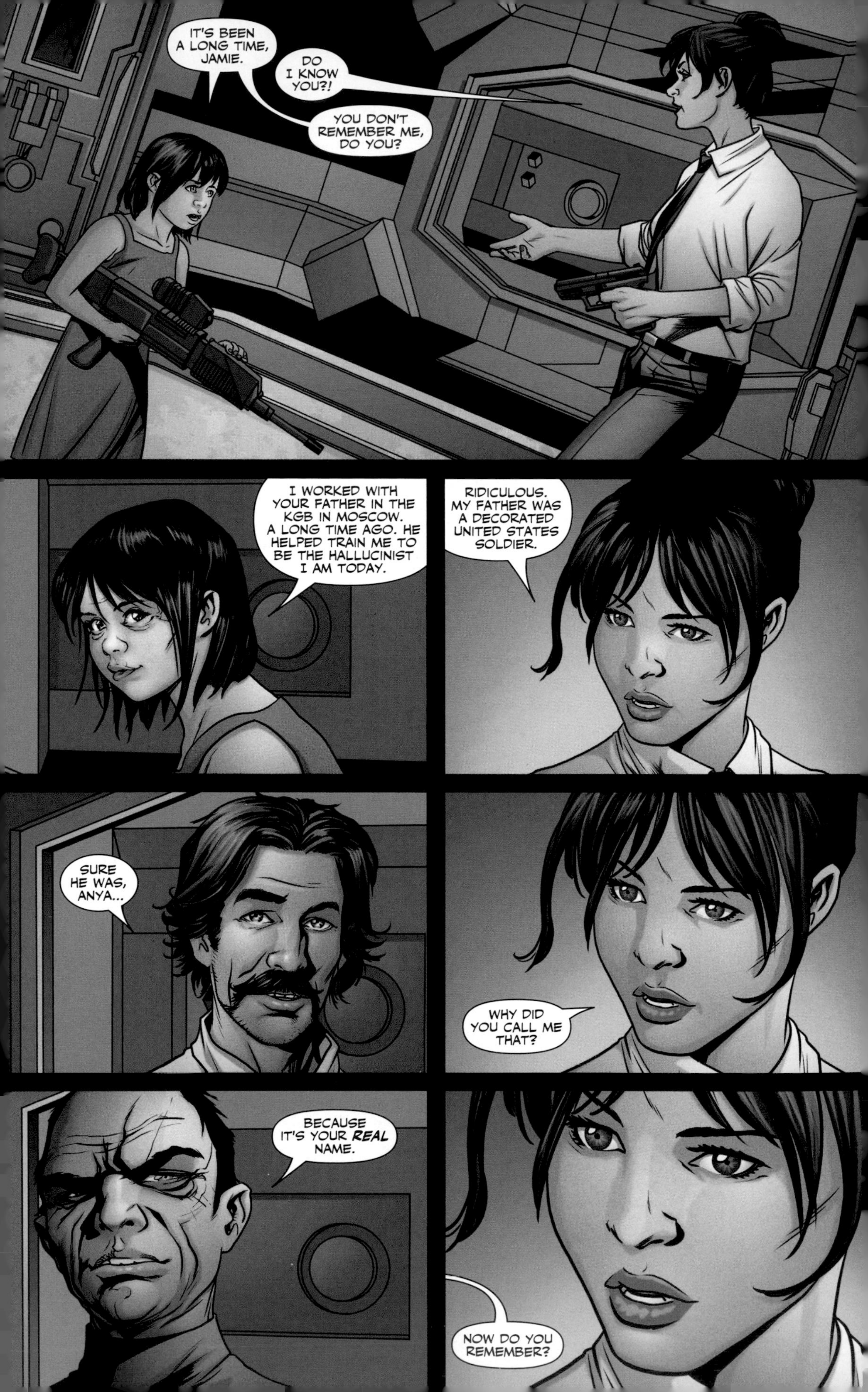
IT'S BEEN A LONG TIME, JAMIE.
DO I KNOW YOU?!
YOU DON'T REMEMBER ME, DO YOU?
I WORKED WITH YOUR FATHER IN THE KGB IN MOSCOW. A LONG TIME AGO. HE HELPED TRAIN ME TO BE THE HALLUCINIST I AM TODAY.
RIDICULOUS. MY FATHER WAS A DECORATED UNITED STATES SOLDIER.
SURE HE WAS, ANYA...
WHY DID YOU CALL ME THAT?
BECAUSE IT'S YOUR *REAL* NAME.
NOW DO YOU REMEMBER?

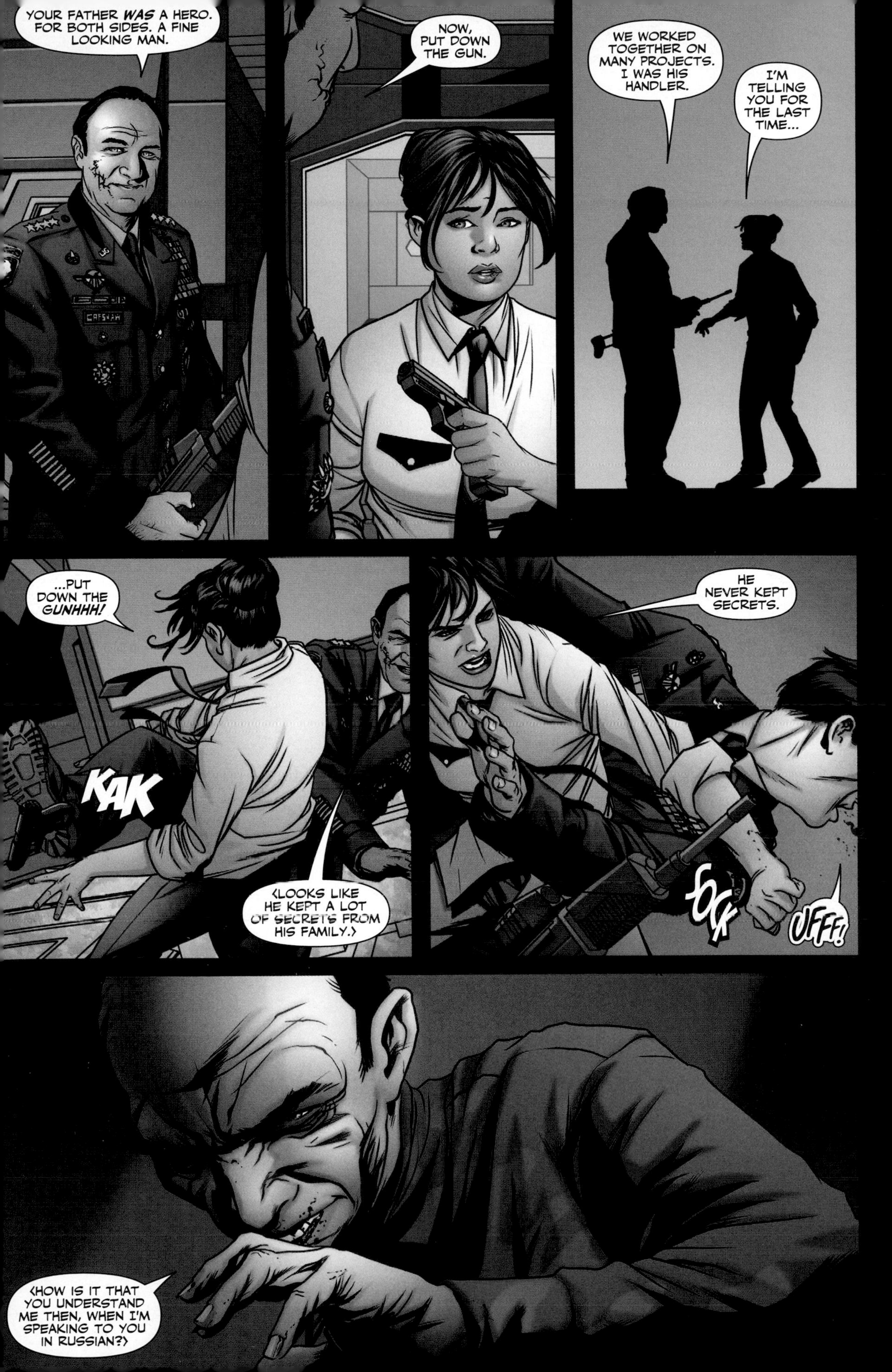
YOUR FATHER WAS A HERO. FOR BOTH SIDES. A FINE LOOKING MAN.
NOW, PUT DOWN THE GUN.
WE WORKED TOGETHER ON MANY PROJECTS. I WAS HIS HANDLER.
I'M TELLING YOU FOR THE LAST TIME...
...PUT DOWN THE GUNHHH!
KAK
‹LOOKS LIKE HE KEPT A LOT OF SECRETS FROM HIS FAMILY.›
HE NEVER KEPT SECRETS.
SOCK
UFFF!
‹HOW IS IT THAT YOU UNDERSTAND ME THEN, WHEN I'M SPEAKING TO YOU IN RUSSIAN?›

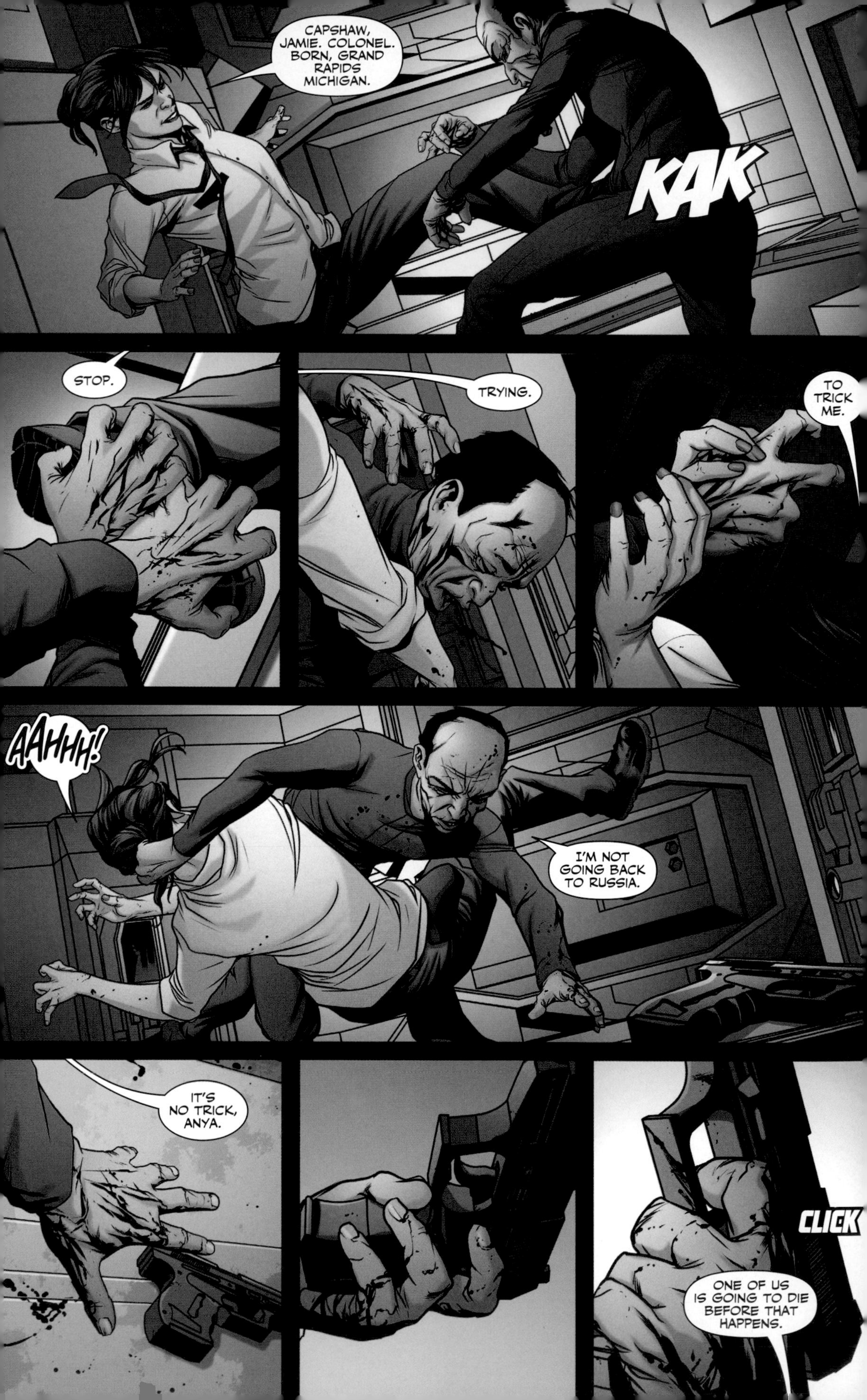
CAPSHAW, JAMIE. COLONEL. BORN, GRAND RAPIDS MICHIGAN.
KAK
STOP.
TRYING.
TO TRICK ME.
AAHHH!
I'M NOT GOING BACK TO RUSSIA.
IT'S NO TRICK, ANYA.
CLICK
ONE OF US IS GOING TO DIE BEFORE THAT HAPPENS.

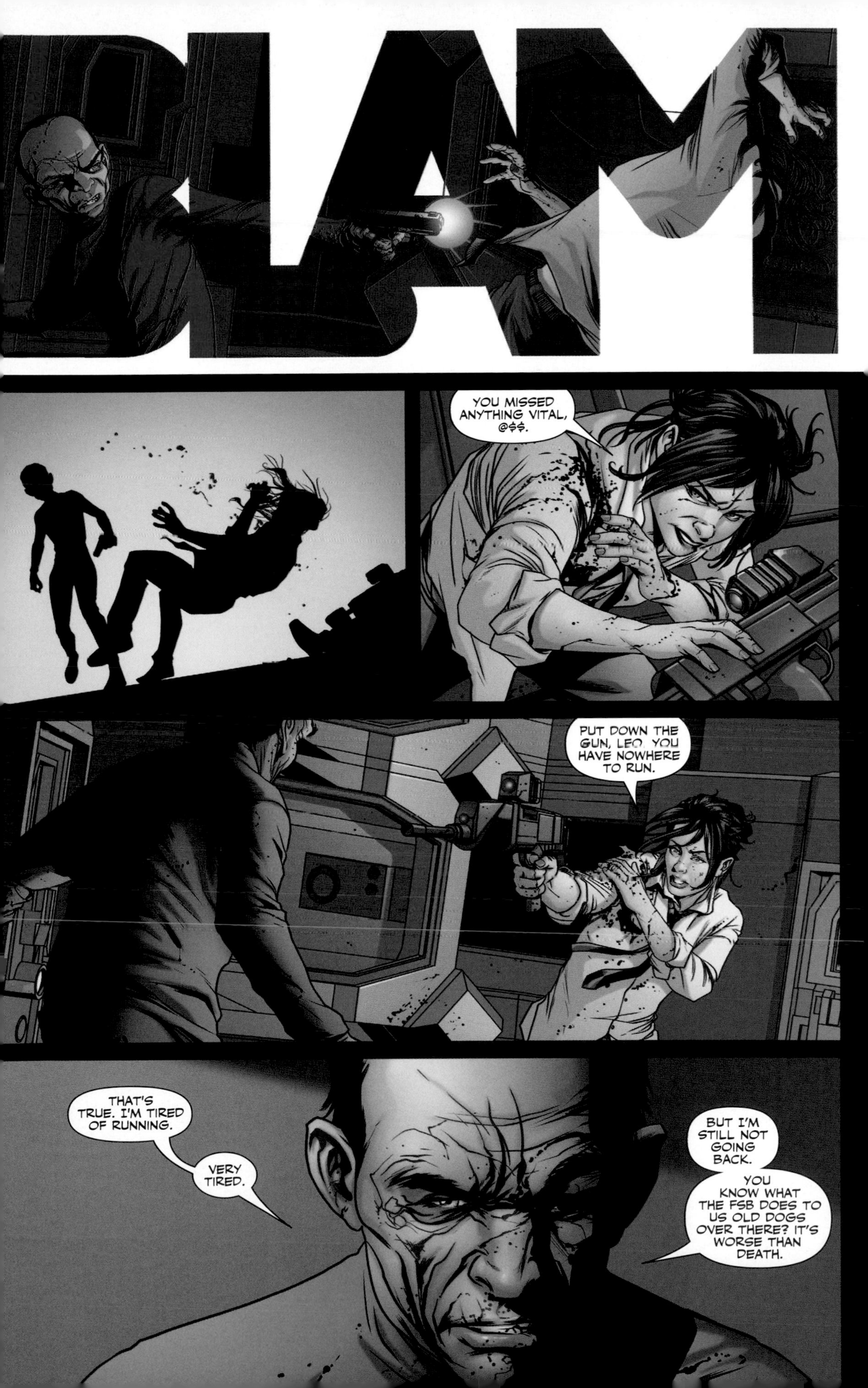
BLAM
YOU MISSED ANYTHING VITAL, @$$.
PUT DOWN THE GUN, LEO. YOU HAVE NOWHERE TO RUN.
THAT'S TRUE. I'M TIRED OF RUNNING.
VERY TIRED.
BUT I'M STILL NOT GOING BACK.
YOU KNOW WHAT THE FSB DOES TO US OLD DOGS OVER THERE? IT'S WORSE THAN DEATH.

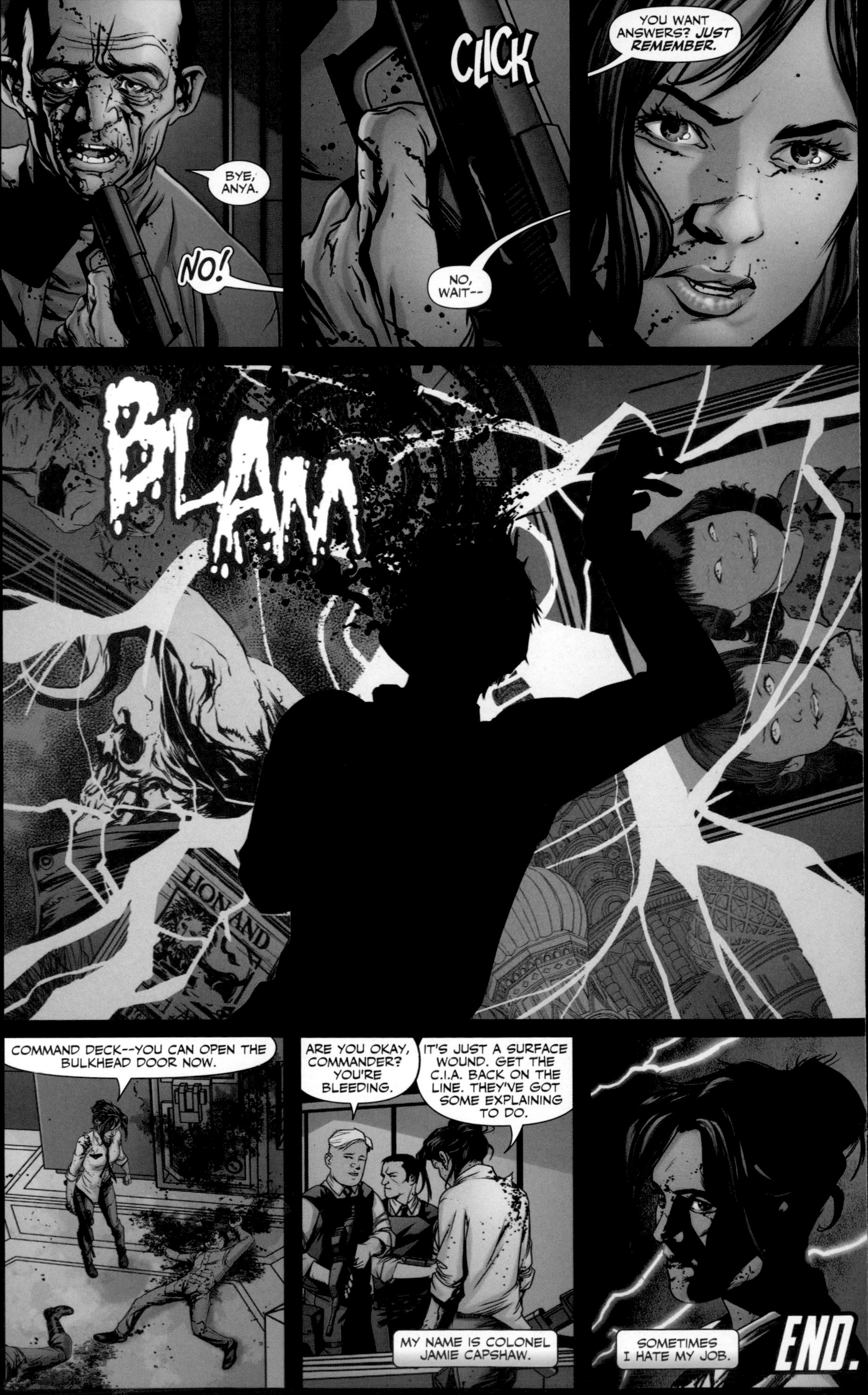
BYE, ANYA.
NO!
CLICK
NO, WAIT--
YOU WANT ANSWERS? JUST REMEMBER.
BLAM
COMMAND DECK--YOU CAN OPEN THE BULKHEAD DOOR NOW.
ARE YOU OKAY, COMMANDER? YOU'RE BLEEDING.
IT'S JUST A SURFACE WOUND. GET THE C.I.A. BACK ON THE LINE. THEY'VE GOT SOME EXPLAINING TO DO.
MY NAME IS COLONEL JAMIE CAPSHAW.
SOMETIMES I HATE MY JOB.
END.

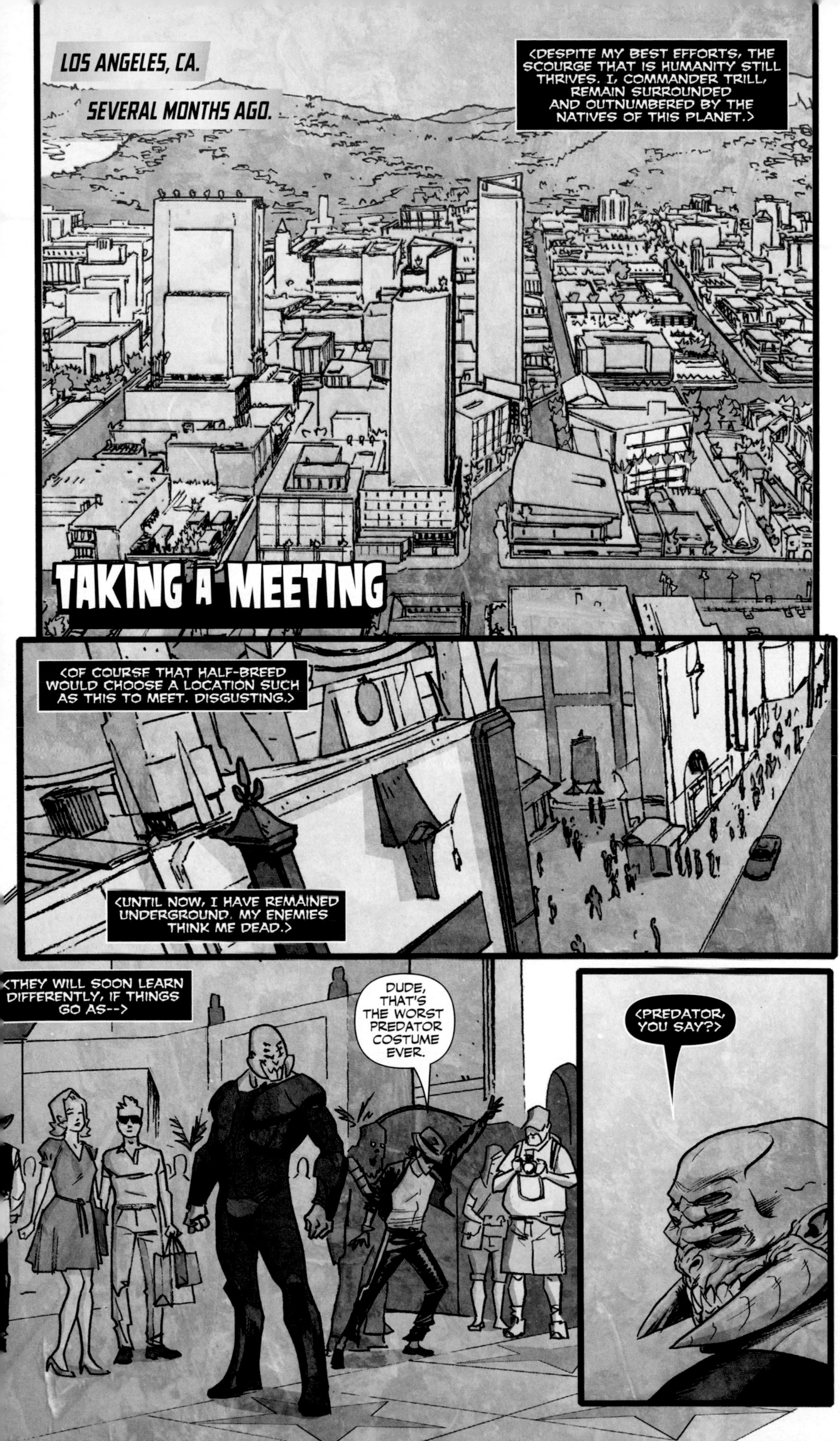
LOS ANGELES, CA.
SEVERAL MONTHS AGO.
<DESPITE MY BEST EFFORTS, THE SCOURGE THAT IS HUMANITY STILL THRIVES. I, COMMANDER TRILL, REMAIN SURROUNDED AND OUTNUMBERED BY THE NATIVES OF THIS PLANET.>
TAKING A MEETING
<OF COURSE THAT HALF-BREED WOULD CHOOSE A LOCATION SUCH AS THIS TO MEET. DISGUSTING.>
<UNTIL NOW, I HAVE REMAINED UNDERGROUND. MY ENEMIES THINK ME DEAD.>
<THEY WILL SOON LEARN DIFFERENTLY, IF THINGS GO AS-->
DUDE, THAT'S THE WORST PREDATOR COSTUME EVER.
<PREDATOR, YOU SAY?>

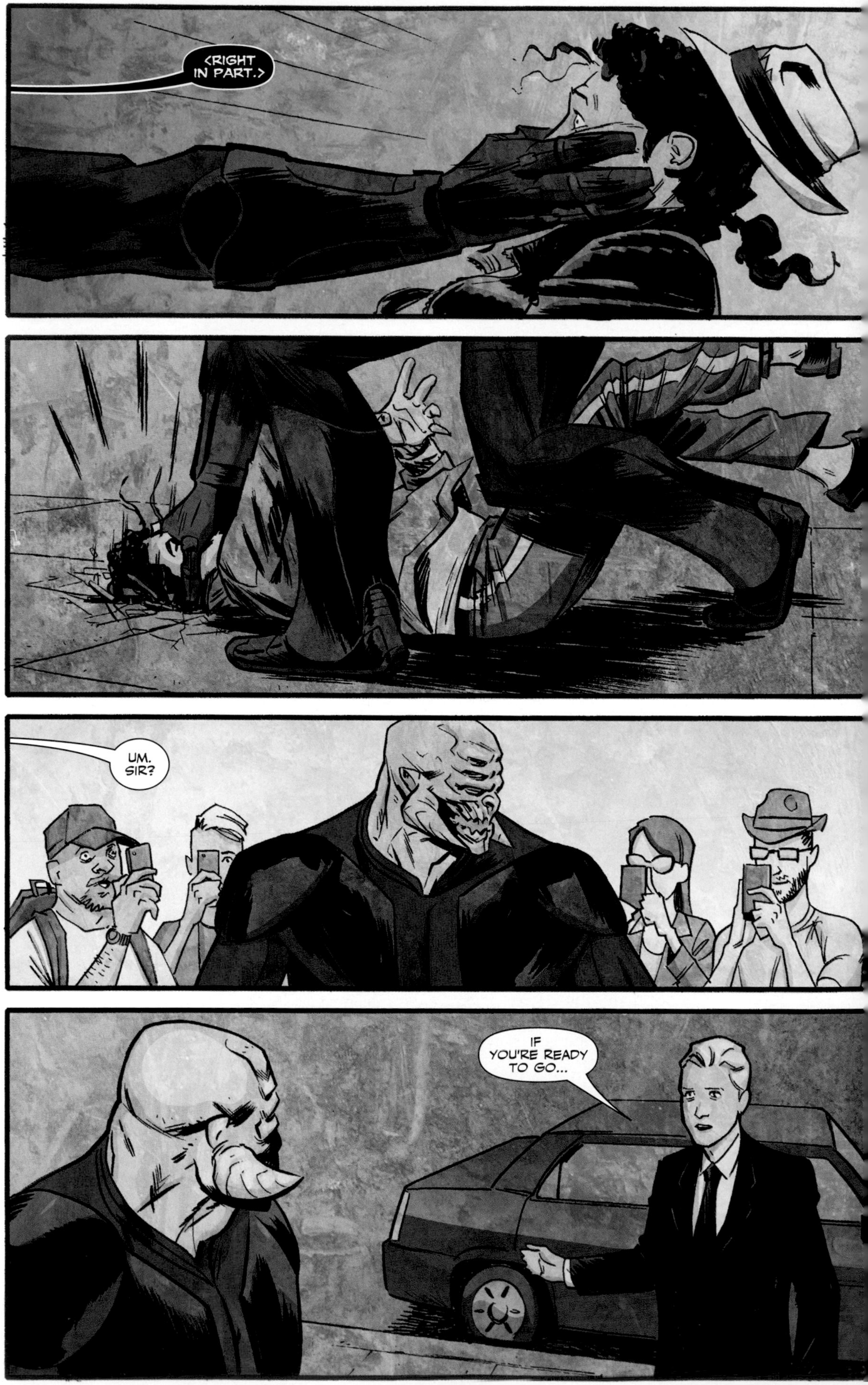
<RIGHT IN PART.>
UM. SIR?
IF YOU'RE READY TO GO...

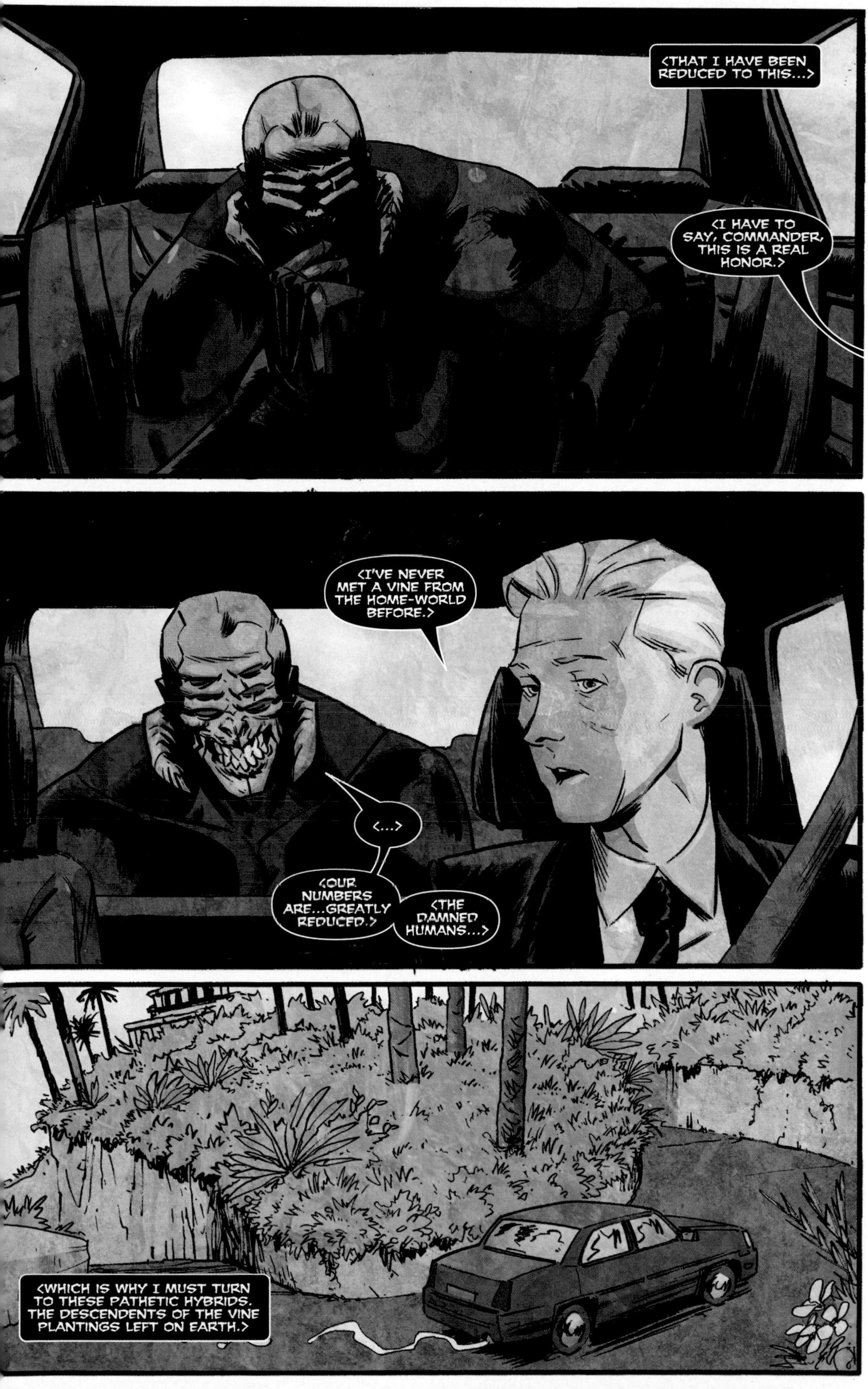
<THAT I HAVE BEEN REDUCED TO THIS...>
<I HAVE TO SAY, COMMANDER, THIS IS A REAL HONOR.>
<I'VE NEVER MET A VINE FROM THE HOME-WORLD BEFORE.>
<...>
<OUR NUMBERS ARE...GREATLY REDUCED.>
<THE DAMNED HUMANS...>
<WHICH IS WHY I MUST TURN TO THESE PATHETIC HYBRIDS. THE DESCENDENTS OF THE VINE PLANTINGS LEFT ON EARTH.>

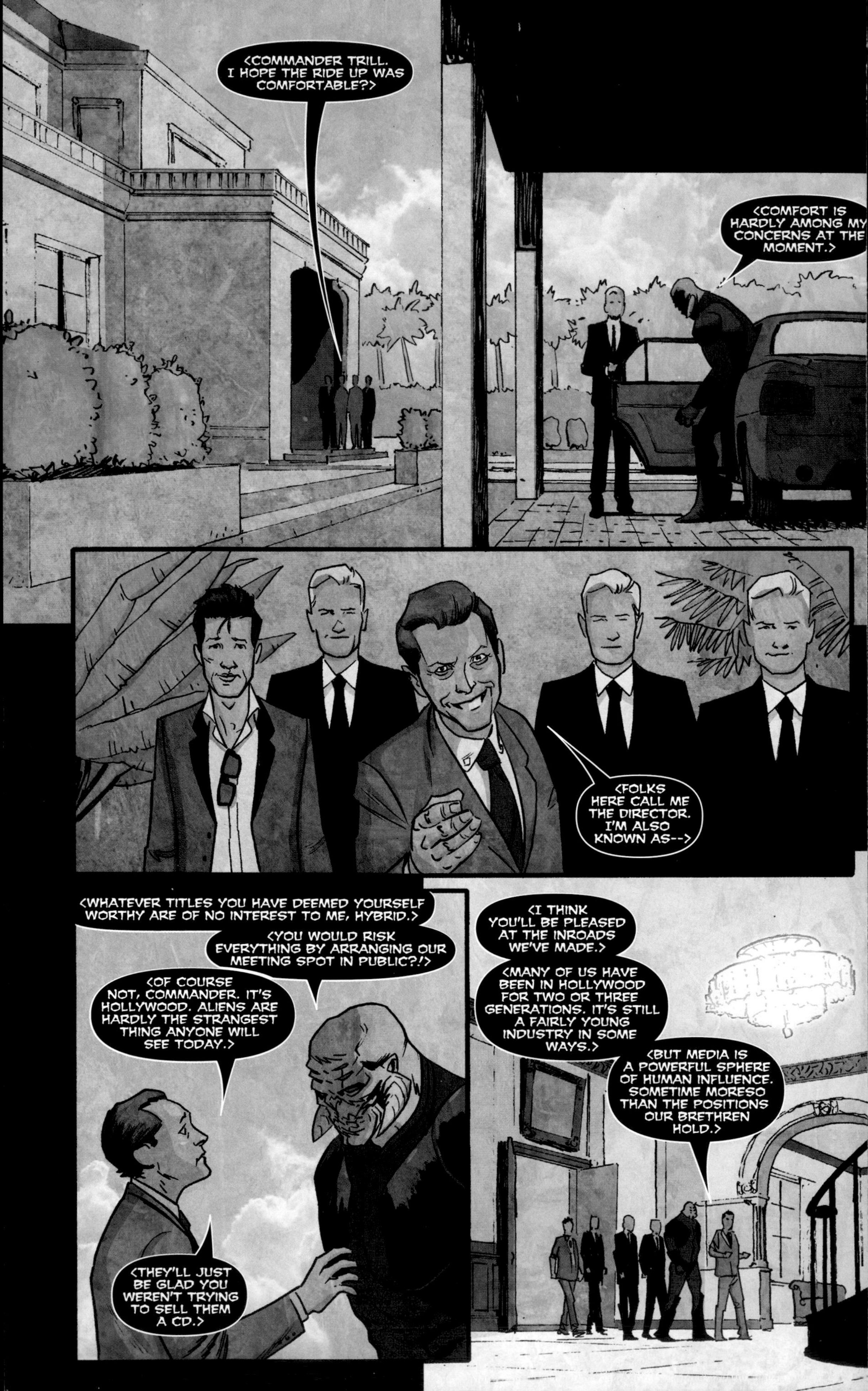
<COMMANDER TRILL. I HOPE THE RIDE UP WAS COMFORTABLE?>
<COMFORT IS HARDLY AMONG MY CONCERNS AT THE MOMENT.>
<FOLKS HERE CALL ME THE DIRECTOR. I'M ALSO KNOWN AS-->
<WHATEVER TITLES YOU HAVE DEEMED YOURSELF WORTHY ARE OF NO INTEREST TO ME, HYBRID.>
<YOU WOULD RISK EVERYTHING BY ARRANGING OUR MEETING SPOT IN PUBLIC?!>
<OF COURSE NOT, COMMANDER. IT'S HOLLYWOOD. ALIENS ARE HARDLY THE STRANGEST THING ANYONE WILL SEE TODAY.>
<THEY'LL JUST BE GLAD YOU WEREN'T TRYING TO SELL THEM A CD.>
<I THINK YOU'LL BE PLEASED AT THE INROADS WE'VE MADE.>
<MANY OF US HAVE BEEN IN HOLLYWOOD FOR TWO OR THREE GENERATIONS. IT'S STILL A FAIRLY YOUNG INDUSTRY IN SOME WAYS.>
<BUT MEDIA IS A POWERFUL SPHERE OF HUMAN INFLUENCE. SOMETIME MORESO THAN THE POSITIONS OUR BRETHREN HOLD.>

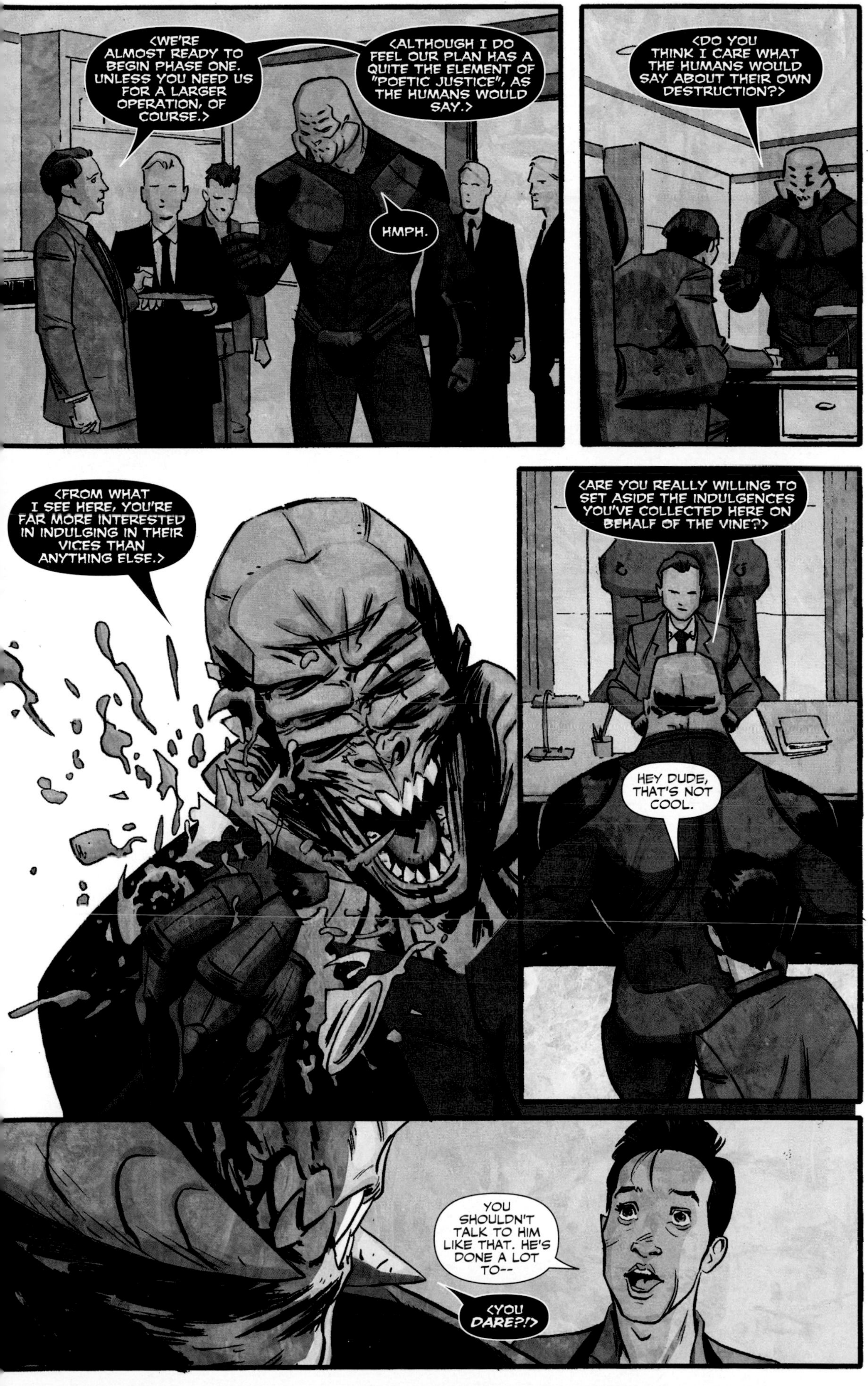

<WE'RE ALMOST READY TO BEGIN PHASE ONE. UNLESS YOU NEED US FOR A LARGER OPERATION, OF COURSE.>
<ALTHOUGH I DO FEEL OUR PLAN HAS A QUITE THE ELEMENT OF "POETIC JUSTICE", AS THE HUMANS WOULD SAY.>
HMPH.
<DO YOU THINK I CARE WHAT THE HUMANS WOULD SAY ABOUT THEIR OWN DESTRUCTION?>
<FROM WHAT I SEE HERE, YOU'RE FAR MORE INTERESTED IN INDULGING IN THEIR VICES THAN ANYTHING ELSE.>
<ARE YOU REALLY WILLING TO SET ASIDE THE INDULGENCES YOU'VE COLLECTED HERE ON BEHALF OF THE VINE?>
HEY DUDE, THAT'S NOT COOL.
YOU SHOULDN'T TALK TO HIM LIKE THAT. HE'S DONE A LOT TO--
<YOU DARE?!>

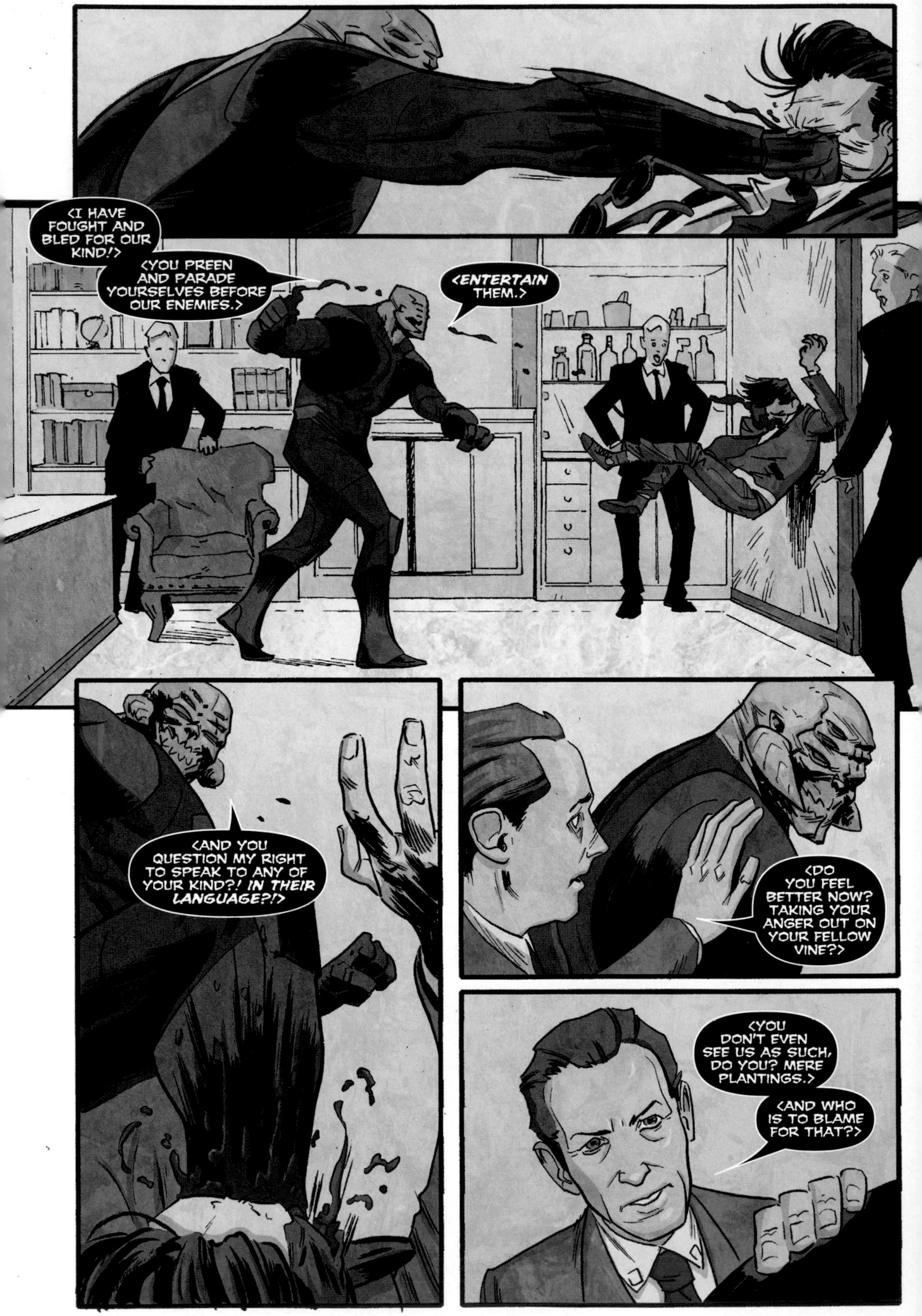
<I HAVE FOUGHT AND BLED FOR OUR KIND!>
<YOU PREEN AND PARADE YOURSELVES BEFORE OUR ENEMIES.>
<*ENTERTAIN* THEM.>
<AND YOU QUESTION MY RIGHT TO SPEAK TO ANY OF YOUR KIND?! *IN THEIR LANGUAGE?!*>
<DO YOU FEEL BETTER NOW? TAKING YOUR ANGER OUT ON YOUR FELLOW VINE?>
<YOU DON'T EVEN SEE US AS SUCH, DO YOU? MERE PLANTINGS.>
<AND WHO IS TO BLAME FOR THAT?>

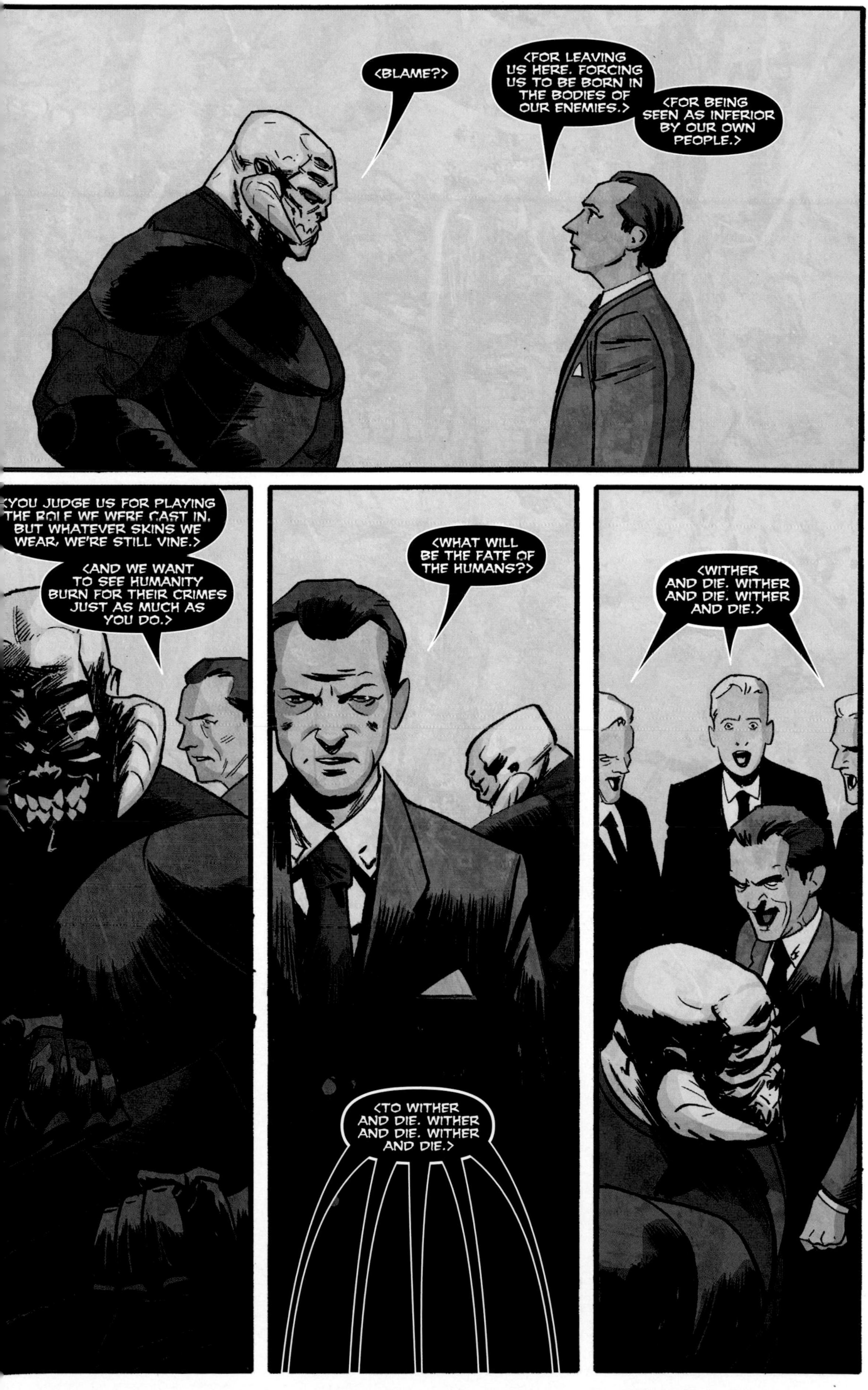
<BLAME?>
<FOR LEAVING US HERE. FORCING US TO BE BORN IN THE BODIES OF OUR ENEMIES.>
<FOR BEING SEEN AS INFERIOR BY OUR OWN PEOPLE.>
<YOU JUDGE US FOR PLAYING THE ROLE WE WERE CAST IN. BUT WHATEVER SKINS WE WEAR, WE'RE STILL VINE.>
<AND WE WANT TO SEE HUMANITY BURN FOR THEIR CRIMES JUST AS MUCH AS YOU DO.>
<WHAT WILL BE THE FATE OF THE HUMANS?>
<TO WITHER AND DIE. WITHER AND DIE. WITHER AND DIE.>
<WITHER AND DIE. WITHER AND DIE. WITHER AND DIE.>

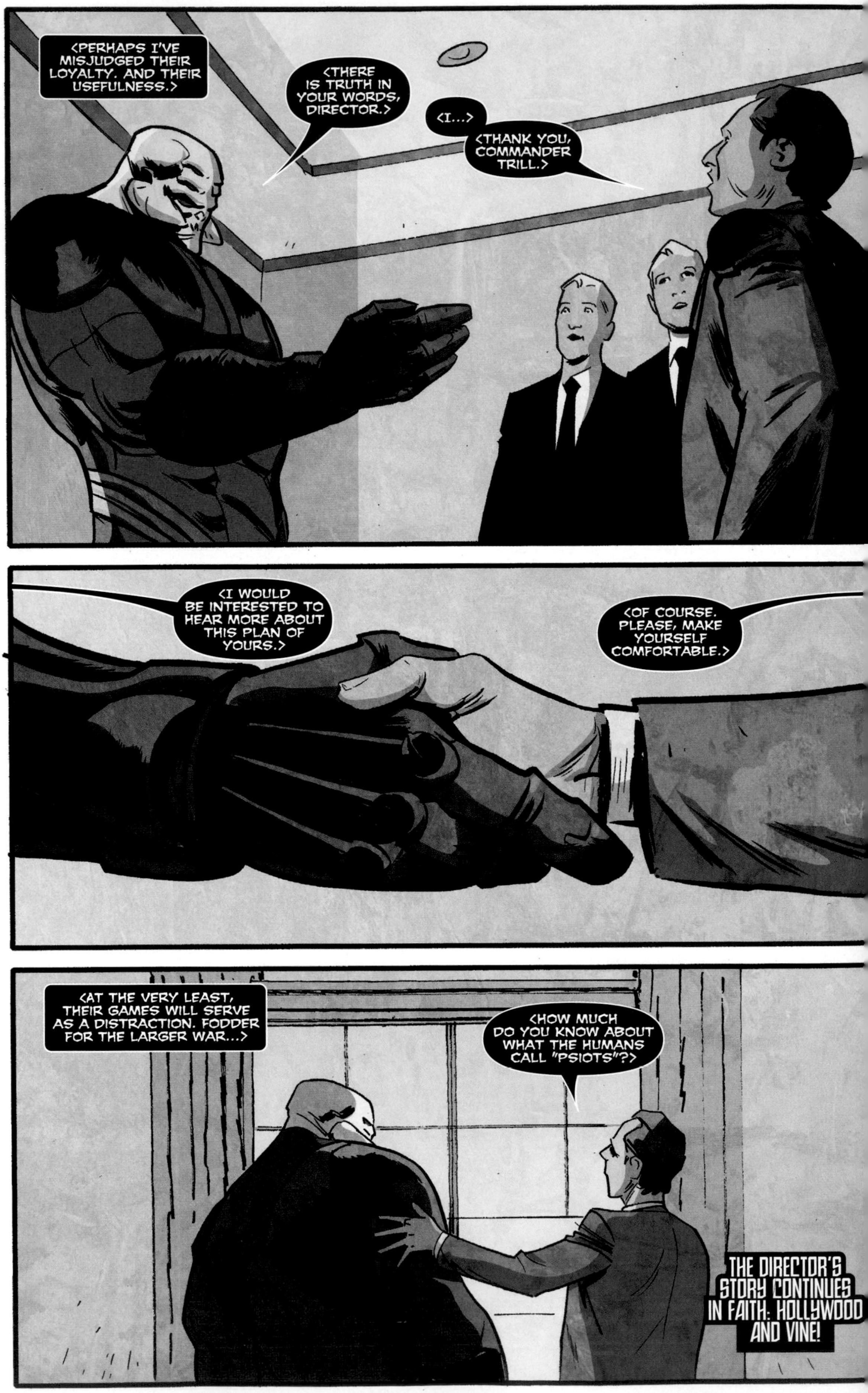

<PERHAPS I'VE MISJUDGED THEIR LOYALTY. AND THEIR USEFULNESS.>
<THERE IS TRUTH IN YOUR WORDS, DIRECTOR.>
<I...>
<THANK YOU, COMMANDER TRILL.>
<I WOULD BE INTERESTED TO HEAR MORE ABOUT THIS PLAN OF YOURS.>
<OF COURSE. PLEASE, MAKE YOURSELF COMFORTABLE.>
<AT THE VERY LEAST, THEIR GAMES WILL SERVE AS A DISTRACTION. FODDER FOR THE LARGER WAR...>
<HOW MUCH DO YOU KNOW ABOUT WHAT THE HUMANS CALL "PSIOTS"?>
THE DIRECTOR'S STORY CONTINUES IN FAITH: HOLLYWOOD AND VINE!

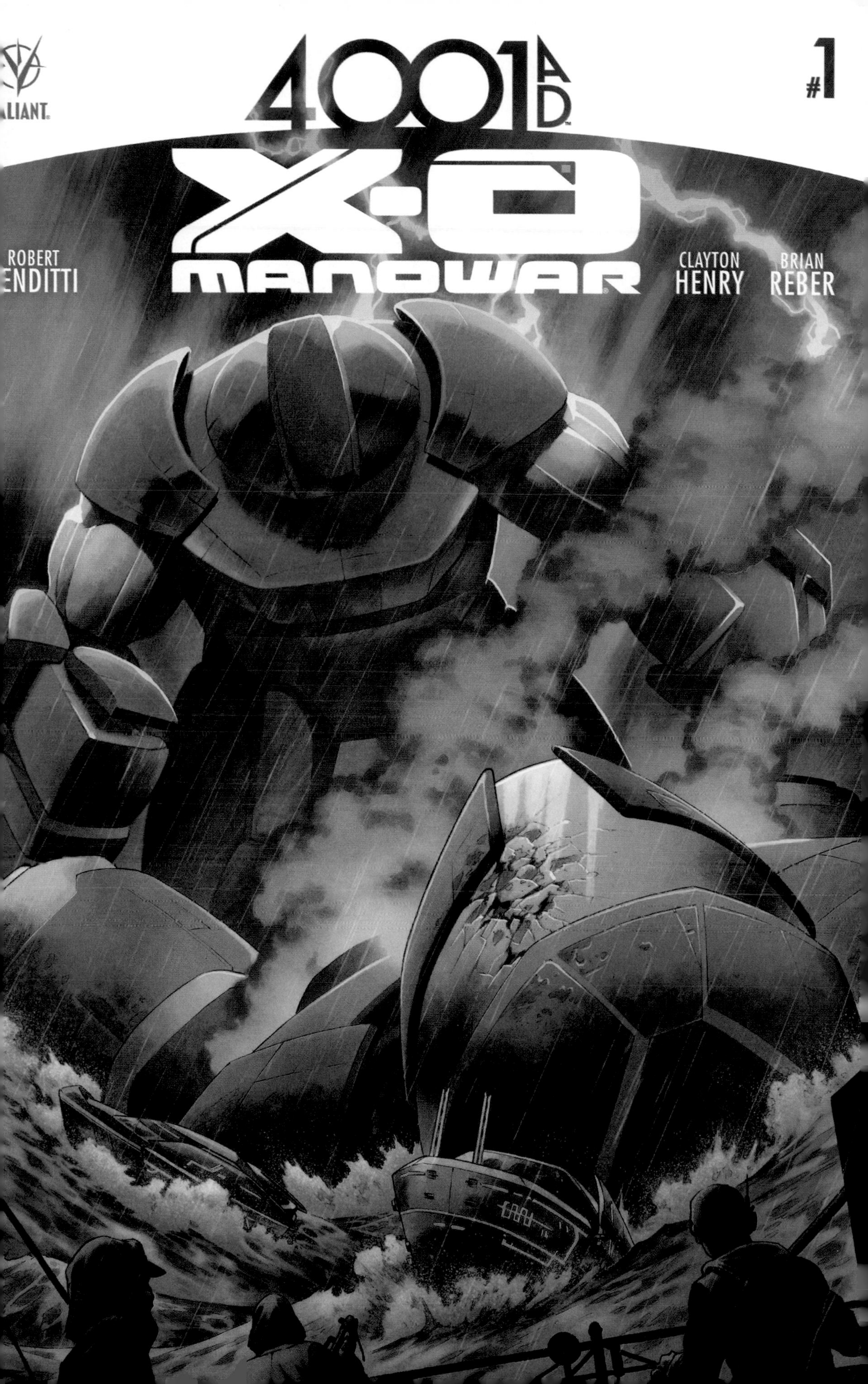

LIANT.
4001 A D
#1
X-O
MANOWAR
ROBERT
ENDITTI
CLAYTON
HENRY
BRIAN
REBER

4001 A.D.™

Rai was once the spirit guardian of New Japan.

Created by a sentient A.I. named Father, he was tasked with protecting New Japan. But when Rai learned of Father's corruption and cruelty, he joined a rebellion.

Father learned of Rai's betrayal and cast him down to Earth.

In Rai's absence, the rebels struck a blow to Father when they planted a viral bomb in his control center, damaging his ability to maintain total rule over New Japan.

Now, Rai has made his way back to New Japan with the help of The Eternal Warrior and Lemur, and hopes to save the country from Father's tyranny.

The consequences of their rebellion are felt even on the surface of the Earth, thousands of miles below...

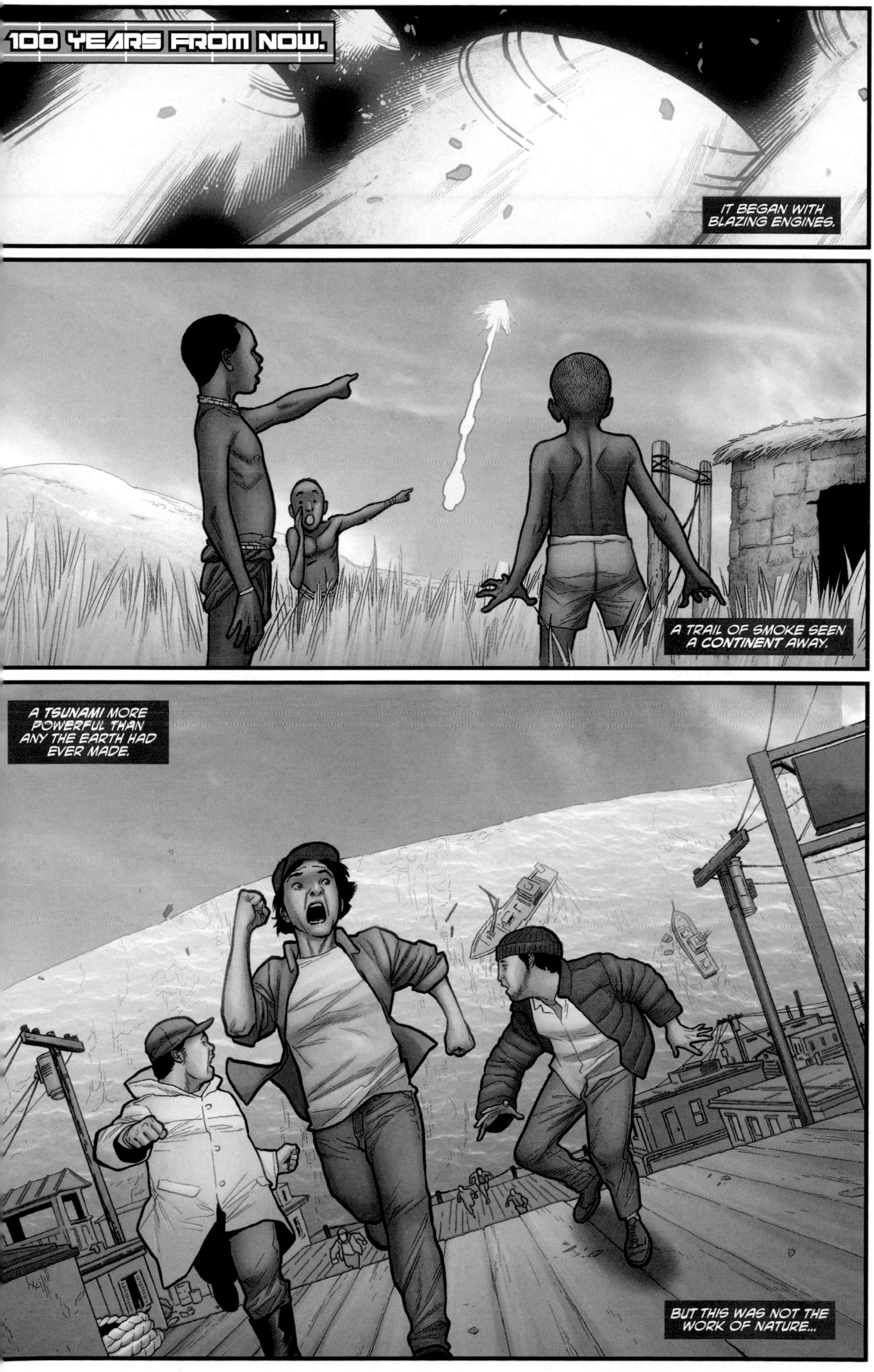
100 YEARS FROM NOW.
IT BEGAN WITH BLAZING ENGINES.
A TRAIL OF SMOKE SEEN A CONTINENT AWAY.
A TSUNAMI MORE POWERFUL THAN ANY THE EARTH HAD EVER MADE.
BUT THIS WAS NOT THE WORK OF NATURE...

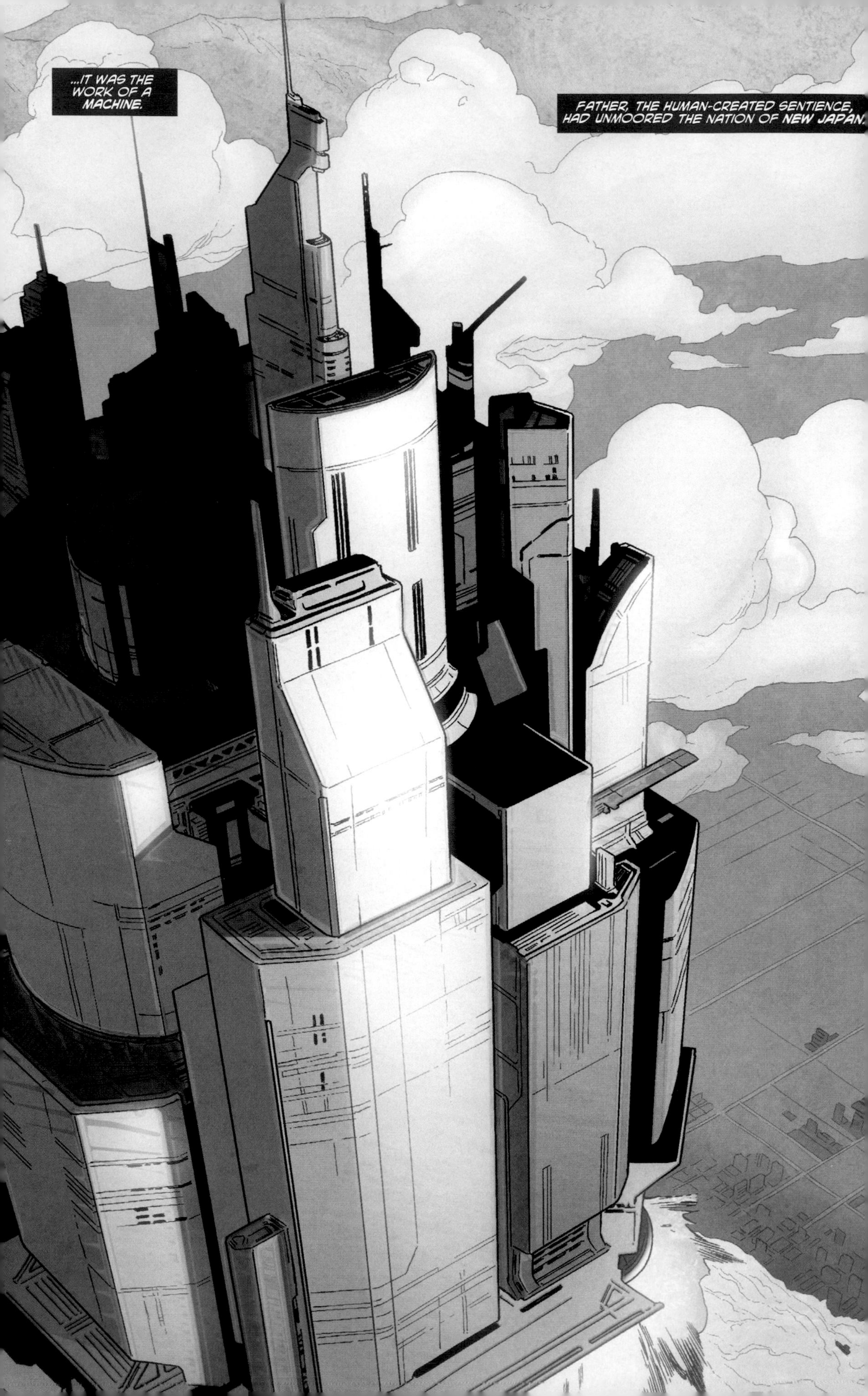
...IT WAS THE WORK OF A MACHINE.
FATHER, THE HUMAN-CREATED SENTIENCE, HAD UNMOORED THE NATION OF NEW JAPAN.

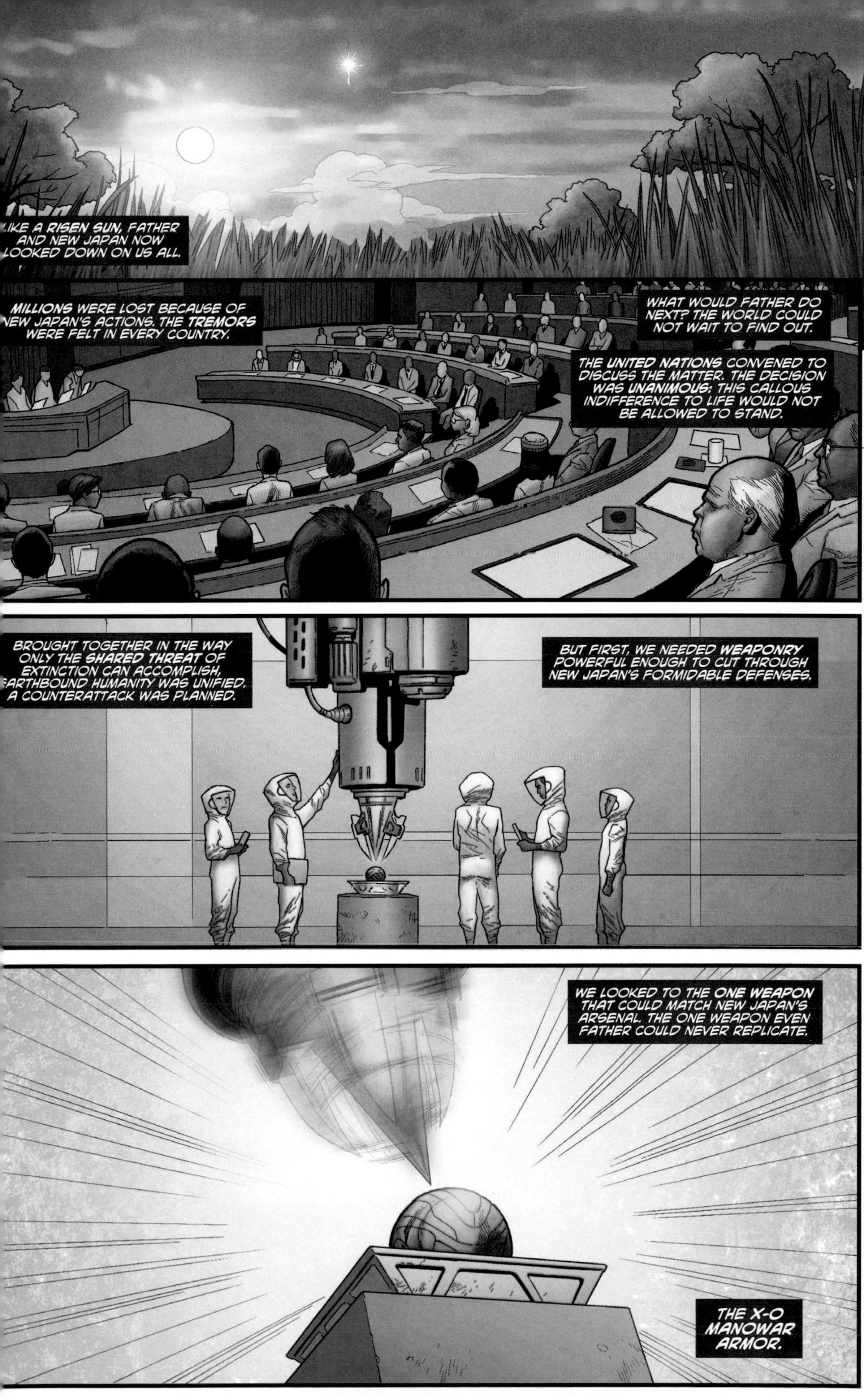
LIKE A RISEN SUN, FATHER AND NEW JAPAN NOW LOOKED DOWN ON US ALL.
MILLIONS WERE LOST BECAUSE OF NEW JAPAN'S ACTIONS. THE TREMORS WERE FELT IN EVERY COUNTRY.
WHAT WOULD FATHER DO NEXT? THE WORLD COULD NOT WAIT TO FIND OUT.
THE UNITED NATIONS CONVENED TO DISCUSS THE MATTER. THE DECISION WAS UNANIMOUS: THIS CALLOUS INDIFFERENCE TO LIFE WOULD NOT BE ALLOWED TO STAND.
BROUGHT TOGETHER IN THE WAY ONLY THE SHARED THREAT OF EXTINCTION CAN ACCOMPLISH, EARTHBOUND HUMANITY WAS UNIFIED. A COUNTERATTACK WAS PLANNED.
BUT FIRST, WE NEEDED WEAPONRY POWERFUL ENOUGH TO CUT THROUGH NEW JAPAN'S FORMIDABLE DEFENSES.
WE LOOKED TO THE ONE WEAPON THAT COULD MATCH NEW JAPAN'S ARSENAL. THE ONE WEAPON EVEN FATHER COULD NEVER REPLICATE.
THE X-O MANOWAR ARMOR.

X-O MANOWAR, WHO HAD ONCE CHALLENGED HUMANITY'S SOVEREIGN STATES.

X-O MANOWAR, WHO LATER *DEFENDED* THOSE SOVEREIGN STATES FROM EXTRA-TERRESTRIAL INVASIONS.

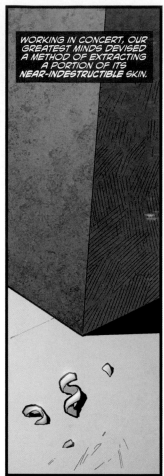

WORKING IN CONCERT, OUR GREATEST MINDS DEVISED A METHOD OF EXTRACTING A PORTION OF ITS *NEAR-INDESTRUCTIBLE* SKIN.

AS WITH PENICILLIN, THIS ONE, TINY SAMPLE--ONCE COPIED--WOULD BECOME THE SAVIOR OF *BILLIONS.*

THE MOST INTRICATE PLANS ARE REDUCED TO MERE INTENTION WITHOUT THE BUILDING BLOCKS REQUIRED TO MAKE THEM REALITY.

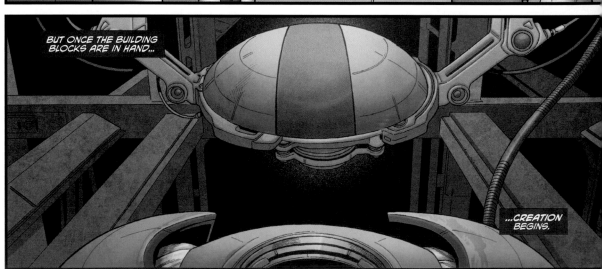

BUT ONCE THE BUILDING BLOCKS ARE IN HAND...

...CREATION BEGINS.

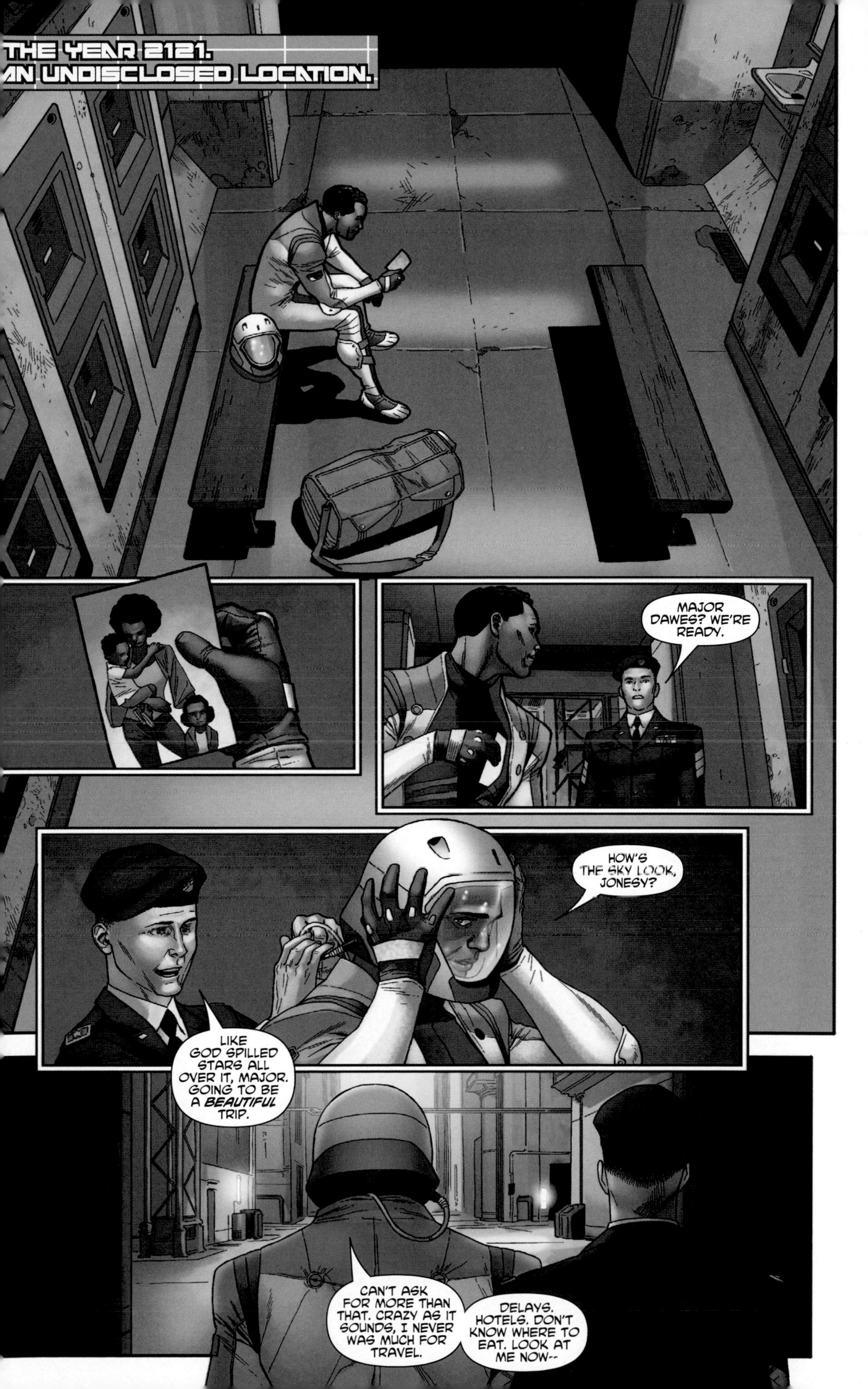
THE YEAR 2121.
AN UNDISCLOSED LOCATION.
MAJOR DAWES? WE'RE READY.
HOW'S THE SKY LOOK, JONESY?
LIKE GOD SPILLED STARS ALL OVER IT, MAJOR. GOING TO BE A *BEAUTIFUL* TRIP.
CAN'T ASK FOR MORE THAN THAT. CRAZY AS IT SOUNDS, I NEVER WAS MUCH FOR TRAVEL.
DELAYS. HOTELS. DON'T KNOW WHERE TO EAT. LOOK AT ME NOW--

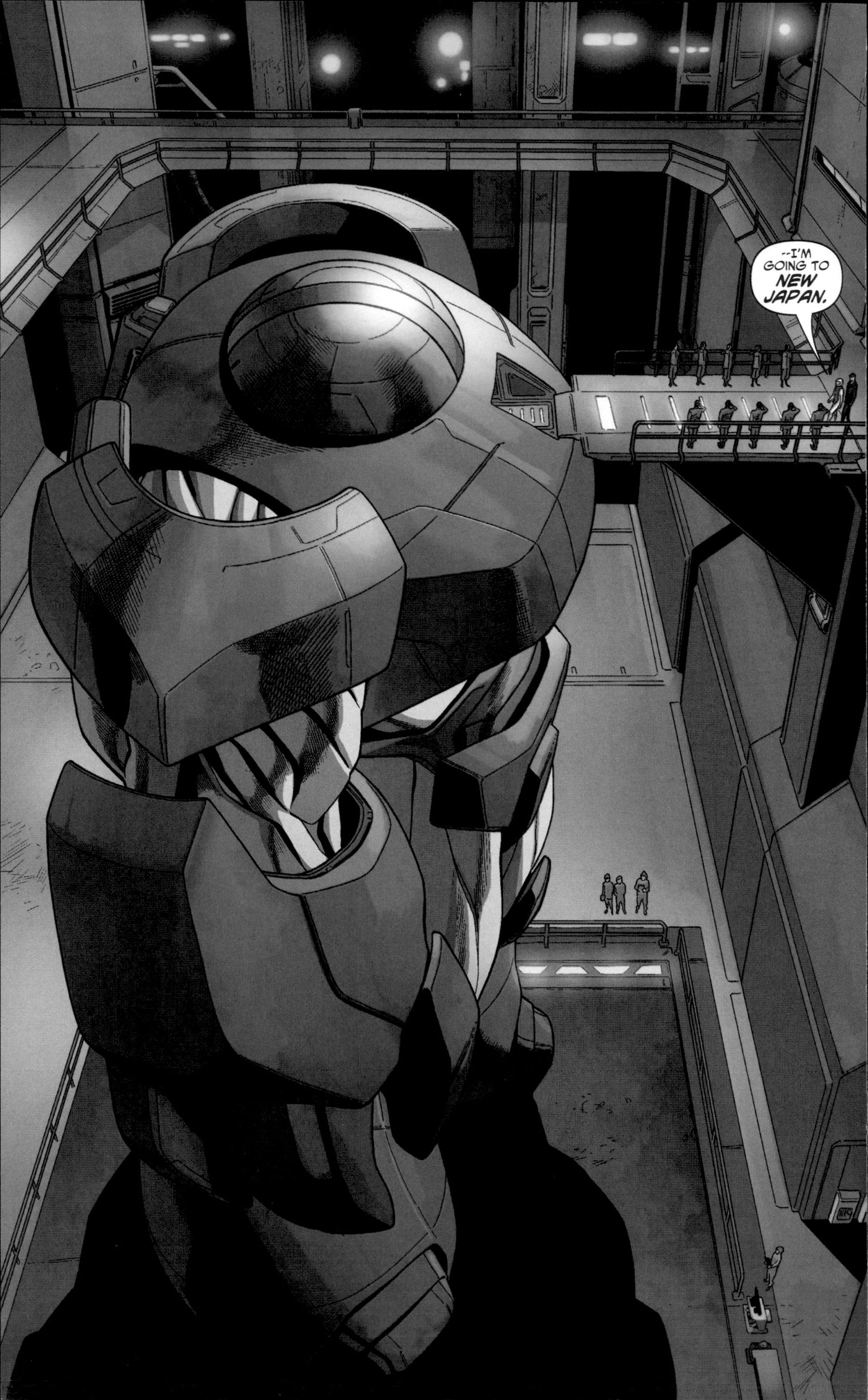
--I'M GOING TO NEW JAPAN.

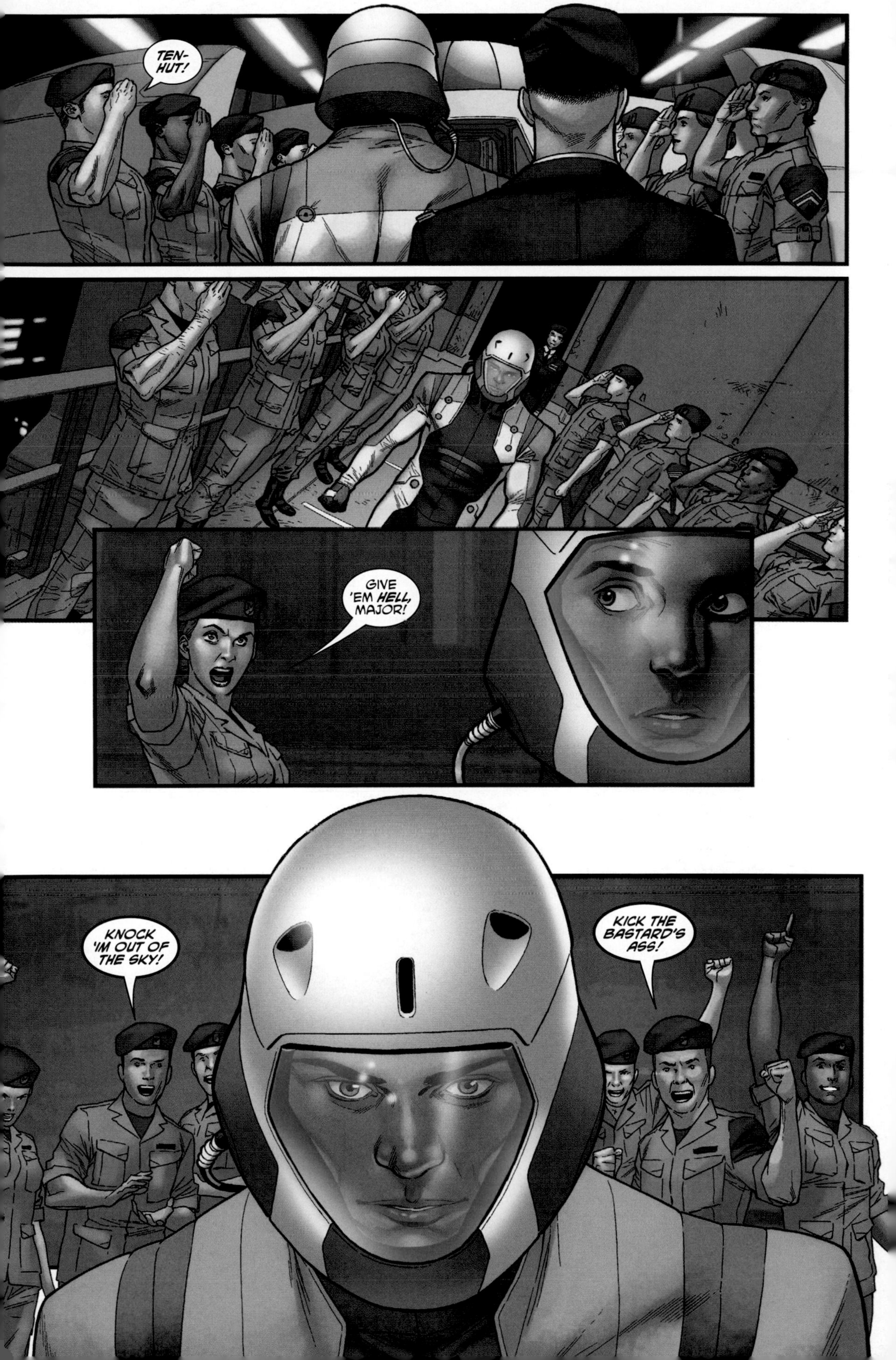
TEN-HUT!
GIVE 'EM HELL, MAJOR!
KNOCK 'IM OUT OF THE SKY!
KICK THE BASTARD'S ASS!

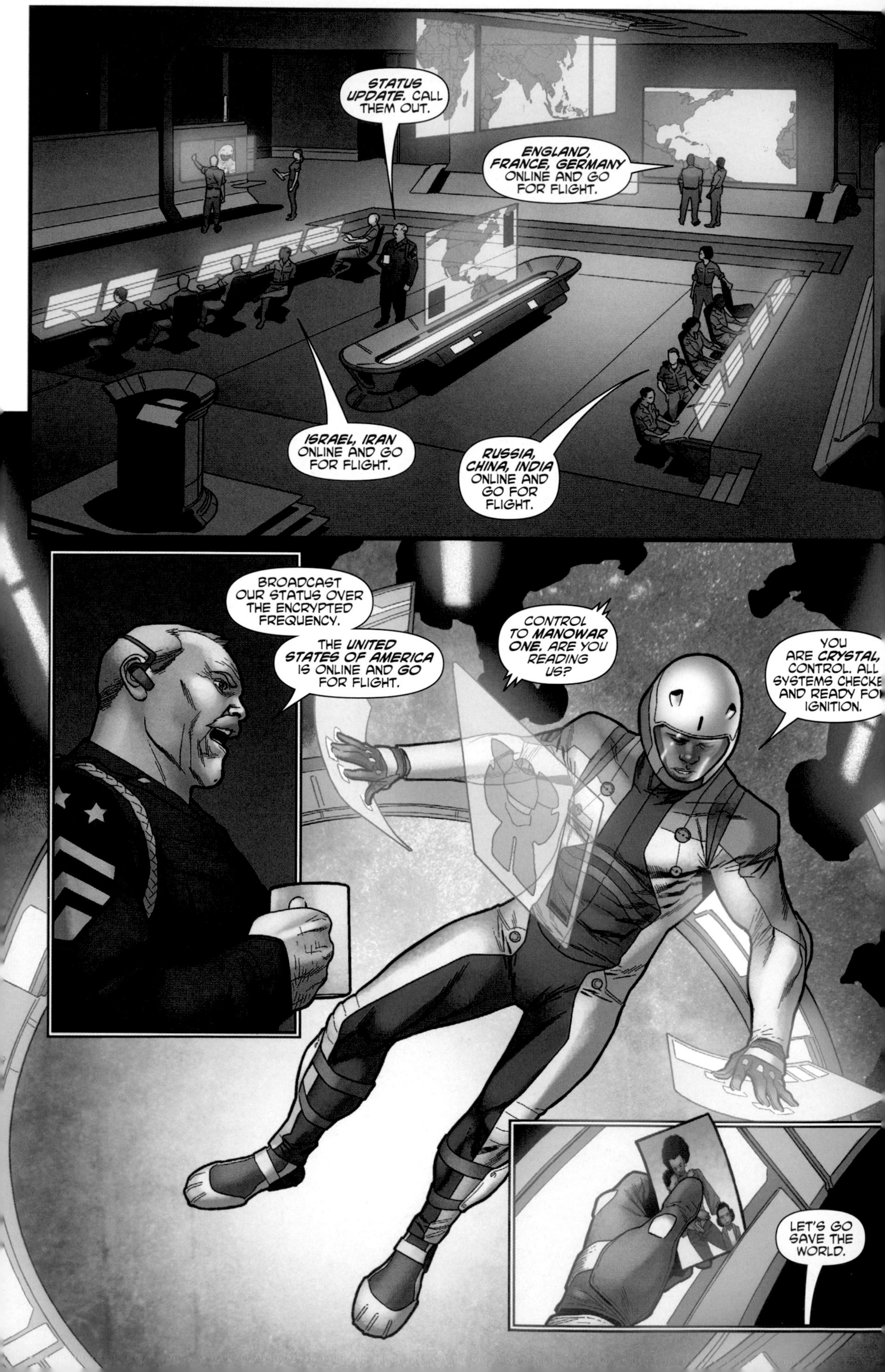
STATUS UPDATE. CALL THEM OUT.
ENGLAND, FRANCE, GERMANY ONLINE AND GO FOR FLIGHT.
ISRAEL, IRAN ONLINE AND GO FOR FLIGHT.
RUSSIA, CHINA, INDIA ONLINE AND GO FOR FLIGHT.
BROADCAST OUR STATUS OVER THE ENCRYPTED FREQUENCY.
THE UNITED STATES OF AMERICA IS ONLINE AND GO FOR FLIGHT.
CONTROL TO MANOWAR ONE. ARE YOU READING US?
YOU ARE CRYSTAL, CONTROL. ALL SYSTEMS CHECKE AND READY FO IGNITION.
LET'S GO SAVE THE WORLD.

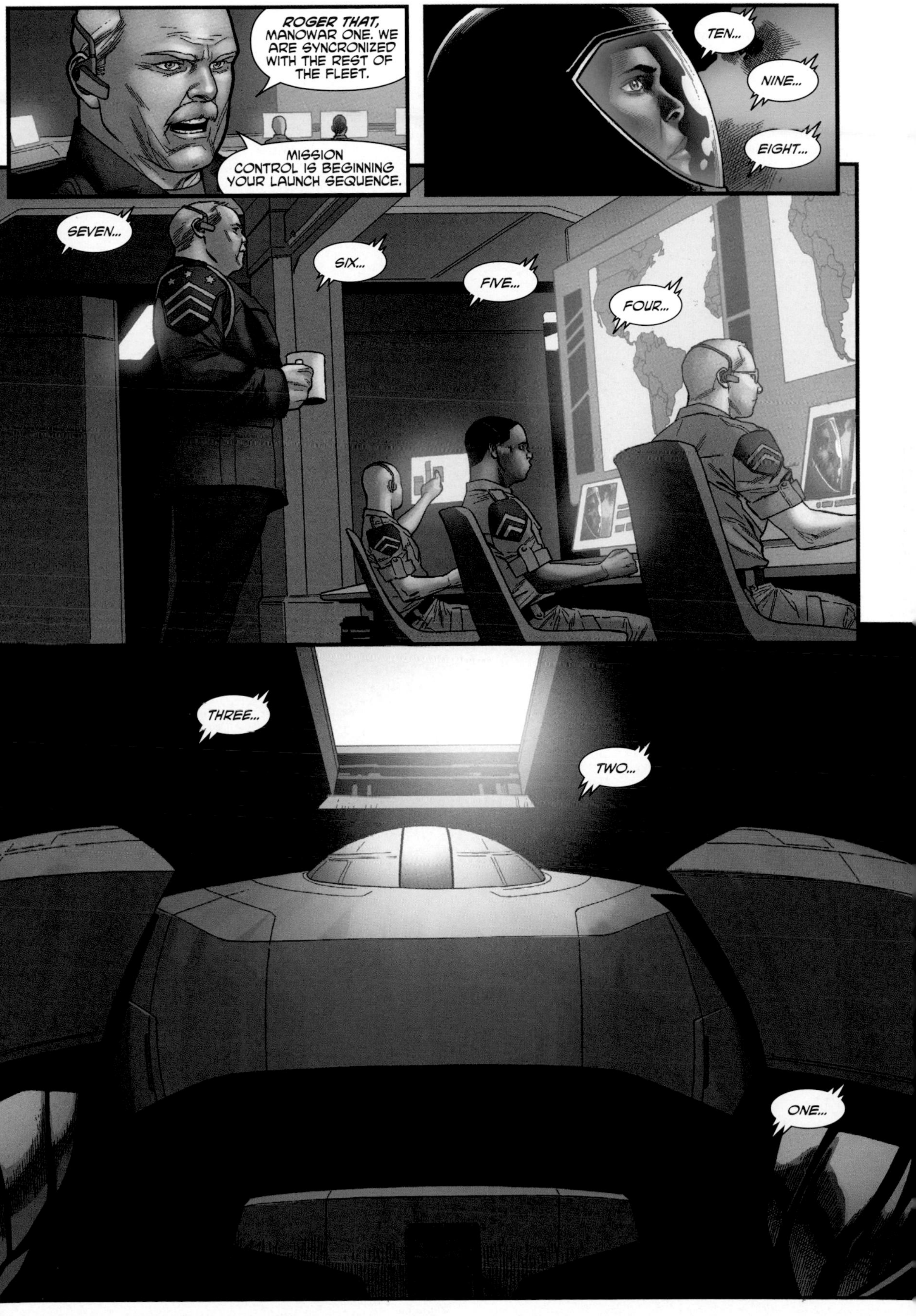
ROGER THAT, MANOWAR ONE. WE ARE SYNCRONIZED WITH THE REST OF THE FLEET.
MISSION CONTROL IS BEGINNING YOUR LAUNCH SEQUENCE.
TEN...
NINE...
EIGHT...
SEVEN...
SIX...
FIVE...
FOUR...
THREE...
TWO...
ONE...

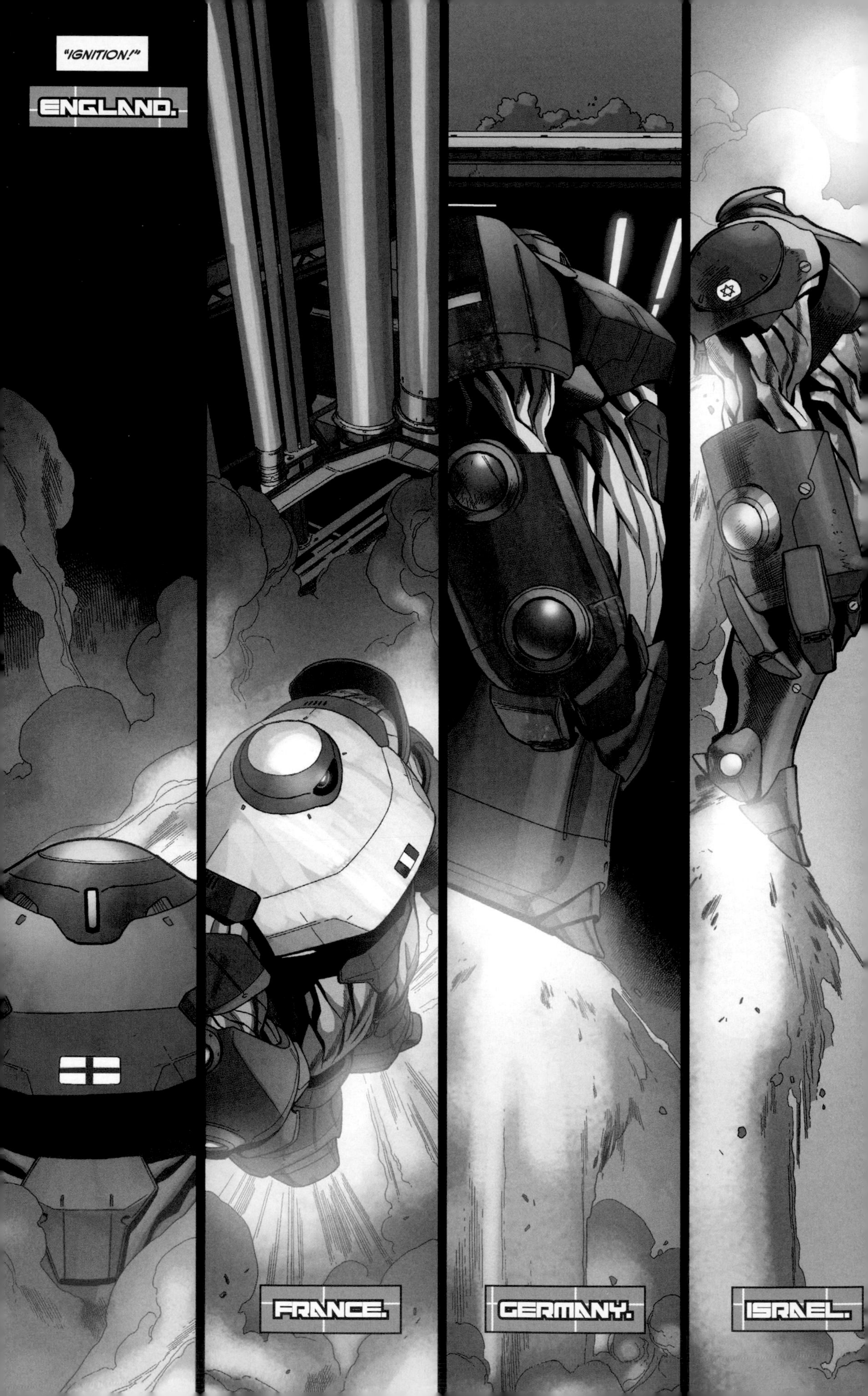
"IGNITION!"
ENGLAND.
FRANCE.
GERMANY.
ISRAEL.

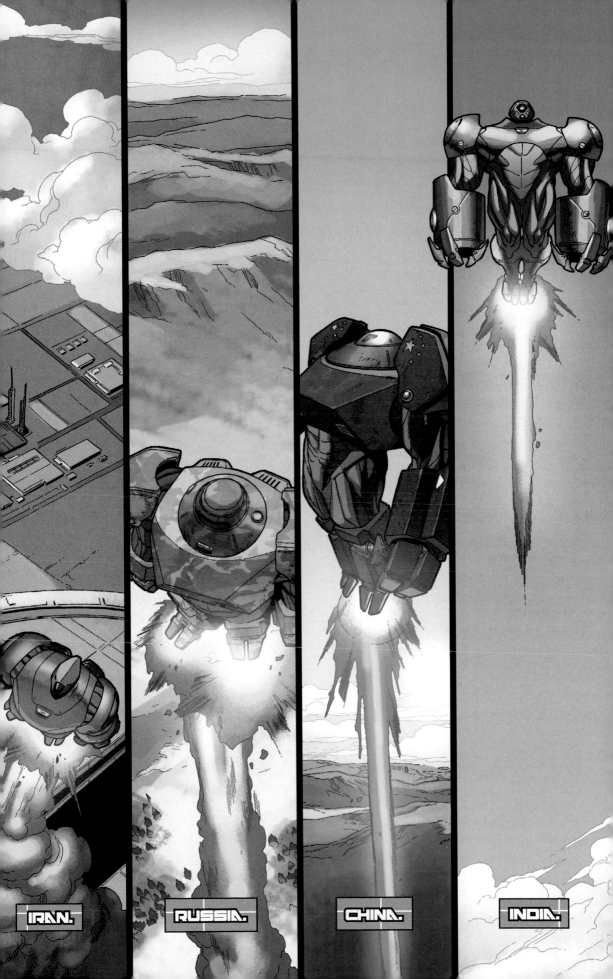

IRAN.

RUSSIA.

CHINA.

INDIA.

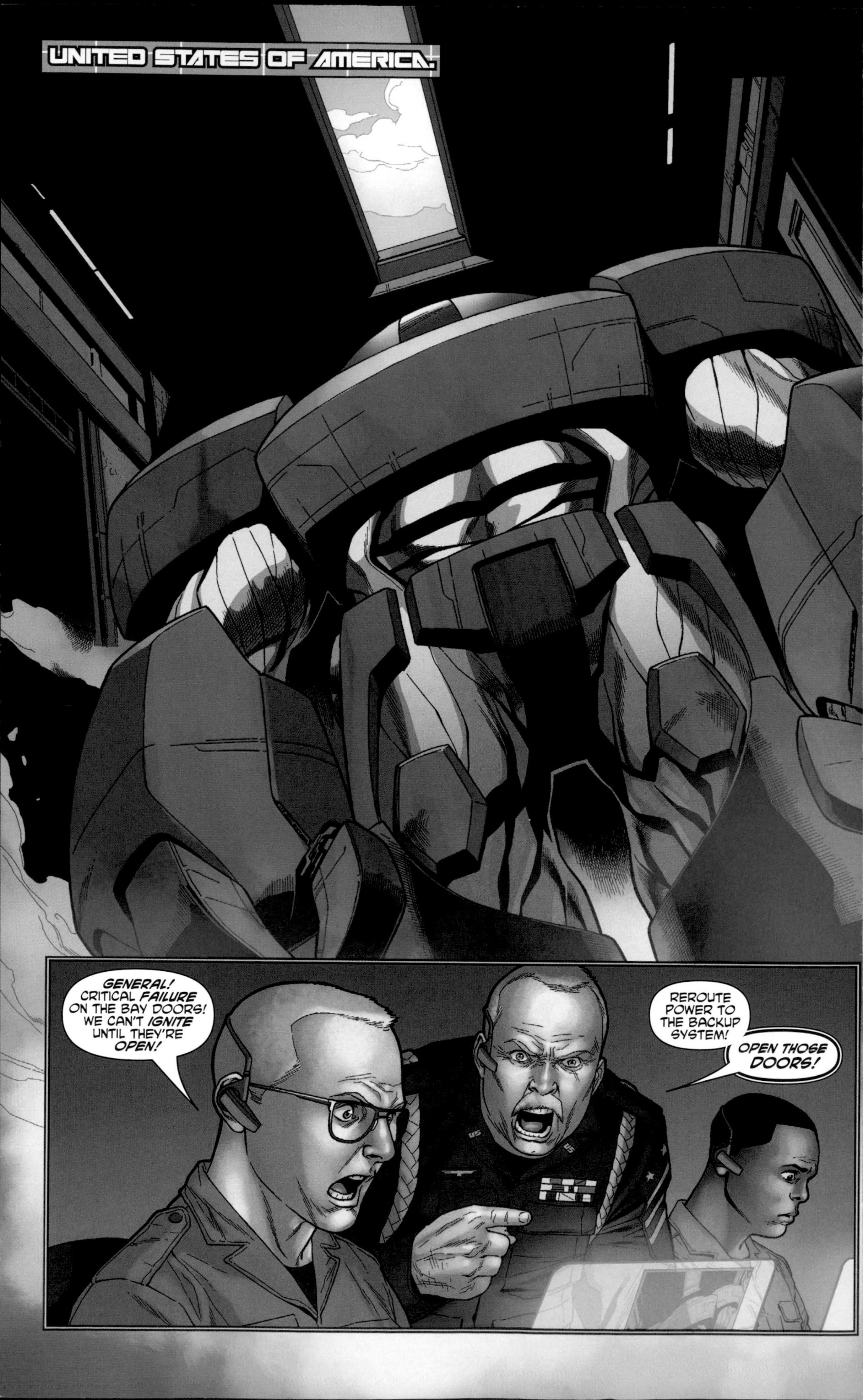
UNITED STATES OF AMERICA.
GENERAL! CRITICAL FAILURE ON THE BAY DOORS! WE CAN'T IGNITE UNTIL THEY'RE OPEN!
REROUTE POWER TO THE BACKUP SYSTEM!
OPEN THOSE DOORS!

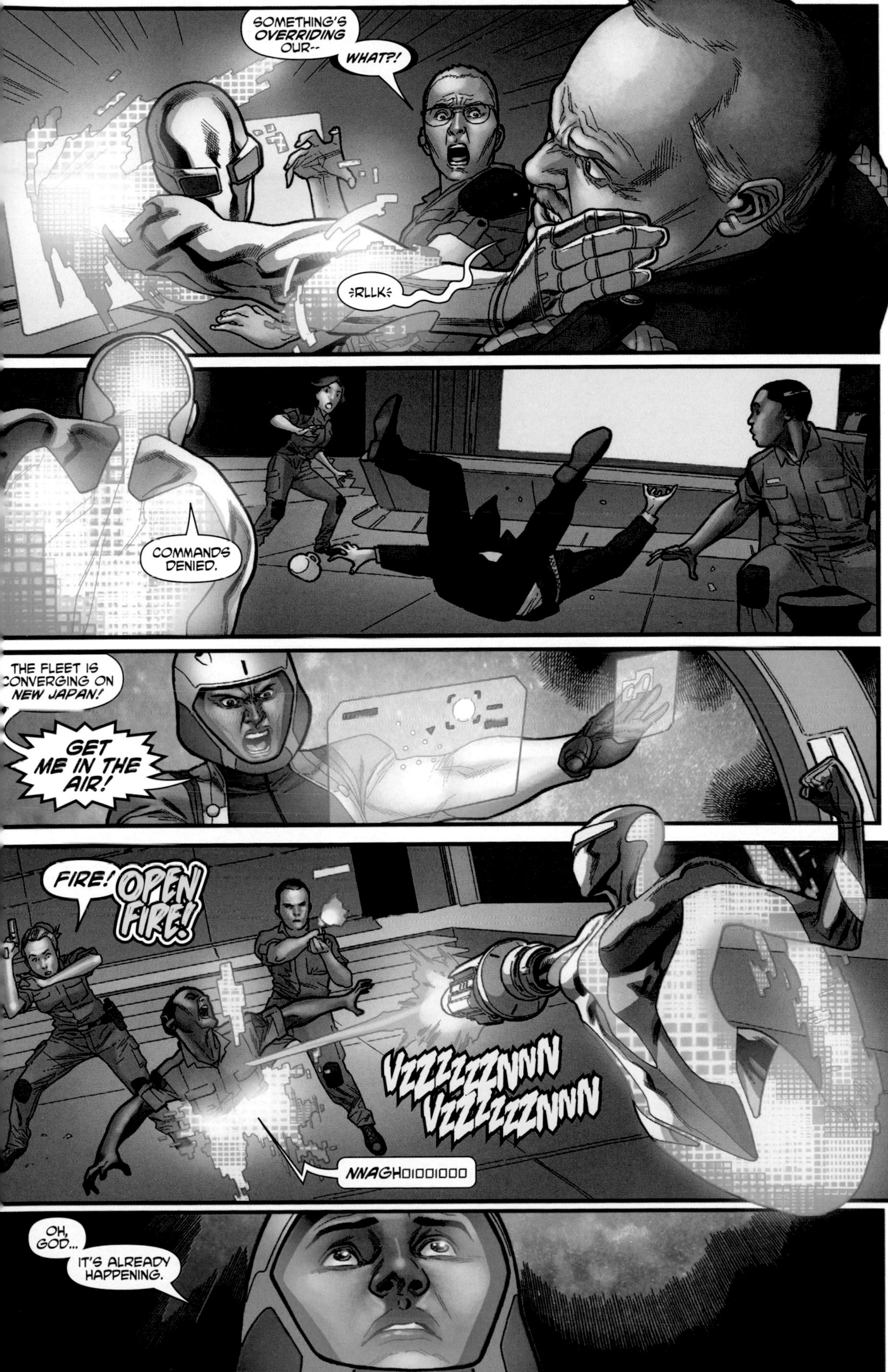
SOMETHING'S OVERRIDING OUR--
WHAT?!
RLLK
COMMANDS DENIED.
THE FLEET IS CONVERGING ON NEW JAPAN!
GET ME IN THE AIR!
FIRE!
OPEN FIRE!
VZZZZZZNNN VZZZZZZNNN
NNAGH01001000
OH, GOD...
IT'S ALREADY HAPPENING.

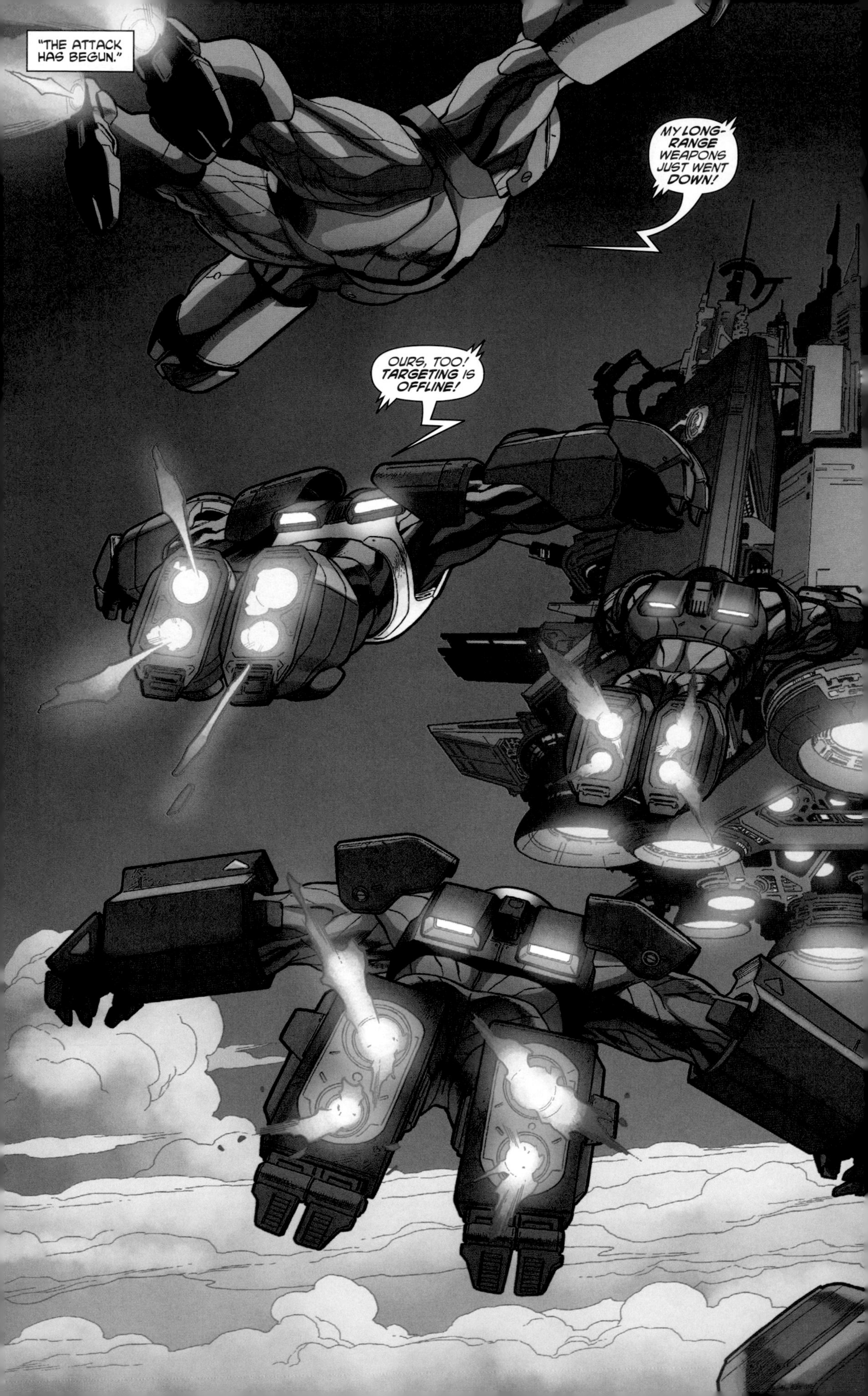
"THE ATTACK HAS BEGUN."
MY LONG-RANGE WEAPONS JUST WENT DOWN!
OURS, TOO! TARGETING IS OFFLINE!

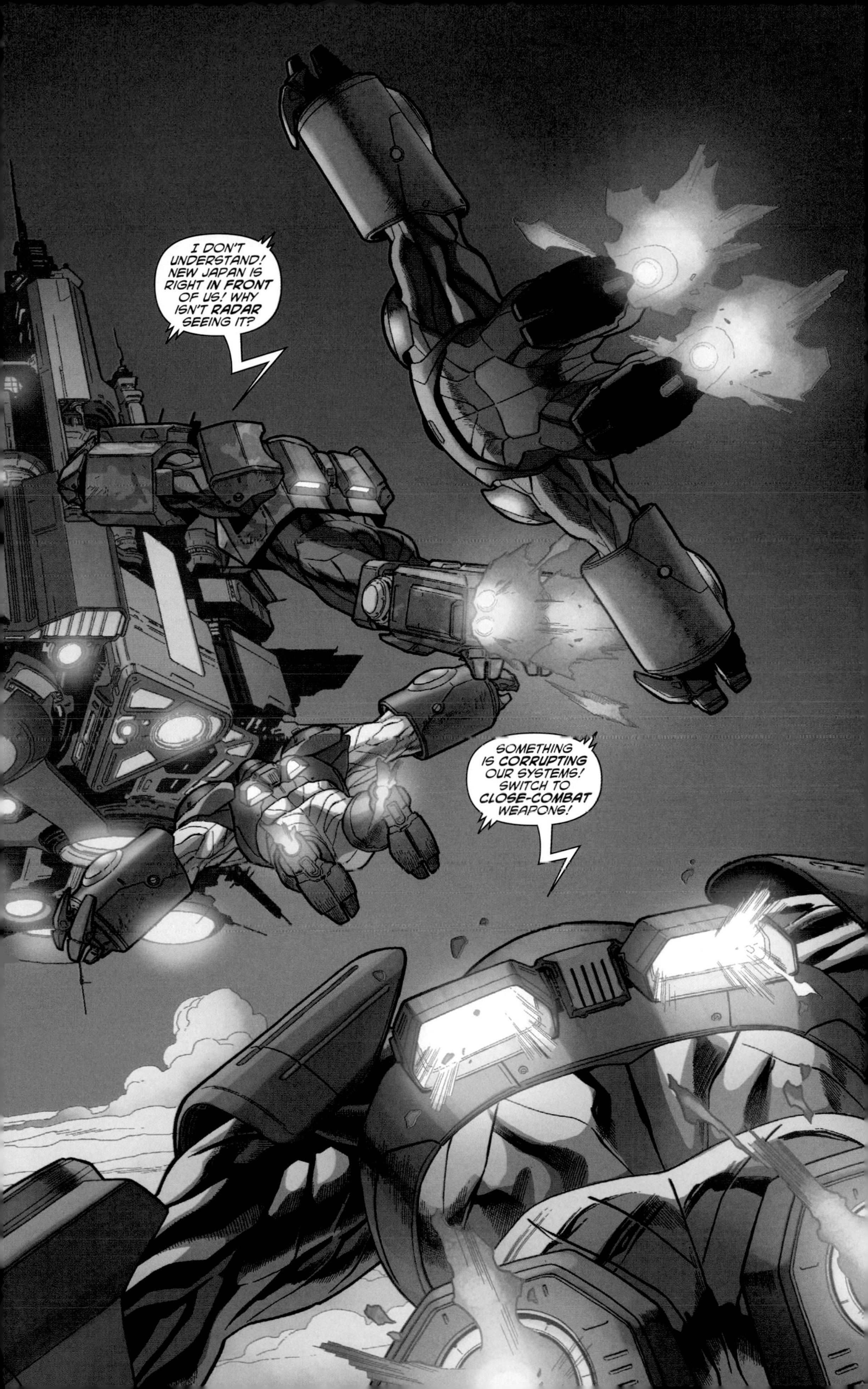
I DON'T UNDERSTAND! NEW JAPAN IS RIGHT IN FRONT OF US! WHY ISN'T RADAR SEEING IT?
SOMETHING IS CORRUPTING OUR SYSTEMS! SWITCH TO CLOSE-COMBAT WEAPONS!

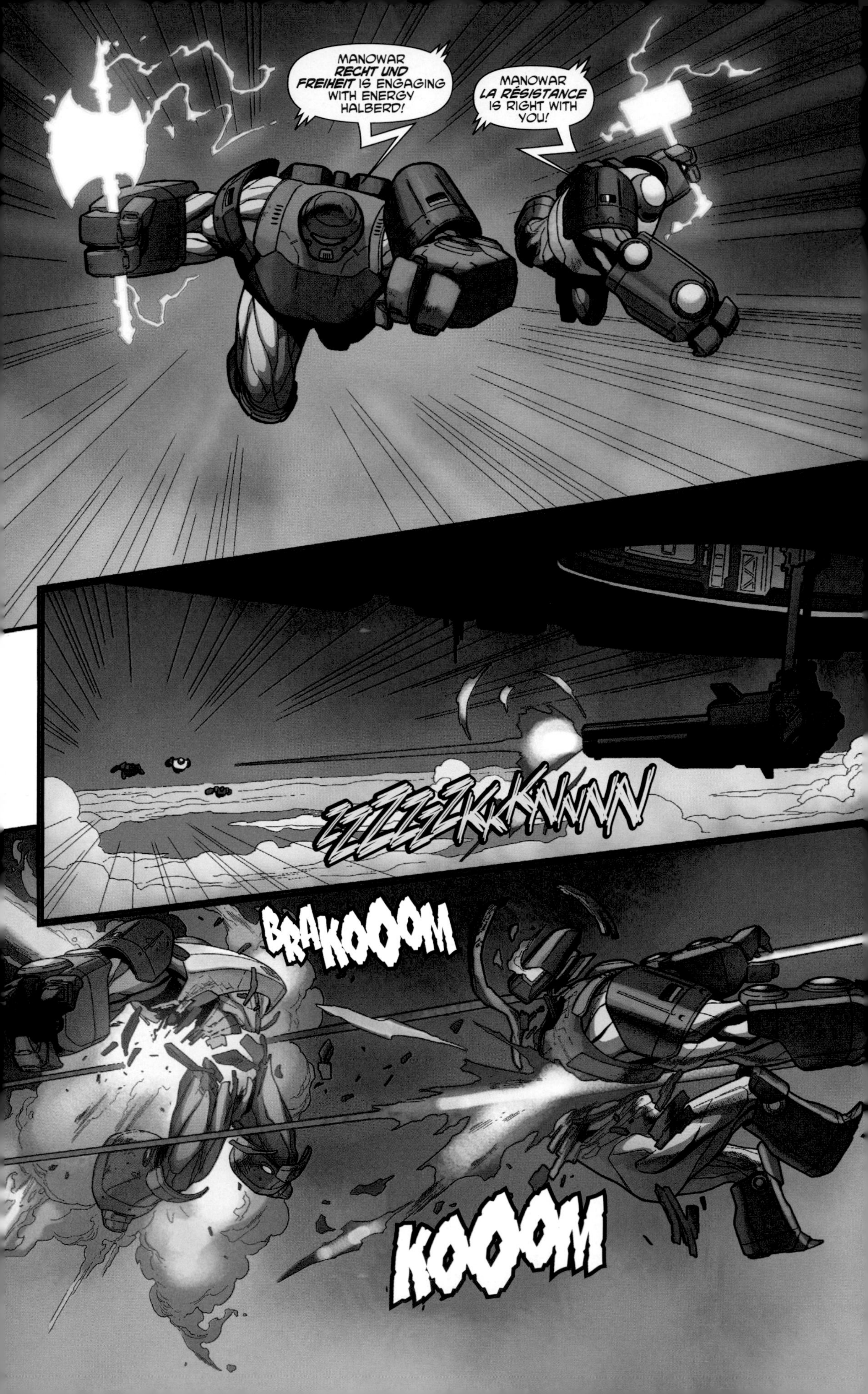

MANOWAR RECHT UND FREIHEIT IS ENGAGING WITH ENERGY HALBERD!
MANOWAR LA RÉSISTANCE IS RIGHT WITH YOU!
ZZZZZZKKKKNNNN
BRAKOOOOM
KOOOM

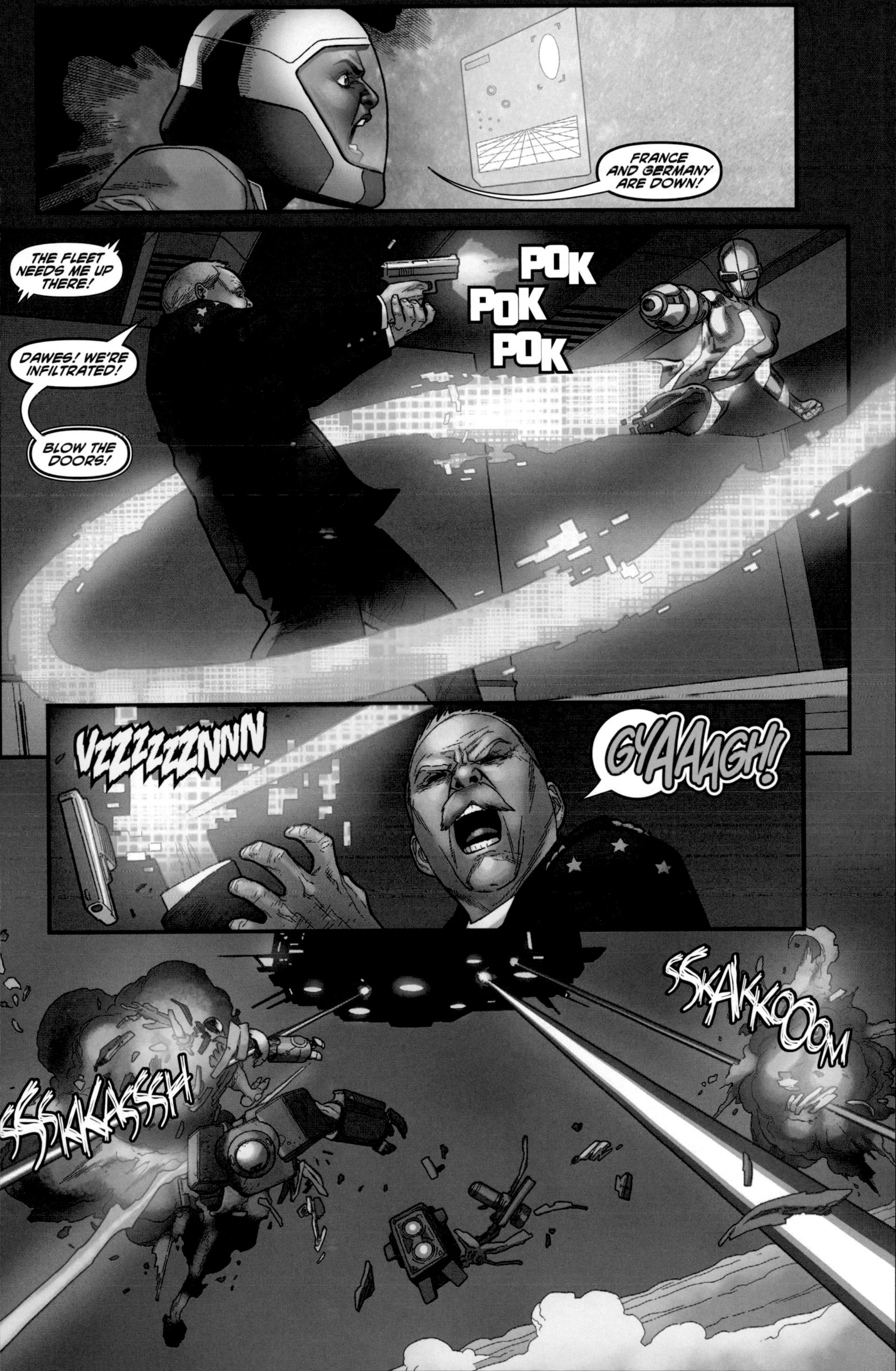
FRANCE AND GERMANY ARE DOWN!
THE FLEET NEEDS ME UP THERE!
POK
POK
POK
DAWES! WE'RE INFILTRATED!
BLOW THE DOORS!
VZZZZZZNNN
GYAAAGH!
SSKAKKOOOM
SSSKAKASSSH

PREPARING FOR SELF-LAUNCH!

THAT *BASTARD* "FATHER" SENT YOU.

HE WON'T STOP US.

ALREADY HAS.

YOUR STRATAGEM: APPARENT.

FATHER SEES ALL.

CHARGING CANNONS!

OPPOSITION NEUTRALIZED.

DOORS TARGETED!

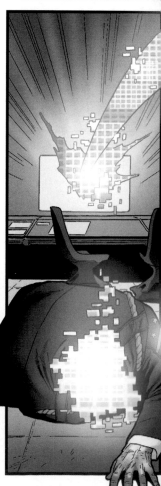

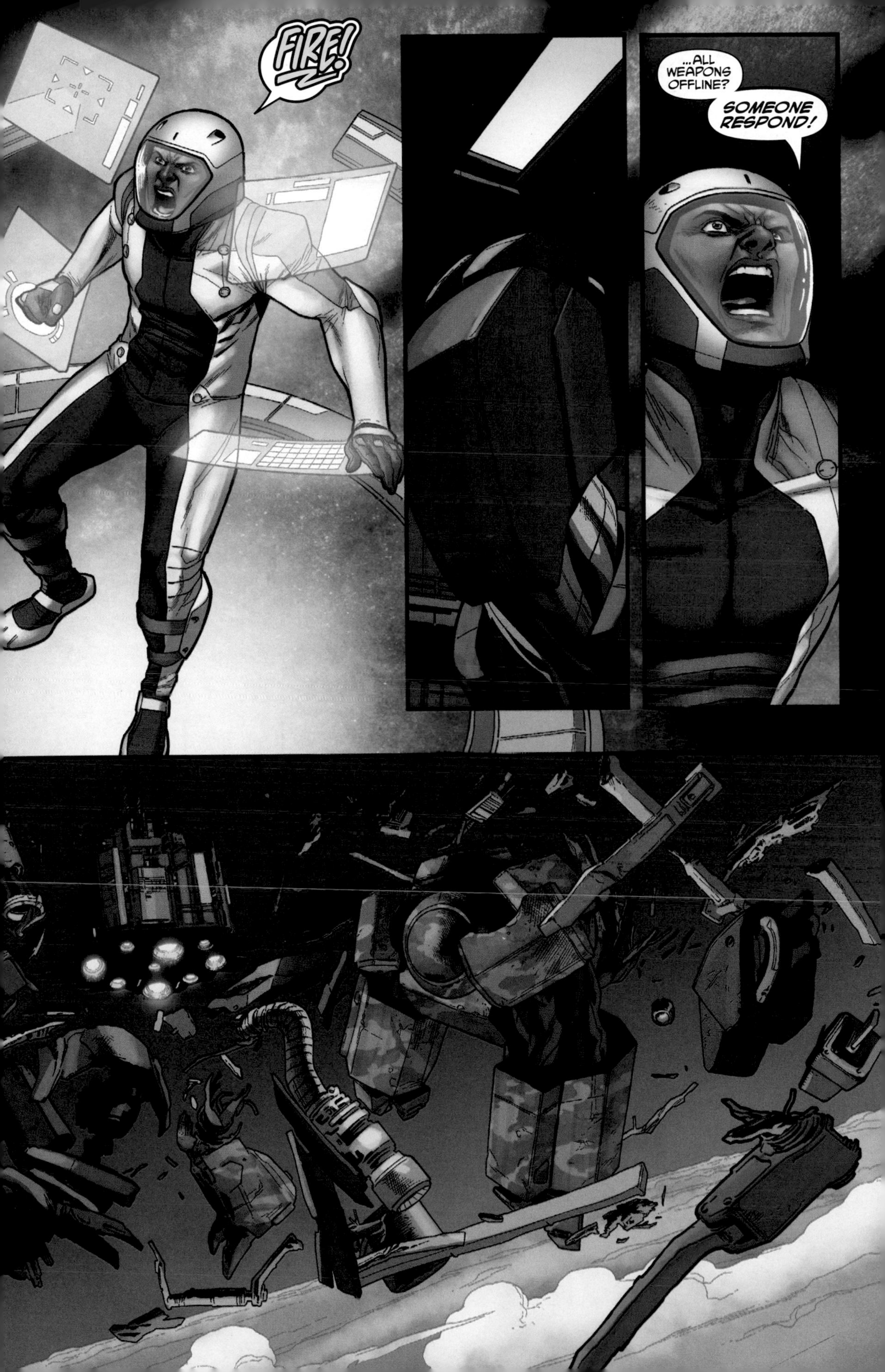
FIRE!
...ALL WEAPONS OFFLINE?
SOMEONE RESPOND!

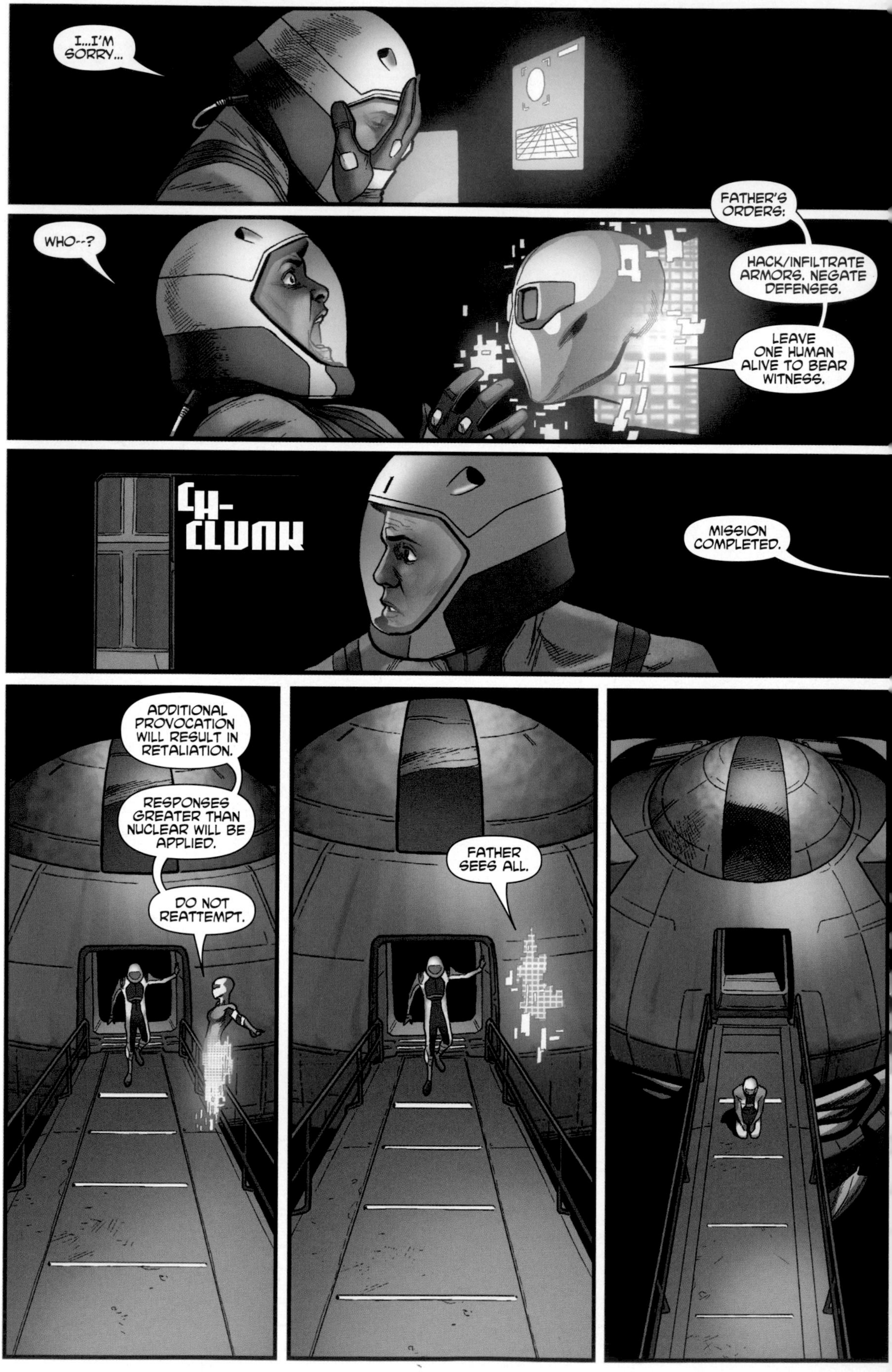
I...I'M SORRY...
WHO--?
FATHER'S ORDERS:
HACK/INFILTRATE ARMORS. NEGATE DEFENSES.
LEAVE ONE HUMAN ALIVE TO BEAR WITNESS.
CH-CLUNK
MISSION COMPLETED.
ADDITIONAL PROVOCATION WILL RESULT IN RETALIATION.
RESPONSES GREATER THAN NUCLEAR WILL BE APPLIED.
DO NOT REATTEMPT.
FATHER SEES ALL.

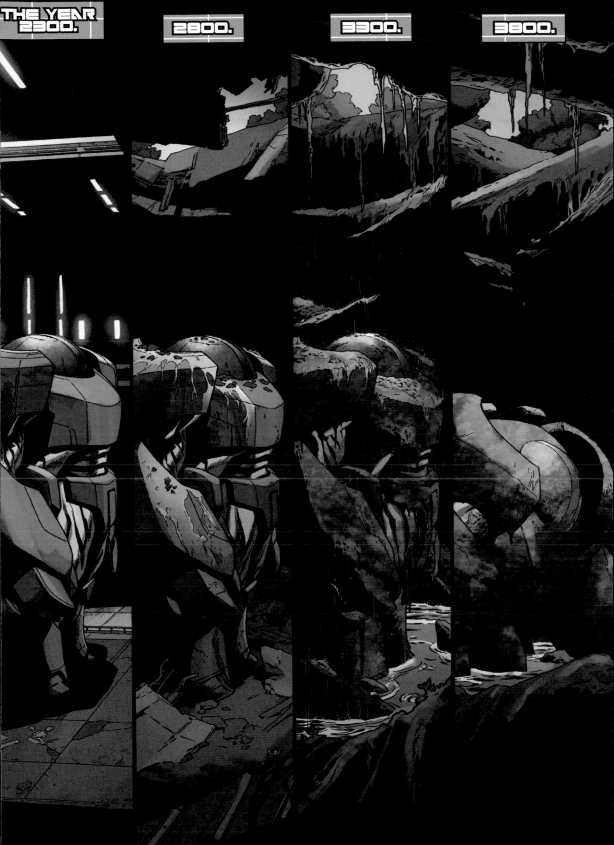

THE YEAR 2300.

2800.

3300.

3800.

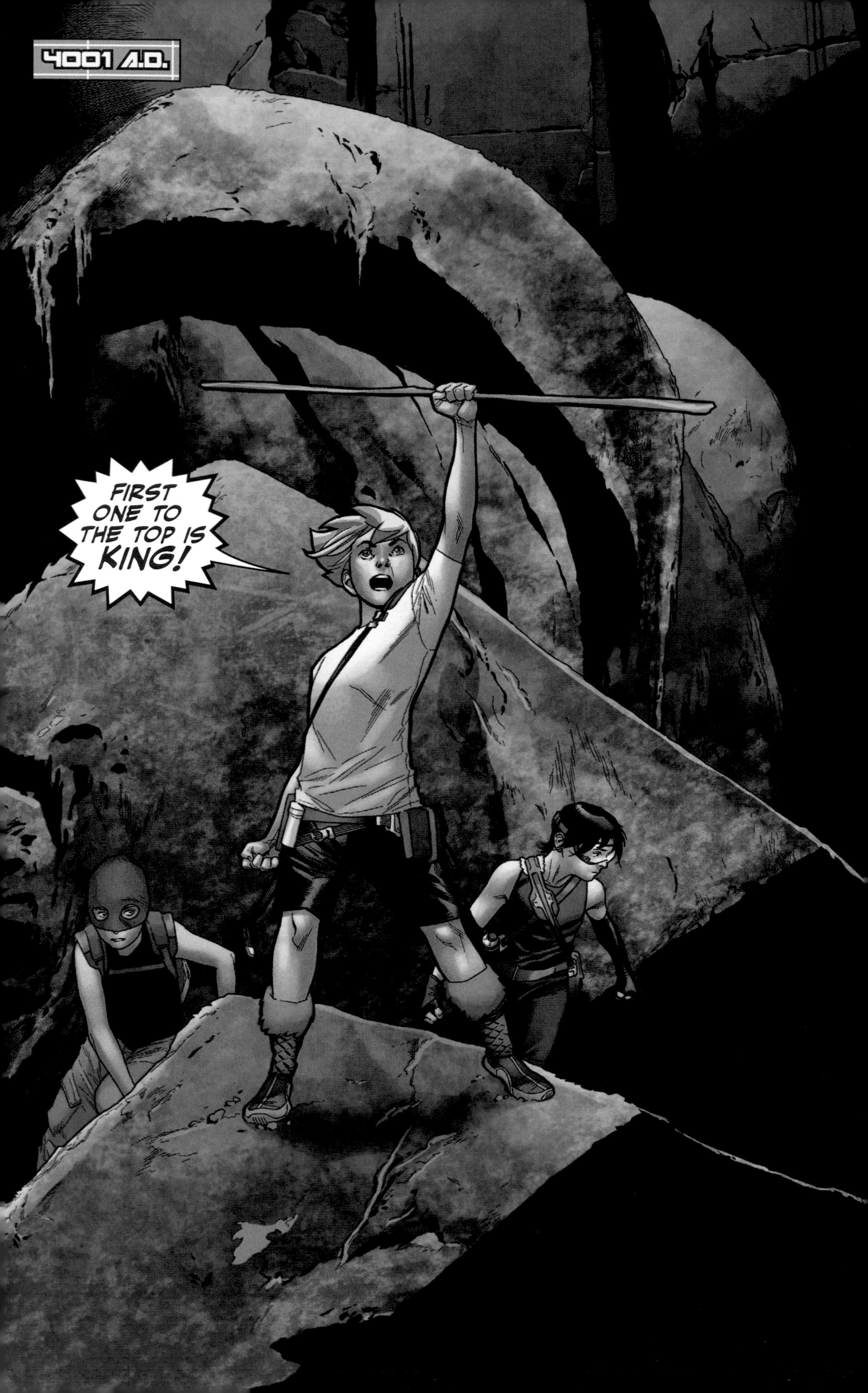
4001 A.D.
FIRST ONE TO THE TOP IS KING!

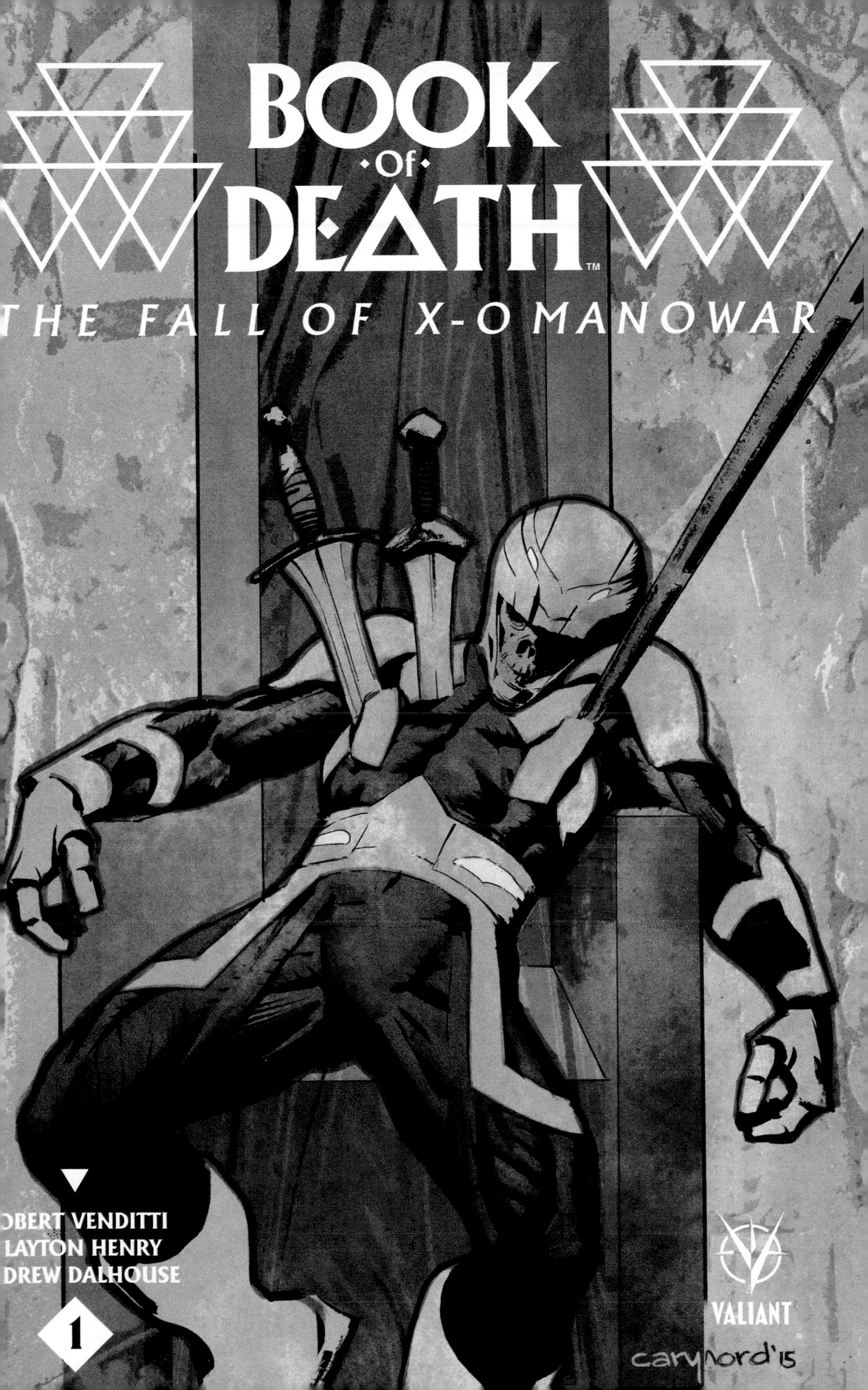
BOOK
Of
DEATH™
THE FALL OF X-O MANOWAR
OBERT VENDITTI
LAYTON HENRY
DREW DALHOUSE
1
VALIANT
carynord'15

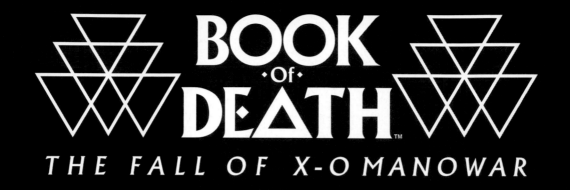

BOOK OF DEATH

THE FALL OF X-O MANOWAR

X-O Manowar is Aric of Dacia, a Visigoth warrior abducted by aliens and the returned to an Earth centuries after the time he left behind.

A slave to the alien race known as The Vine, Aric led a slave uprising and captured the sentient armor Shanhara, a being worshipped as a deity by Th Vine. Bonded to Shanhara, Aric freed his fellow slaves and returned to his home planet - only to discover centuries had passed and the world he knev was gone. He lost his home but found a new purpose as the protector of Earth.

The Book of the Geomancer was brought to the present by a young girl named Tama. The tome foretells a dark future for the Valiant Universe and speaks to the fates of many of its heroes.

This is the story of the fall of X-O Manowar...

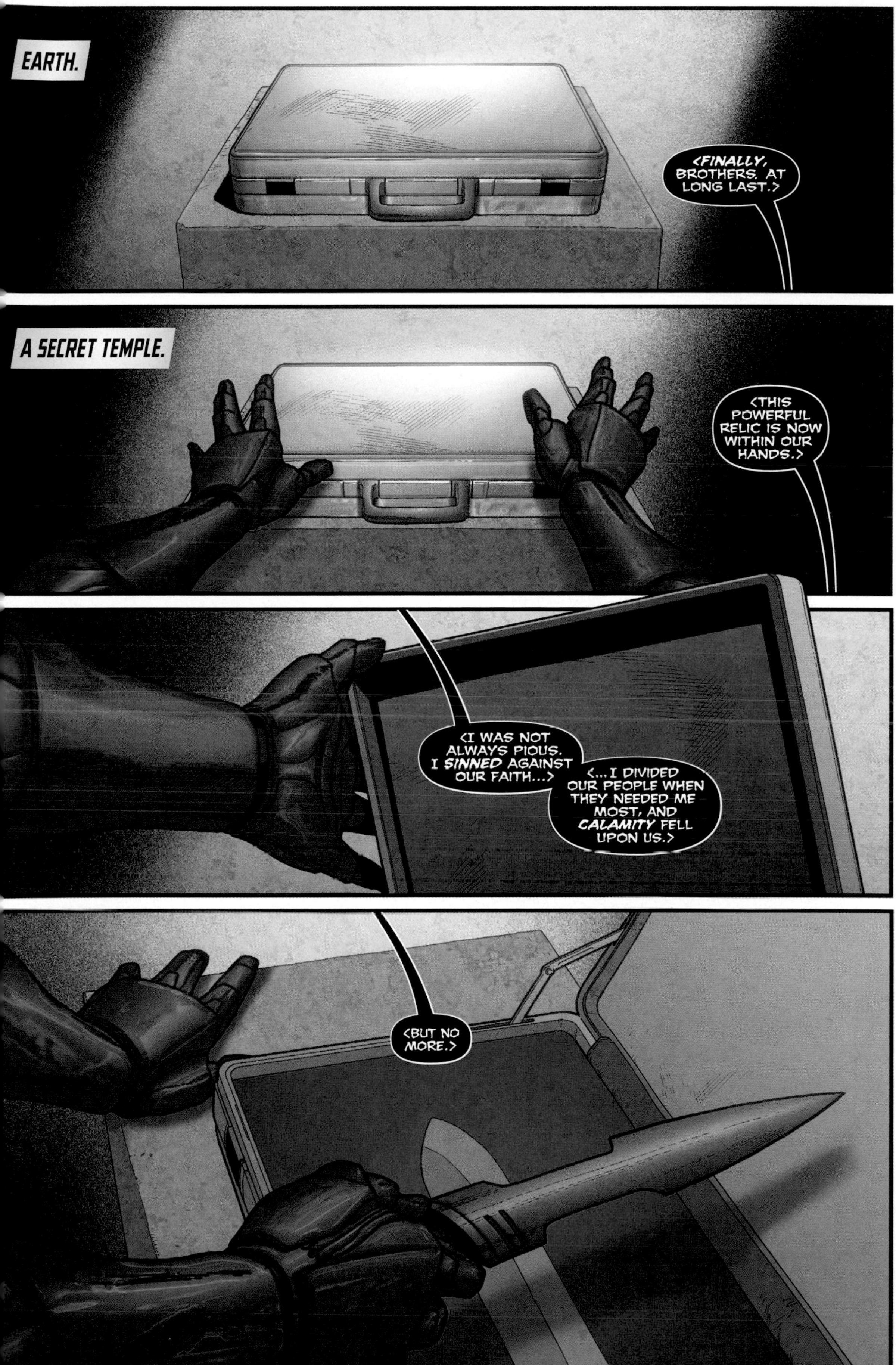
EARTH.
<FINALLY, BROTHERS. AT LONG LAST.>
A SECRET TEMPLE.
<THIS POWERFUL RELIC IS NOW WITHIN OUR HANDS.>
<I WAS NOT ALWAYS PIOUS. I SINNED AGAINST OUR FAITH...>
<...I DIVIDED OUR PEOPLE WHEN THEY NEEDED ME MOST, AND CALAMITY FELL UPON US.>
<BUT NO MORE.>

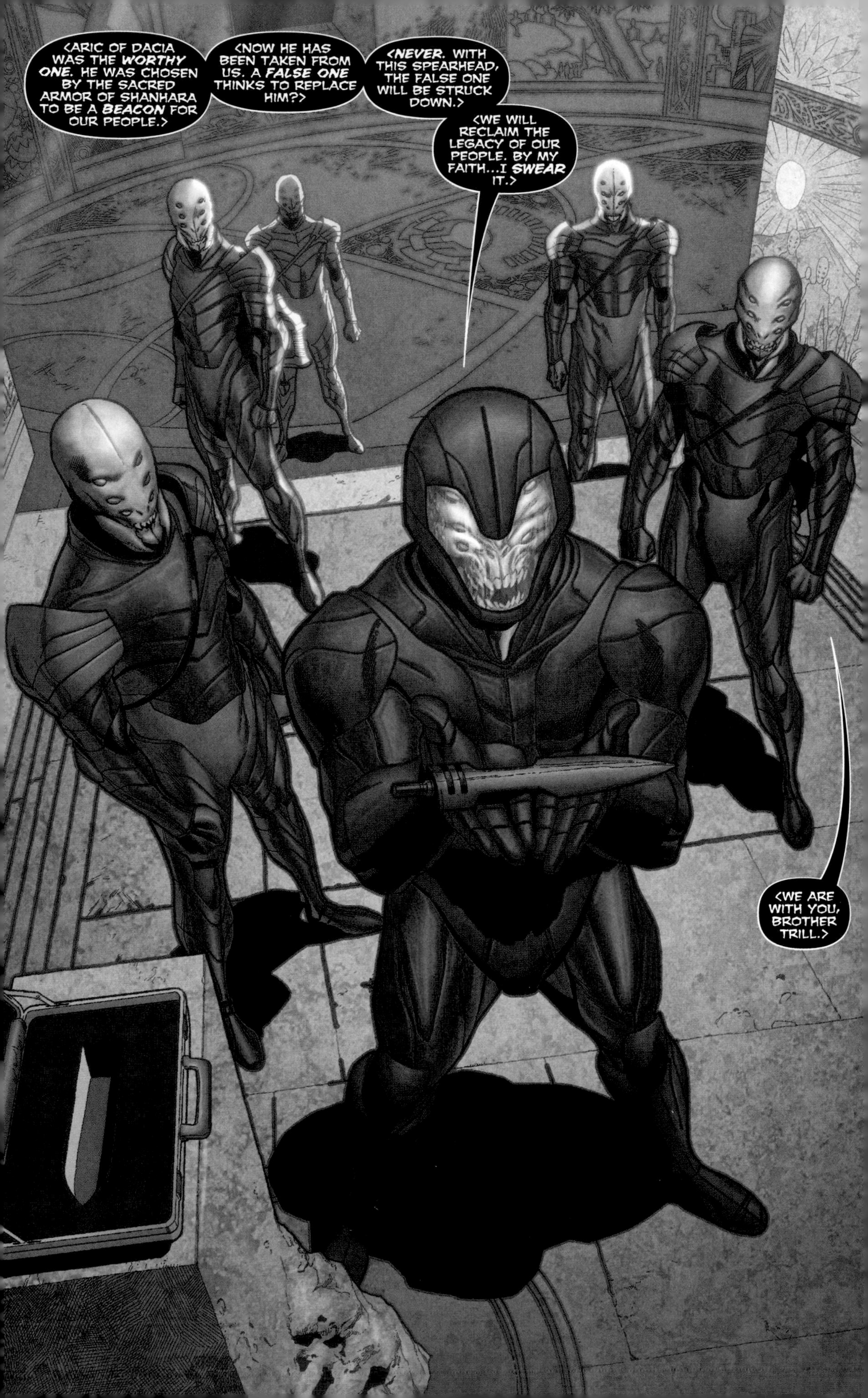
<ARIC OF DACIA WAS THE *WORTHY ONE.* HE WAS CHOSEN BY THE SACRED ARMOR OF SHANHARA TO BE A *BEACON* FOR OUR PEOPLE.>
<NOW HE HAS BEEN TAKEN FROM US. A *FALSE ONE* THINKS TO REPLACE HIM?>
<*NEVER.* WITH THIS SPEARHEAD, THE FALSE ONE WILL BE STRUCK DOWN.>
<WE WILL RECLAIM THE LEGACY OF OUR PEOPLE. BY MY FAITH...I *SWEAR* IT.>
<WE ARE WITH YOU, BROTHER TRILL.>

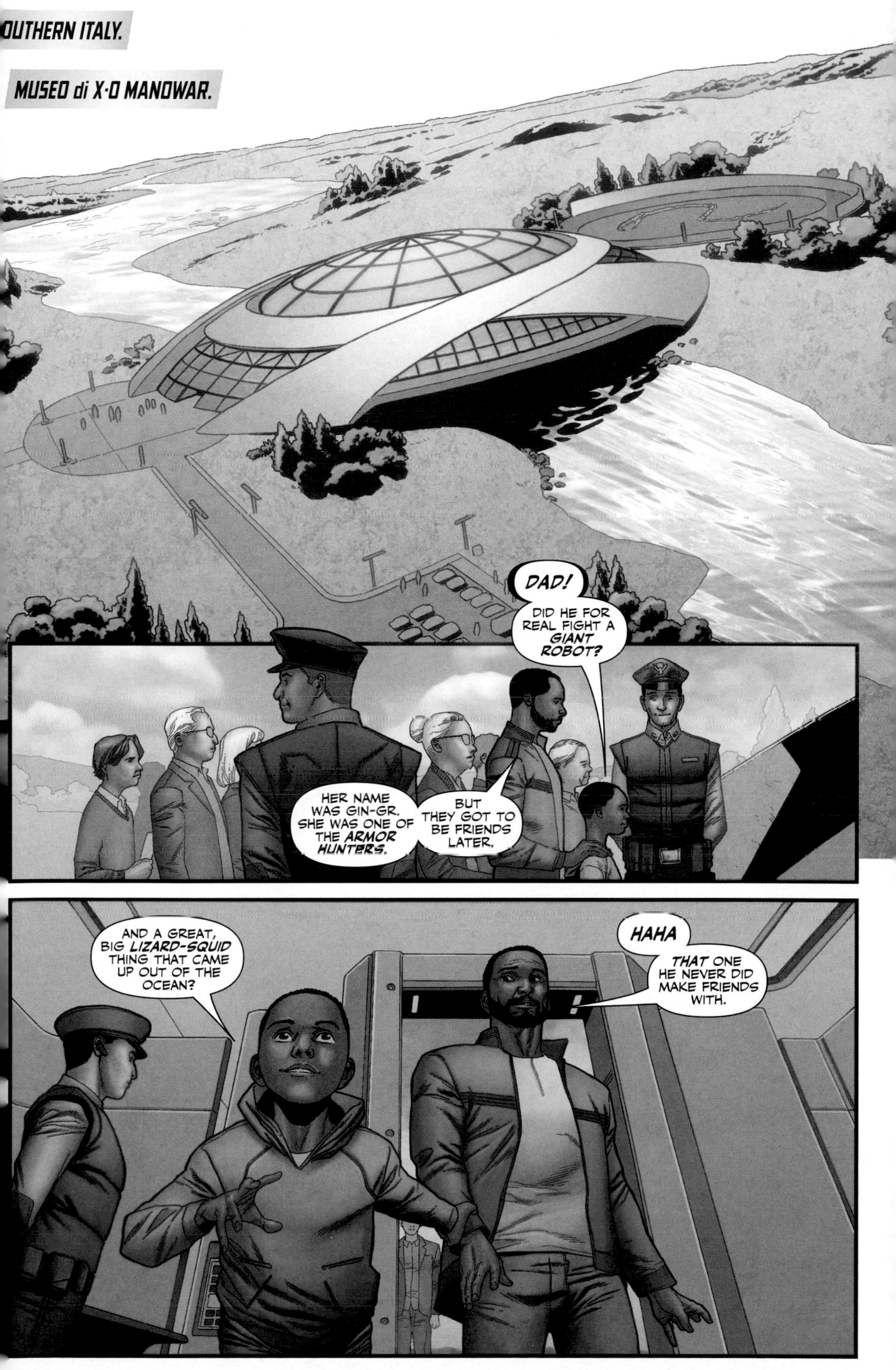
OUTHERN ITALY.
MUSEO di X-O MANOWAR.
DAD!
DID HE FOR REAL FIGHT A GIANT ROBOT?
HER NAME WAS GIN-GR. SHE WAS ONE OF THE ARMOR HUNTERS.
BUT THEY GOT TO BE FRIENDS LATER.
AND A GREAT, BIG LIZARD-SQUID THING THAT CAME UP OUT OF THE OCEAN?
HAHA
THAT ONE HE NEVER DID MAKE FRIENDS WITH.

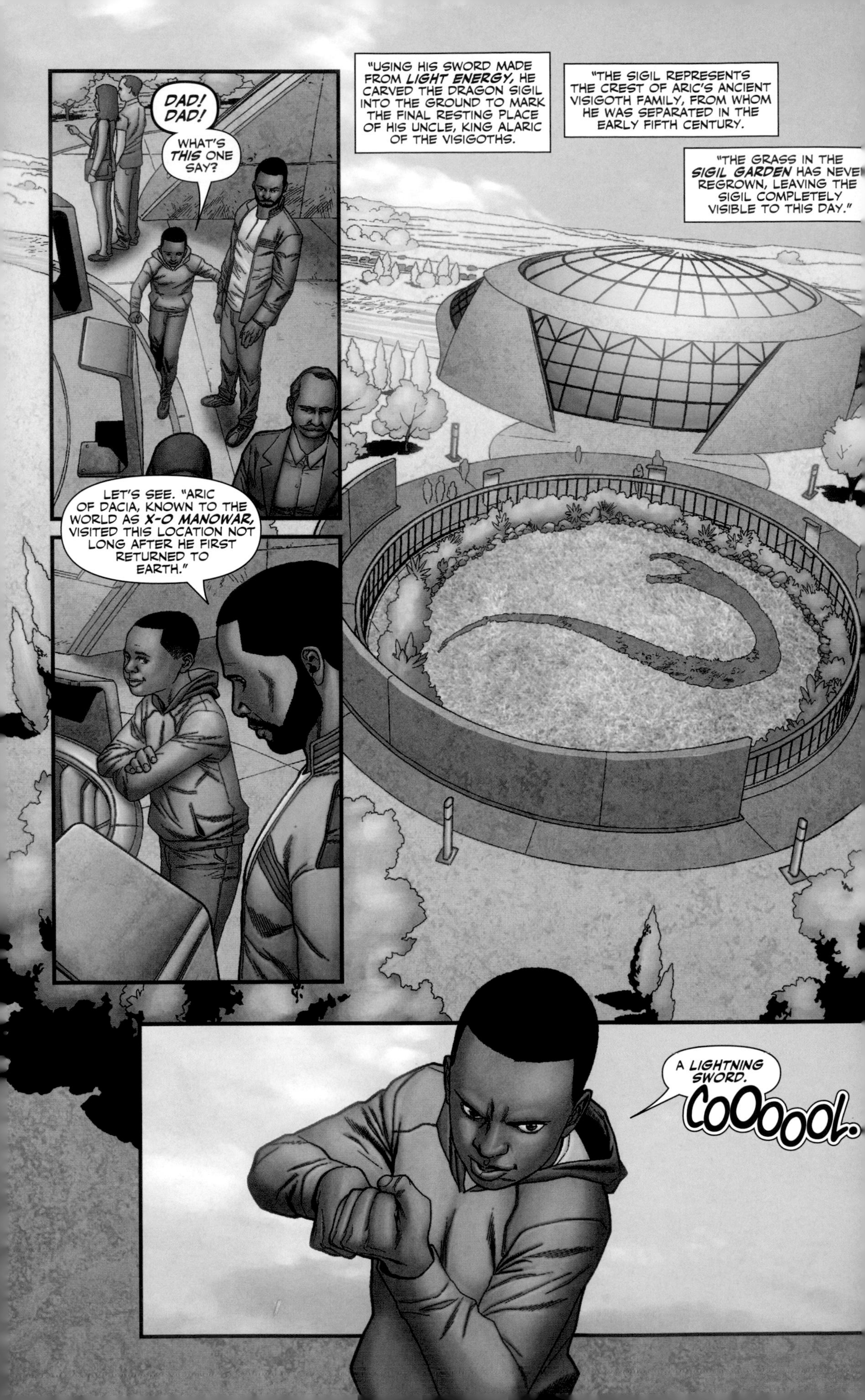
DAD! DAD!
WHAT'S THIS ONE SAY?
"USING HIS SWORD MADE FROM LIGHT ENERGY, HE CARVED THE DRAGON SIGIL INTO THE GROUND TO MARK THE FINAL RESTING PLACE OF HIS UNCLE, KING ALARIC OF THE VISIGOTHS.
"THE SIGIL REPRESENTS THE CREST OF ARIC'S ANCIENT VISIGOTH FAMILY, FROM WHOM HE WAS SEPARATED IN THE EARLY FIFTH CENTURY.
"THE GRASS IN THE SIGIL GARDEN HAS NEVE REGROWN, LEAVING THE SIGIL COMPLETELY VISIBLE TO THIS DAY."
LET'S SEE. "ARIC OF DACIA, KNOWN TO THE WORLD AS X-O MANOWAR, VISITED THIS LOCATION NOT LONG AFTER HE FIRST RETURNED TO EARTH."
A LIGHTNING SWORD.
COOOOOOL.

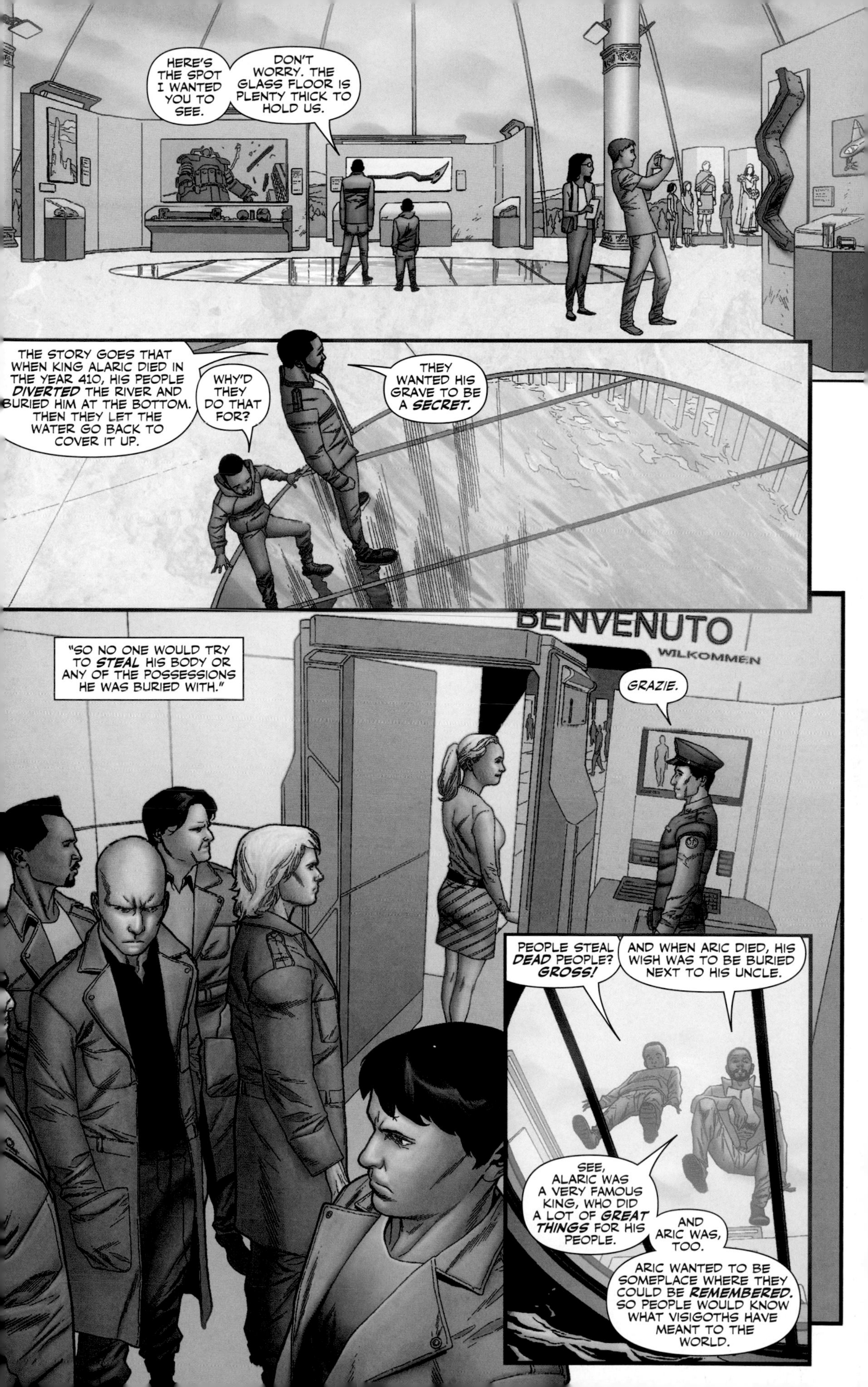
HERE'S THE SPOT I WANTED YOU TO SEE.
DON'T WORRY. THE GLASS FLOOR IS PLENTY THICK TO HOLD US.
THE STORY GOES THAT WHEN KING ALARIC DIED IN THE YEAR 410, HIS PEOPLE DIVERTED THE RIVER AND BURIED HIM AT THE BOTTOM. THEN THEY LET THE WATER GO BACK TO COVER IT UP.
WHY'D THEY DO THAT FOR?
THEY WANTED HIS GRAVE TO BE A SECRET.
BENVENUTO
WILKOMMEN
"SO NO ONE WOULD TRY TO STEAL HIS BODY OR ANY OF THE POSSESSIONS HE WAS BURIED WITH."
GRAZIE.
PEOPLE STEAL DEAD PEOPLE? GROSS!
AND WHEN ARIC DIED, HIS WISH WAS TO BE BURIED NEXT TO HIS UNCLE.
SEE, ALARIC WAS A VERY FAMOUS KING, WHO DID A LOT OF GREAT THINGS FOR HIS PEOPLE.
AND ARIC WAS, TOO.
ARIC WANTED TO BE SOMEPLACE WHERE THEY COULD BE REMEMBERED. SO PEOPLE WOULD KNOW WHAT VISIGOTHS HAVE MEANT TO THE WORLD.

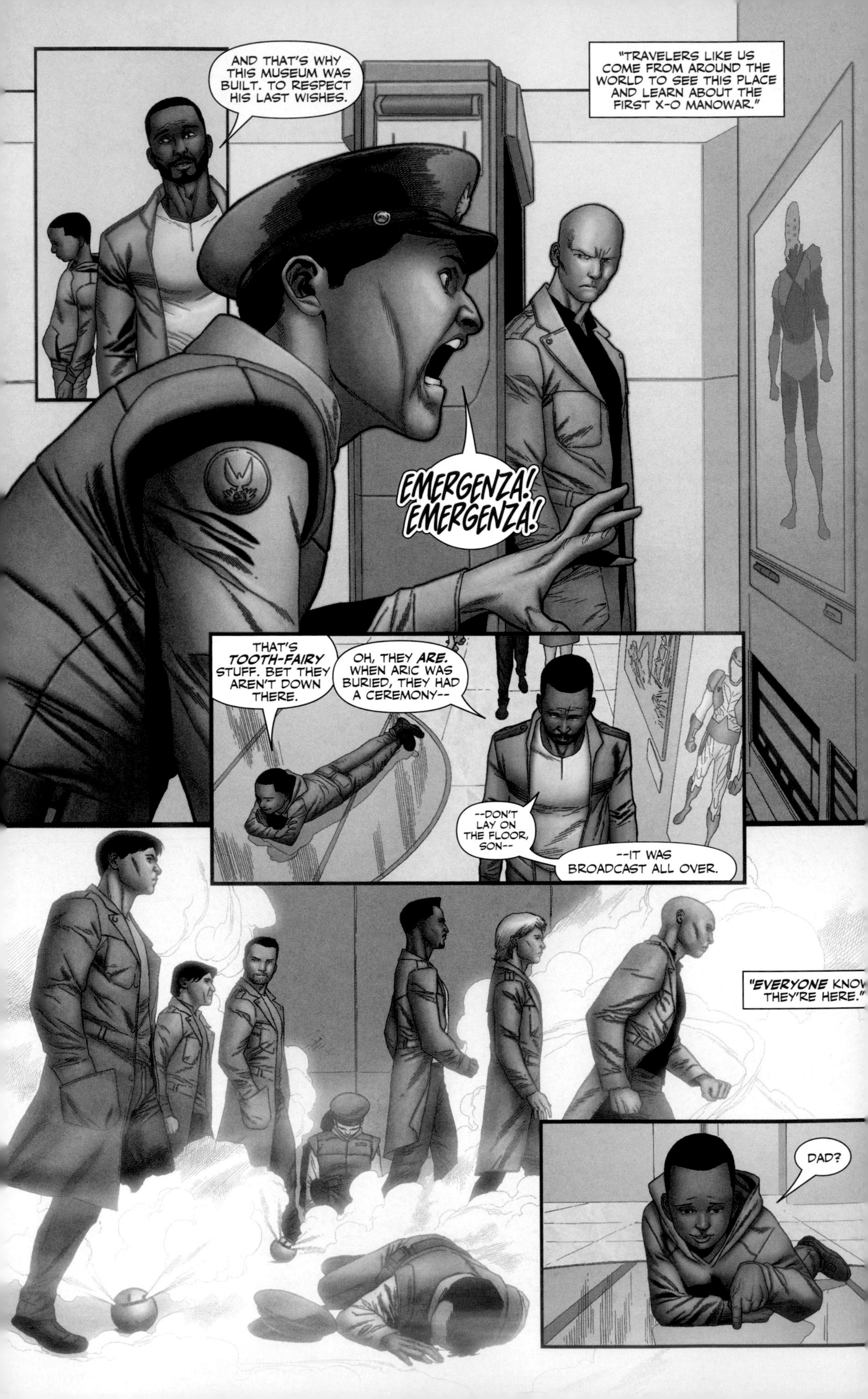

AND THAT'S WHY THIS MUSEUM WAS BUILT. TO RESPECT HIS LAST WISHES.
"TRAVELERS LIKE US COME FROM AROUND THE WORLD TO SEE THIS PLACE AND LEARN ABOUT THE FIRST X-O MANOWAR."
EMERGENZA! EMERGENZA!
THAT'S *TOOTH-FAIRY* STUFF. BET THEY AREN'T DOWN THERE.
OH, THEY *ARE.* WHEN ARIC WAS BURIED, THEY HAD A CEREMONY--
--DON'T LAY ON THE FLOOR, SON--
--IT WAS BROADCAST ALL OVER.
"*EVERYONE* KNOW THEY'RE HERE."
DAD?

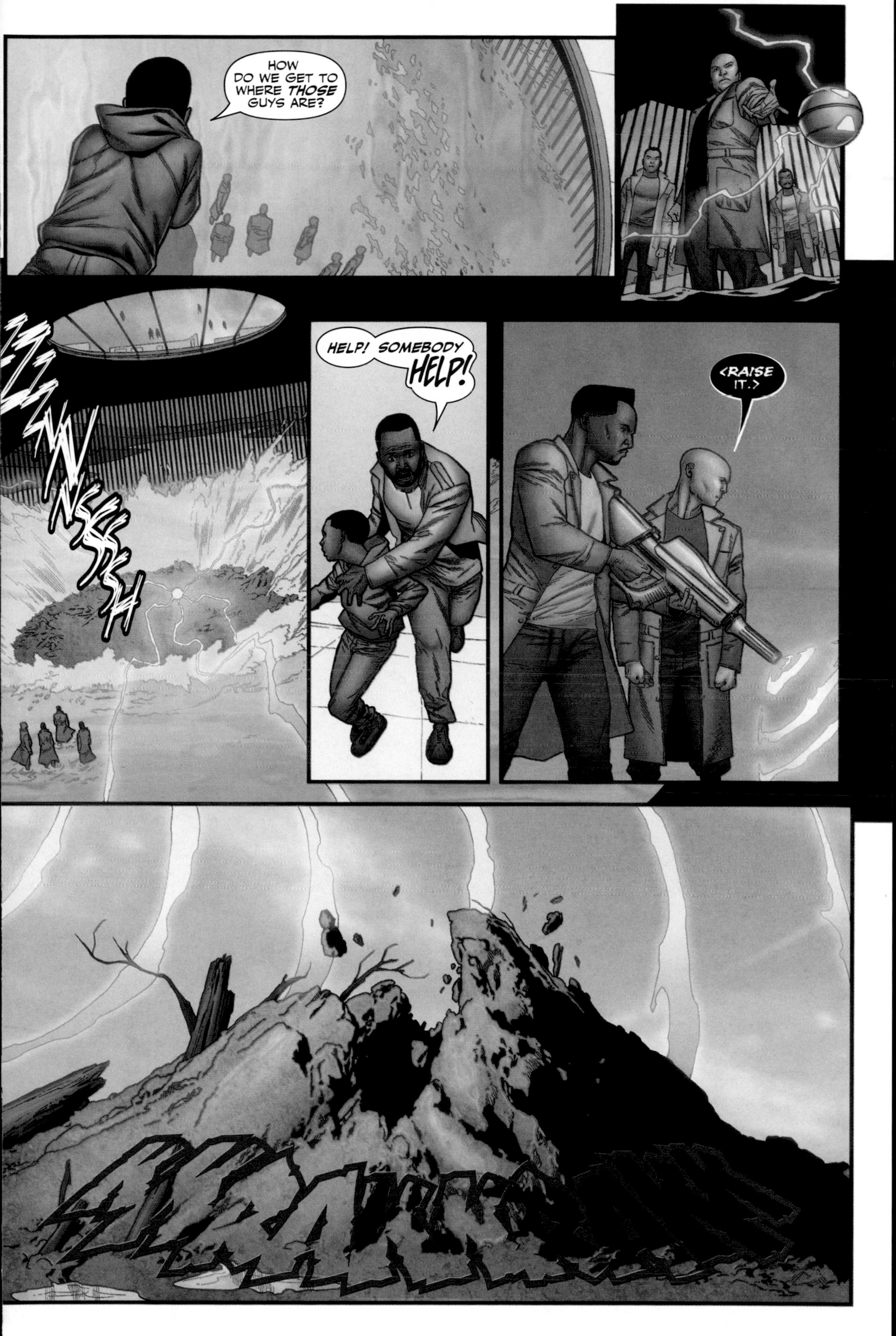
HOW DO WE GET TO WHERE THOSE GUYS ARE?
ZZZNNSSSH
HELP! SOMEBODY HELP!
<RAISE IT.>

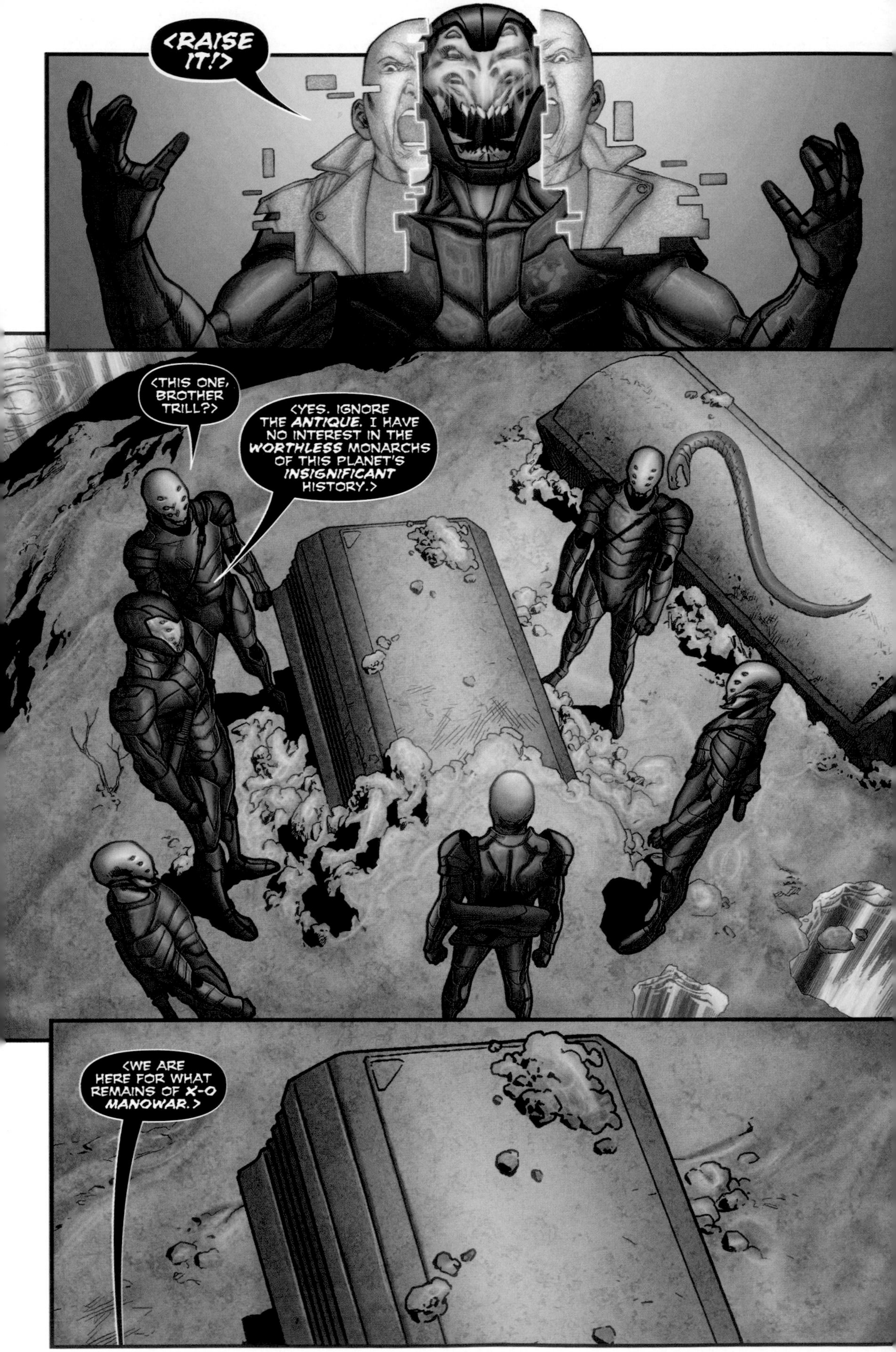
<RAISE IT!>
<THIS ONE, BROTHER TRILL?>
<YES. IGNORE THE ANTIQUE. I HAVE NO INTEREST IN THE WORTHLESS MONARCHS OF THIS PLANET'S INSIGNIFICANT HISTORY.>
<WE ARE HERE FOR WHAT REMAINS OF X-O MANOWAR.>

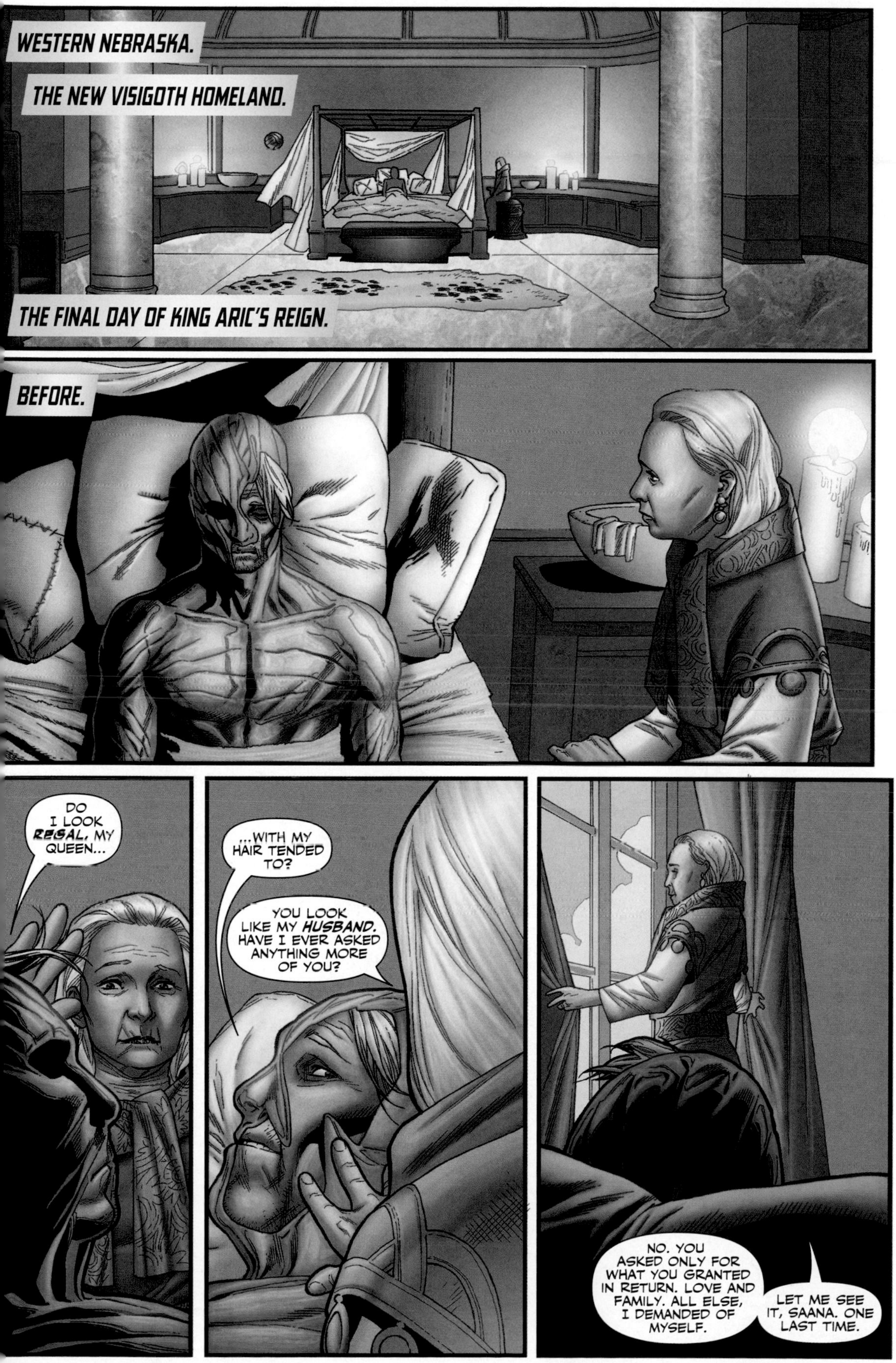

WESTERN NEBRASKA.
THE NEW VISIGOTH HOMELAND.
THE FINAL DAY OF KING ARIC'S REIGN.
BEFORE.
DO I LOOK REGAL, MY QUEEN...
...WITH MY HAIR TENDED TO?
YOU LOOK LIKE MY HUSBAND. HAVE I EVER ASKED ANYTHING MORE OF YOU?
NO. YOU ASKED ONLY FOR WHAT YOU GRANTED IN RETURN. LOVE AND FAMILY. ALL ELSE, I DEMANDED OF MYSELF.
LET ME SEE IT, SAANA. ONE LAST TIME.

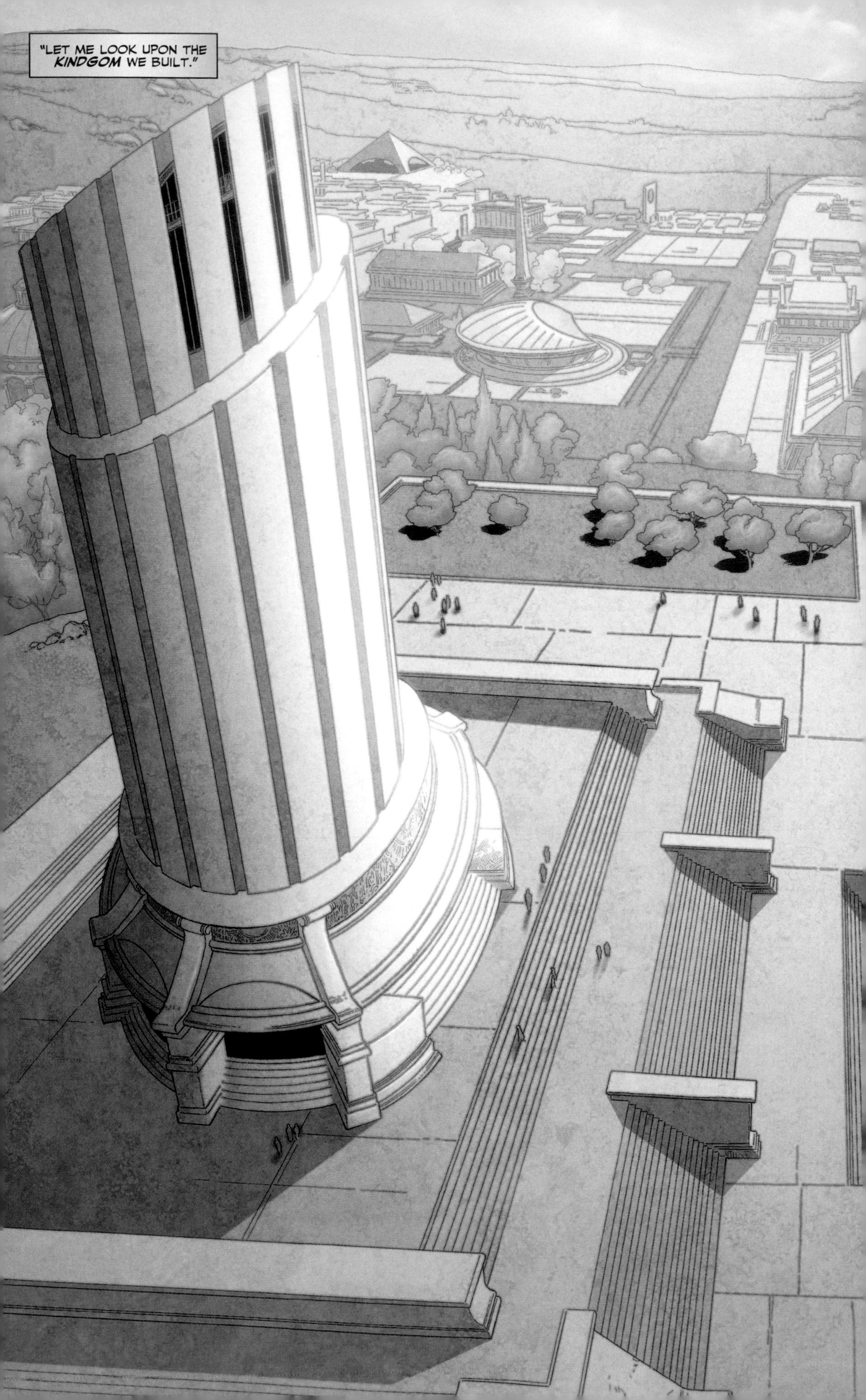
"LET ME LOOK UPON THE *KINDGOM* WE BUILT."

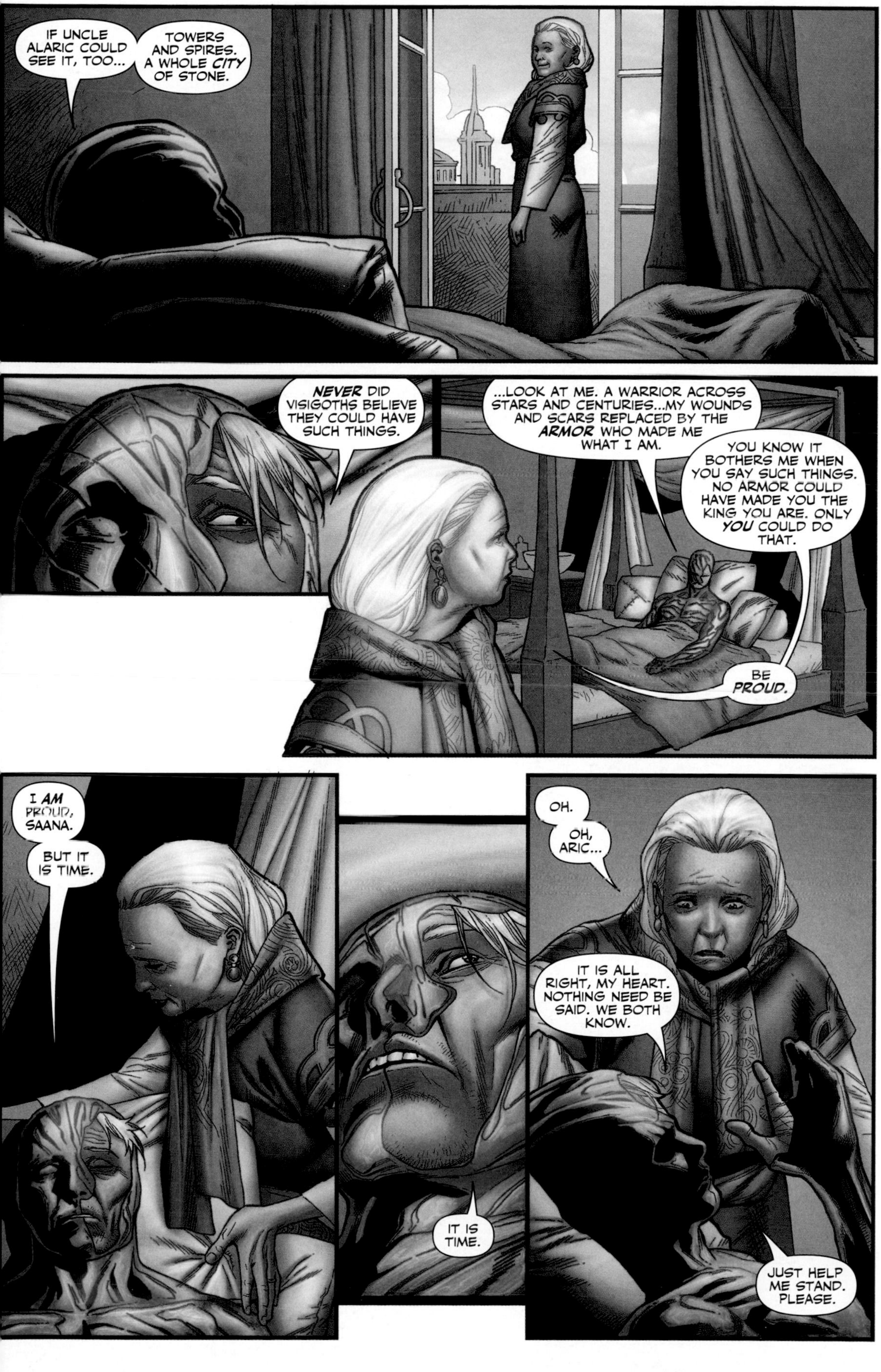
IF UNCLE ALARIC COULD SEE IT, TOO...
TOWERS AND SPIRES. A WHOLE CITY OF STONE.
NEVER DID VISIGOTHS BELIEVE THEY COULD HAVE SUCH THINGS.
...LOOK AT ME. A WARRIOR ACROSS STARS AND CENTURIES...MY WOUNDS AND SCARS REPLACED BY THE ARMOR WHO MADE ME WHAT I AM.
YOU KNOW IT BOTHERS ME WHEN YOU SAY SUCH THINGS. NO ARMOR COULD HAVE MADE YOU THE KING YOU ARE. ONLY YOU COULD DO THAT.
BE PROUD.
I AM PROUD, SAANA.
BUT IT IS TIME.
IT IS TIME.
OH.
OH, ARIC...
IT IS ALL RIGHT, MY HEART. NOTHING NEED BE SAID. WE BOTH KNOW.
JUST HELP ME STAND. PLEASE.

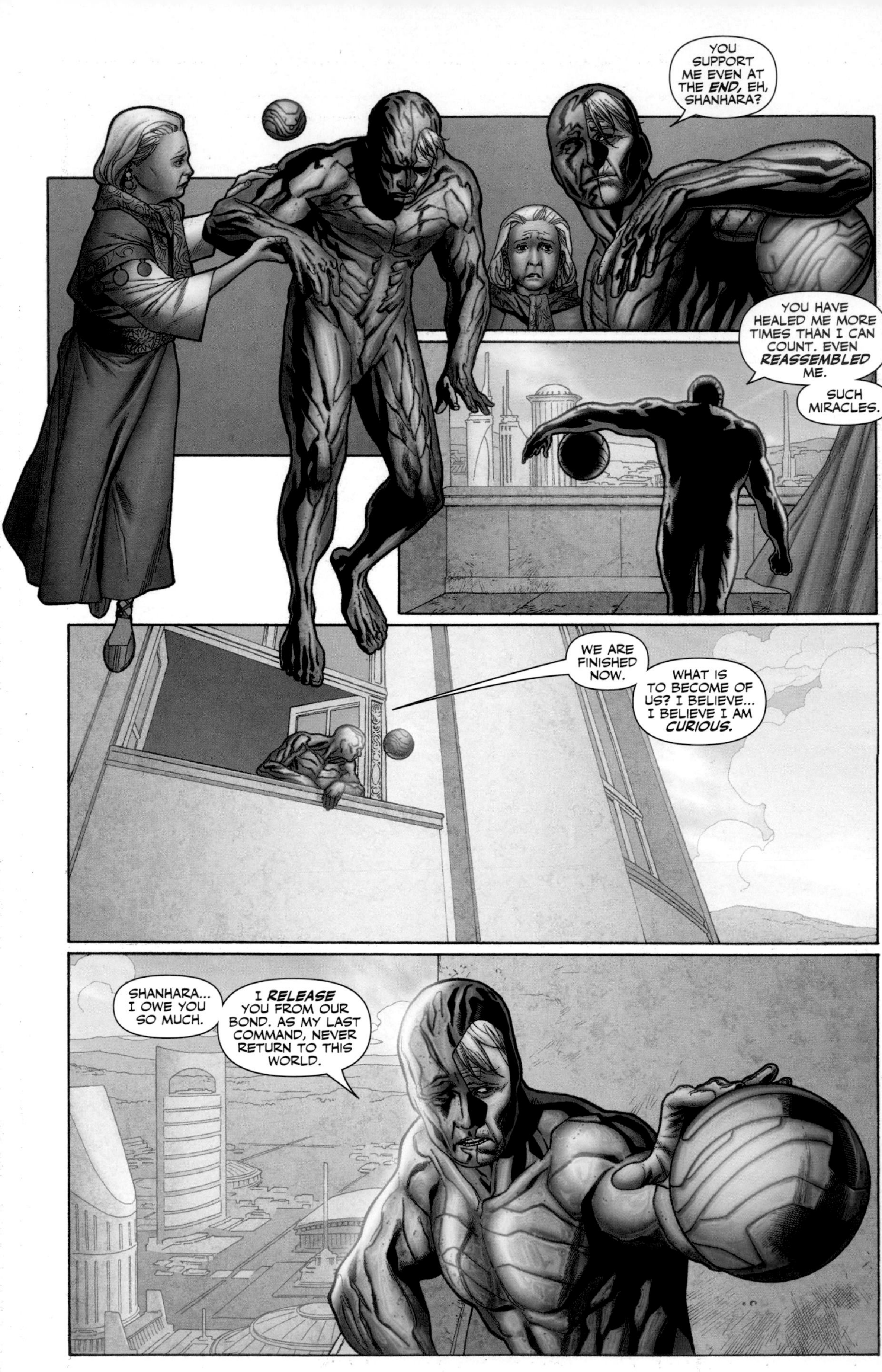
YOU SUPPORT ME EVEN AT THE *END*, EH, SHANHARA?
YOU HAVE HEALED ME MORE TIMES THAN I CAN COUNT. EVEN *REASSEMBLED* ME.
SUCH MIRACLES.
WE ARE FINISHED NOW.
WHAT IS TO BECOME OF US? I BELIEVE... I BELIEVE I AM *CURIOUS.*
SHANHARA... I OWE YOU SO MUCH.
I *RELEASE* YOU FROM OUR BOND. AS MY LAST COMMAND, NEVER RETURN TO THIS WORLD.

I WILL SEE YOU IN ETERNITY.

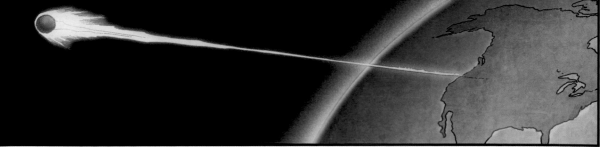

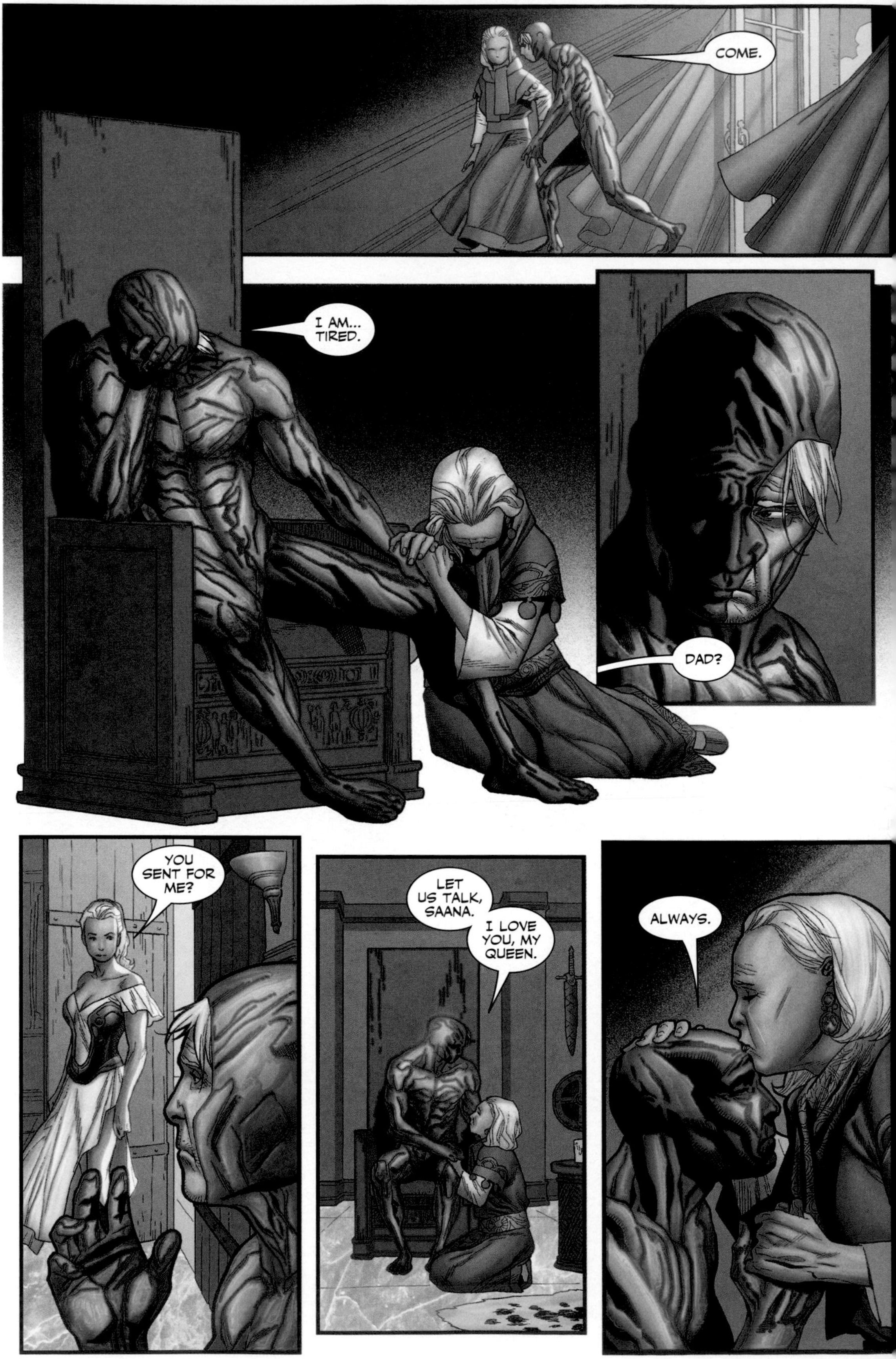
COME.
I AM... TIRED.
DAD?
YOU SENT FOR ME?
LET US TALK, SAANA.
I LOVE YOU, MY QUEEN.
ALWAYS.

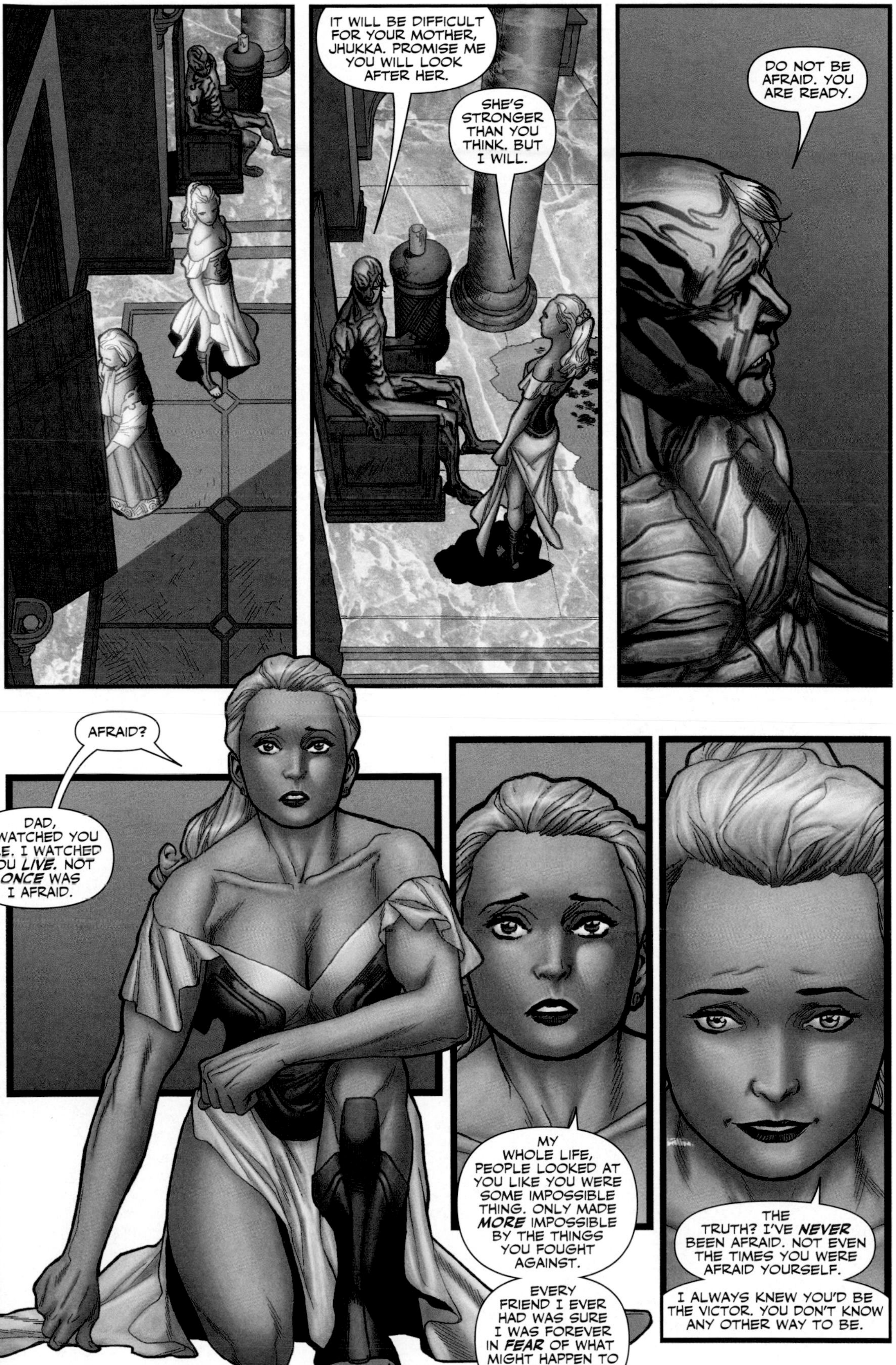
IT WILL BE DIFFICULT FOR YOUR MOTHER, JHUKKA. PROMISE ME YOU WILL LOOK AFTER HER.
SHE'S STRONGER THAN YOU THINK. BUT I WILL.
DO NOT BE AFRAID. YOU ARE READY.
AFRAID?
DAD, WATCHED YOU LE. I WATCHED YOU LIVE. NOT ONCE WAS I AFRAID.
MY WHOLE LIFE, PEOPLE LOOKED AT YOU LIKE YOU WERE SOME IMPOSSIBLE THING. ONLY MADE MORE IMPOSSIBLE BY THE THINGS YOU FOUGHT AGAINST.
EVERY FRIEND I EVER HAD WAS SURE I WAS FOREVER IN FEAR OF WHAT MIGHT HAPPEN TO YOU OR MOTHER OR ME.
THE TRUTH? I'VE NEVER BEEN AFRAID. NOT EVEN THE TIMES YOU WERE AFRAID YOURSELF.
I ALWAYS KNEW YOU'D BE THE VICTOR. YOU DON'T KNOW ANY OTHER WAY TO BE.

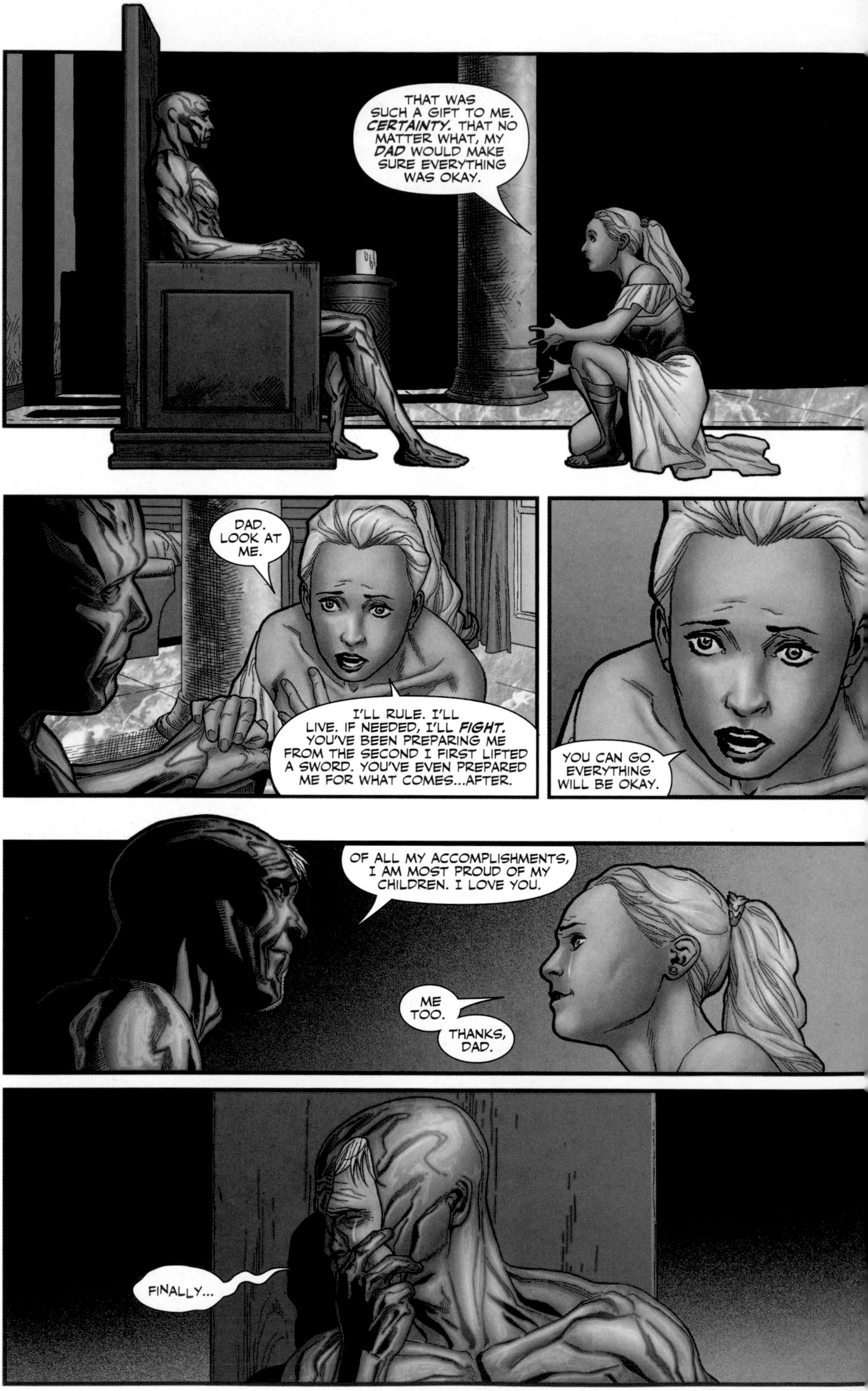
THAT WAS SUCH A GIFT TO ME. CERTAINTY. THAT NO MATTER WHAT, MY DAD WOULD MAKE SURE EVERYTHING WAS OKAY.
DAD. LOOK AT ME.
I'LL RULE. I'LL LIVE. IF NEEDED, I'LL FIGHT. YOU'VE BEEN PREPARING ME FROM THE SECOND I FIRST LIFTED A SWORD. YOU'VE EVEN PREPARED ME FOR WHAT COMES...AFTER.
YOU CAN GO. EVERYTHING WILL BE OKAY.
OF ALL MY ACCOMPLISHMENTS, I AM MOST PROUD OF MY CHILDREN. I LOVE YOU.
ME TOO.
THANKS, DAD.
FINALLY...

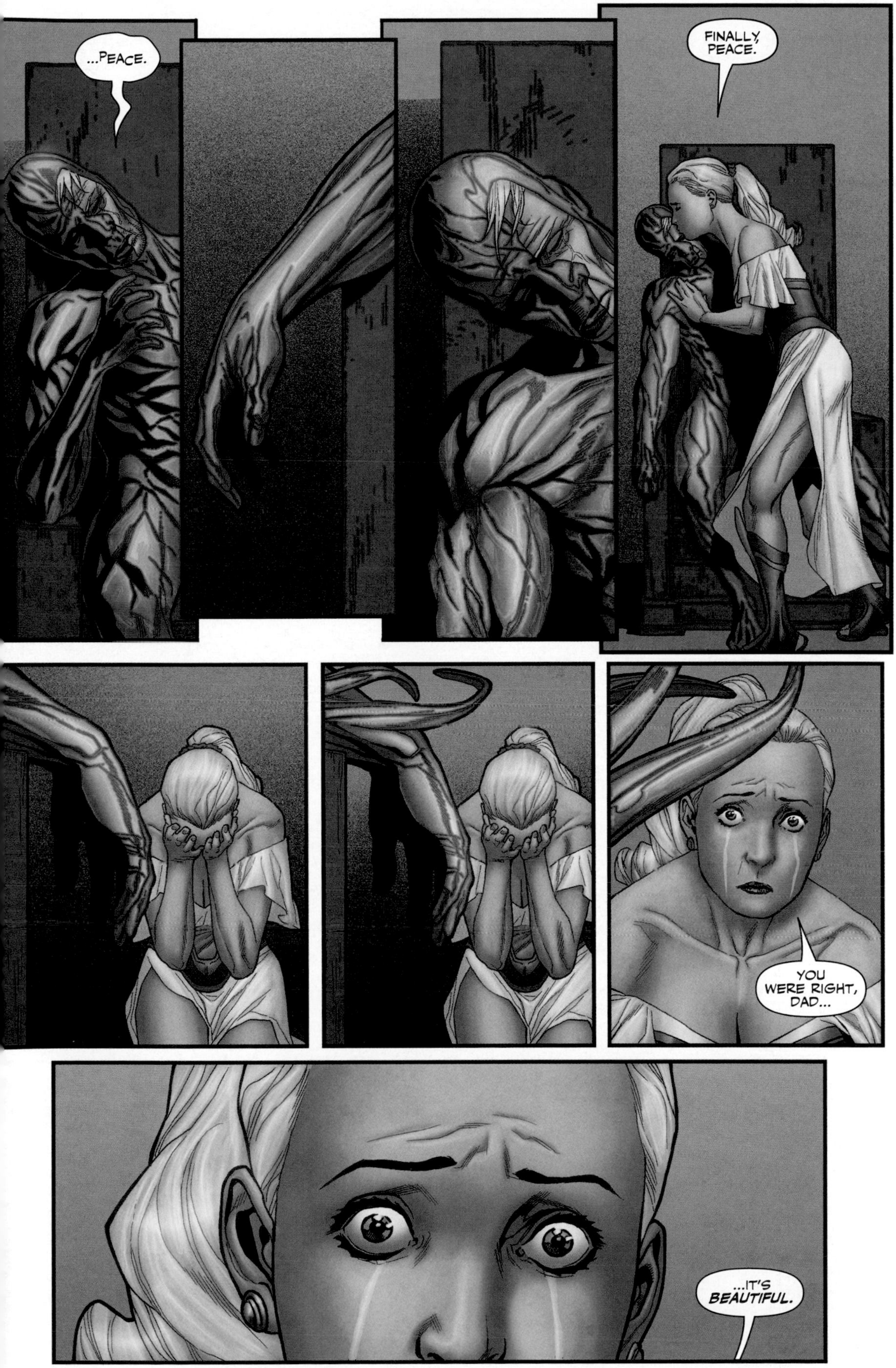

...PEACE.
FINALLY, PEACE.
YOU WERE RIGHT, DAD...
...IT'S *BEAUTIFUL*.

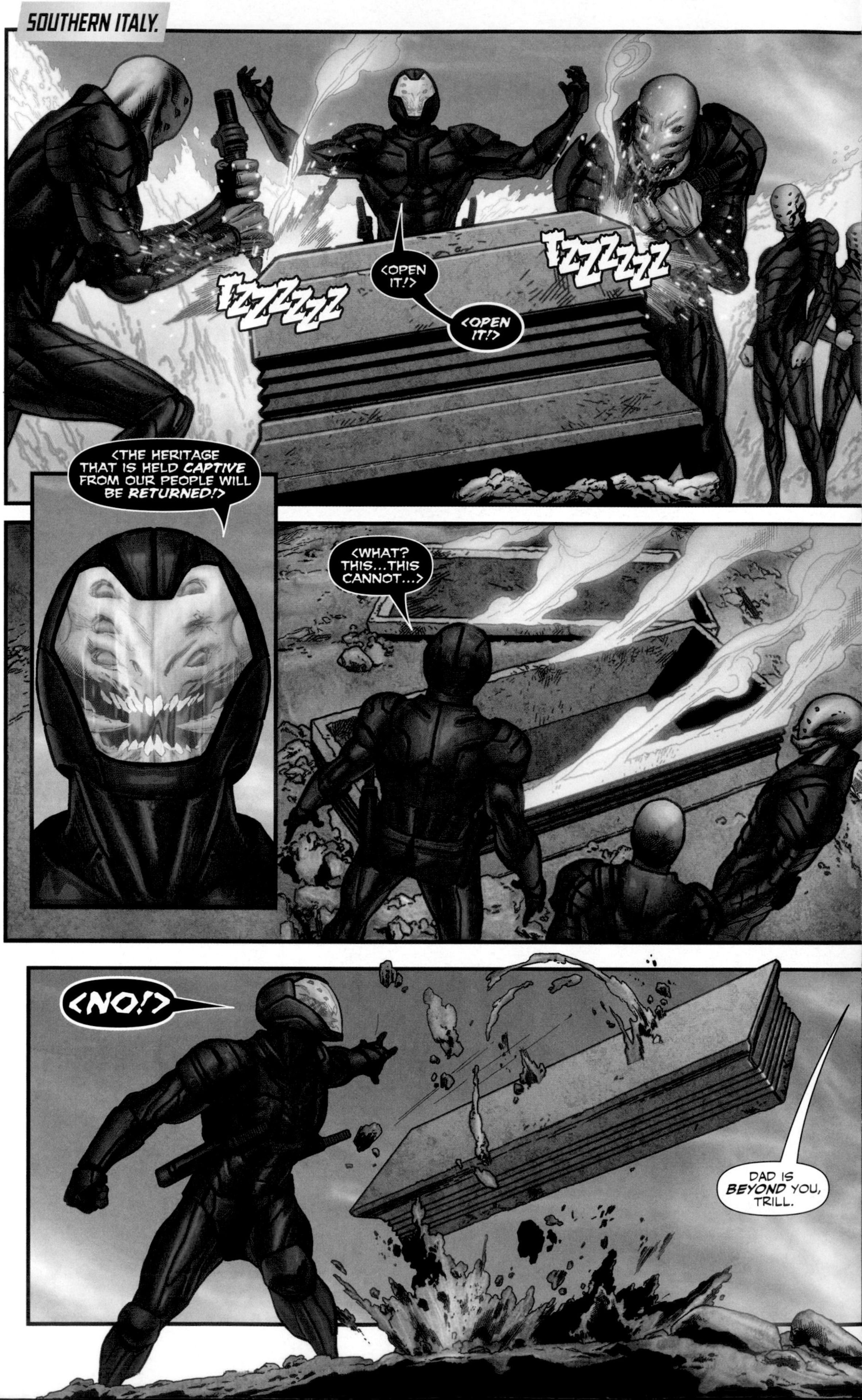
SOUTHERN ITALY.
TZZZZZZ
<OPEN IT!>
<OPEN IT!>
TZZZZZZ
<THE HERITAGE THAT IS HELD CAPTIVE FROM OUR PEOPLE WILL BE RETURNED!>
<WHAT? THIS...THIS CANNOT...>
<NO!>
DAD IS BEYOND YOU, TRILL.

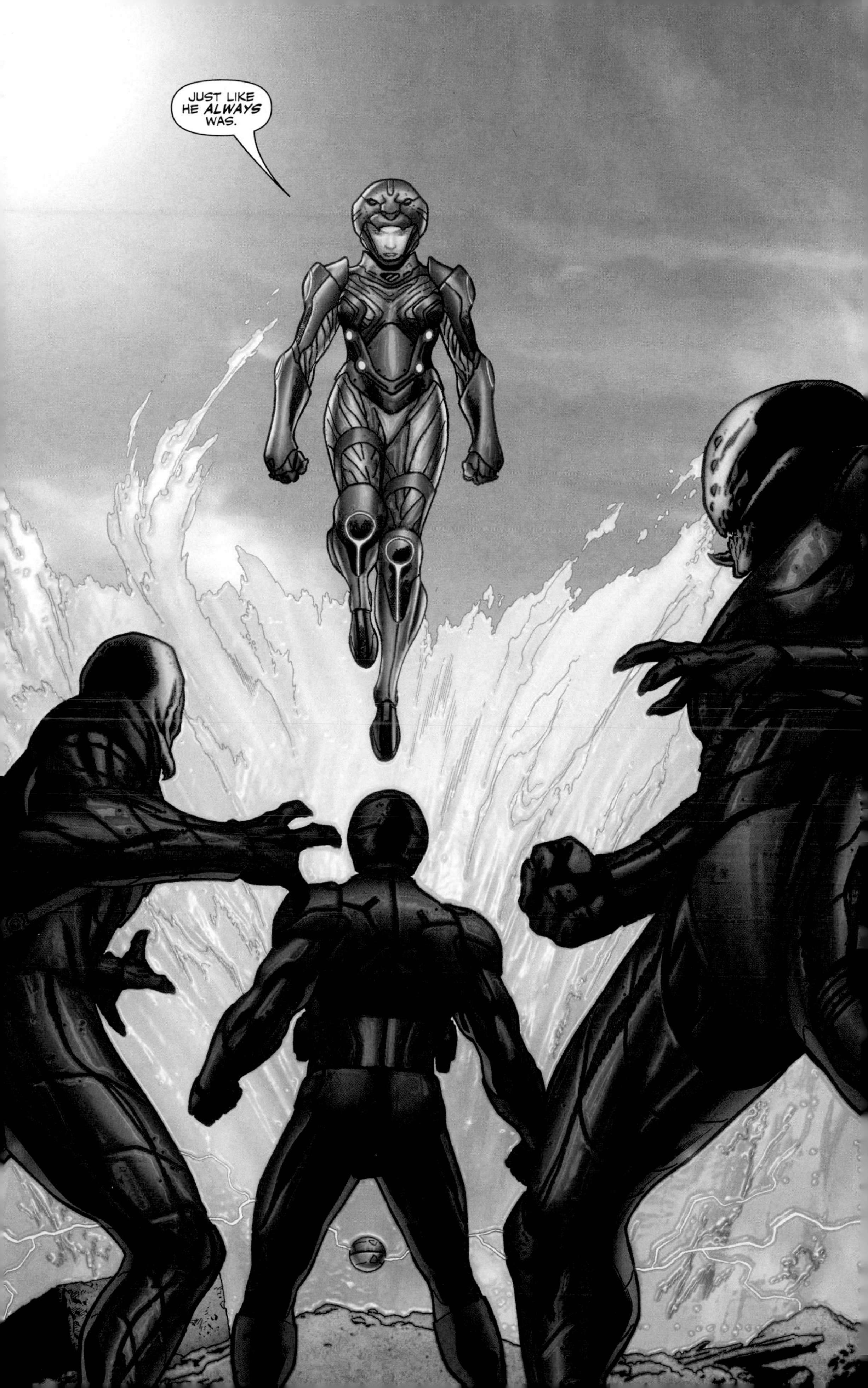
JUST LIKE HE *ALWAYS* WAS.

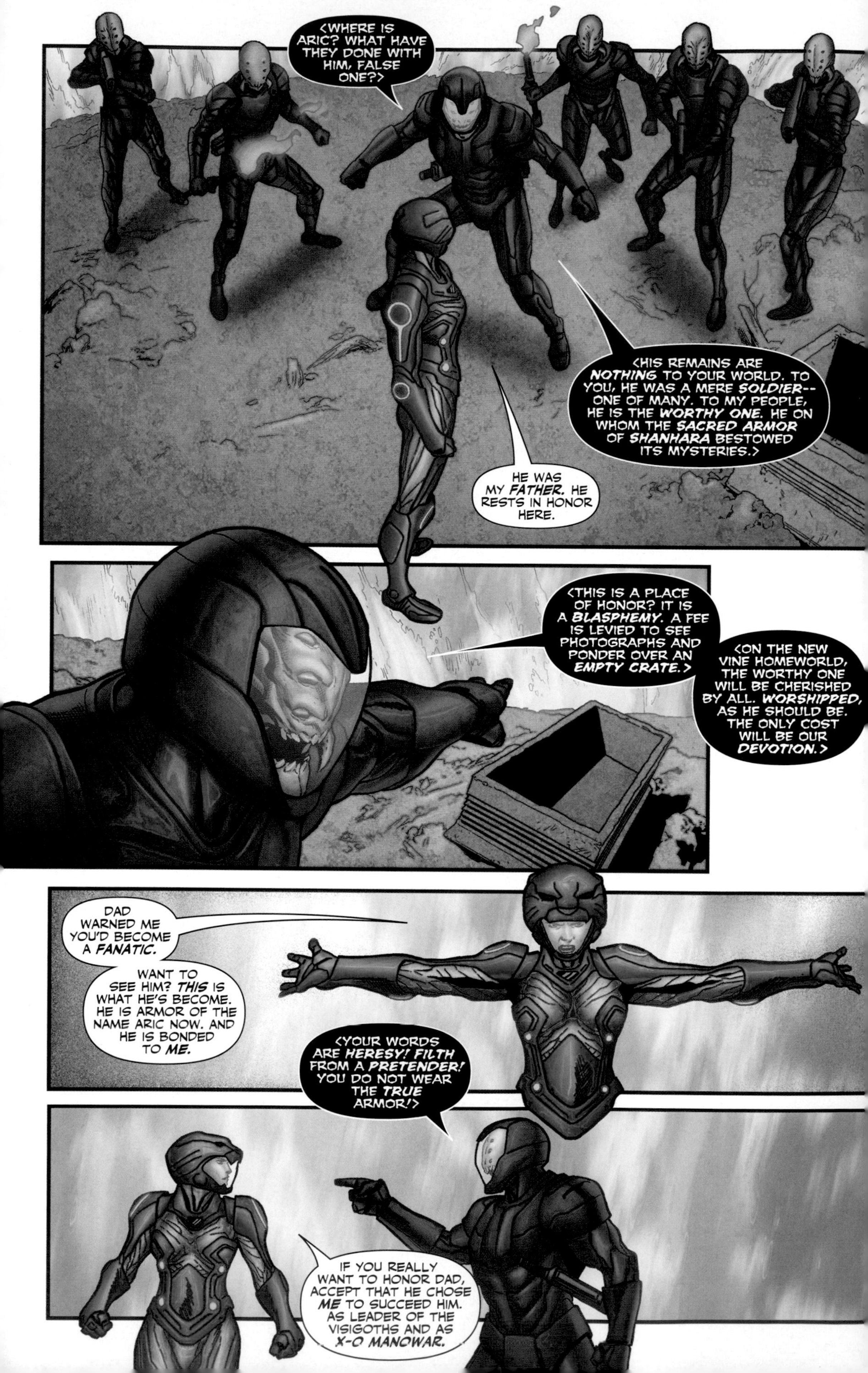

<WHERE IS ARIC? WHAT HAVE THEY DONE WITH HIM, FALSE ONE?>
<HIS REMAINS ARE NOTHING TO YOUR WORLD. TO YOU, HE WAS A MERE SOLDIER-- ONE OF MANY. TO MY PEOPLE, HE IS THE WORTHY ONE. HE ON WHOM THE SACRED ARMOR OF SHANHARA BESTOWED ITS MYSTERIES.>
HE WAS MY FATHER. HE RESTS IN HONOR HERE.
<THIS IS A PLACE OF HONOR? IT IS A BLASPHEMY. A FEE IS LEVIED TO SEE PHOTOGRAPHS AND PONDER OVER AN EMPTY CRATE.>
<ON THE NEW VINE HOMEWORLD, THE WORTHY ONE WILL BE CHERISHED BY ALL. WORSHIPPED, AS HE SHOULD BE. THE ONLY COST WILL BE OUR DEVOTION.>
DAD WARNED ME YOU'D BECOME A FANATIC.
WANT TO SEE HIM? THIS IS WHAT HE'S BECOME. HE IS ARMOR OF THE NAME ARIC NOW. AND HE IS BONDED TO ME.
<YOUR WORDS ARE HERESY! FILTH FROM A PRETENDER! YOU DO NOT WEAR THE TRUE ARMOR!>
IF YOU REALLY WANT TO HONOR DAD, ACCEPT THAT HE CHOSE ME TO SUCCEED HIM. AS LEADER OF THE VISIGOTHS AND AS X-O MANOWAR.

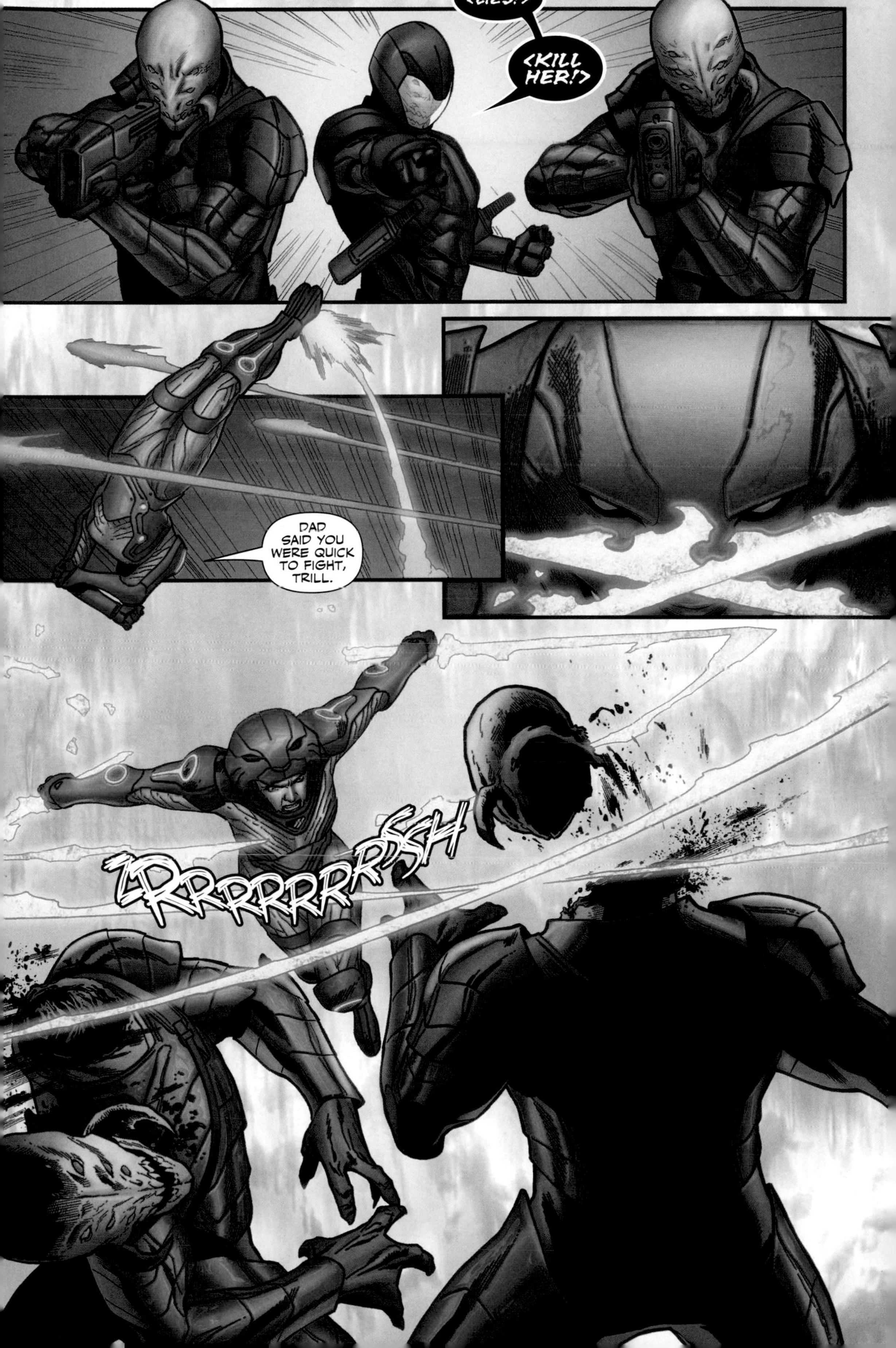
<LIES!>
<KILL HER!>
DAD SAID YOU WERE QUICK TO FIGHT, TRILL.
ZRRRRRRRRSSH

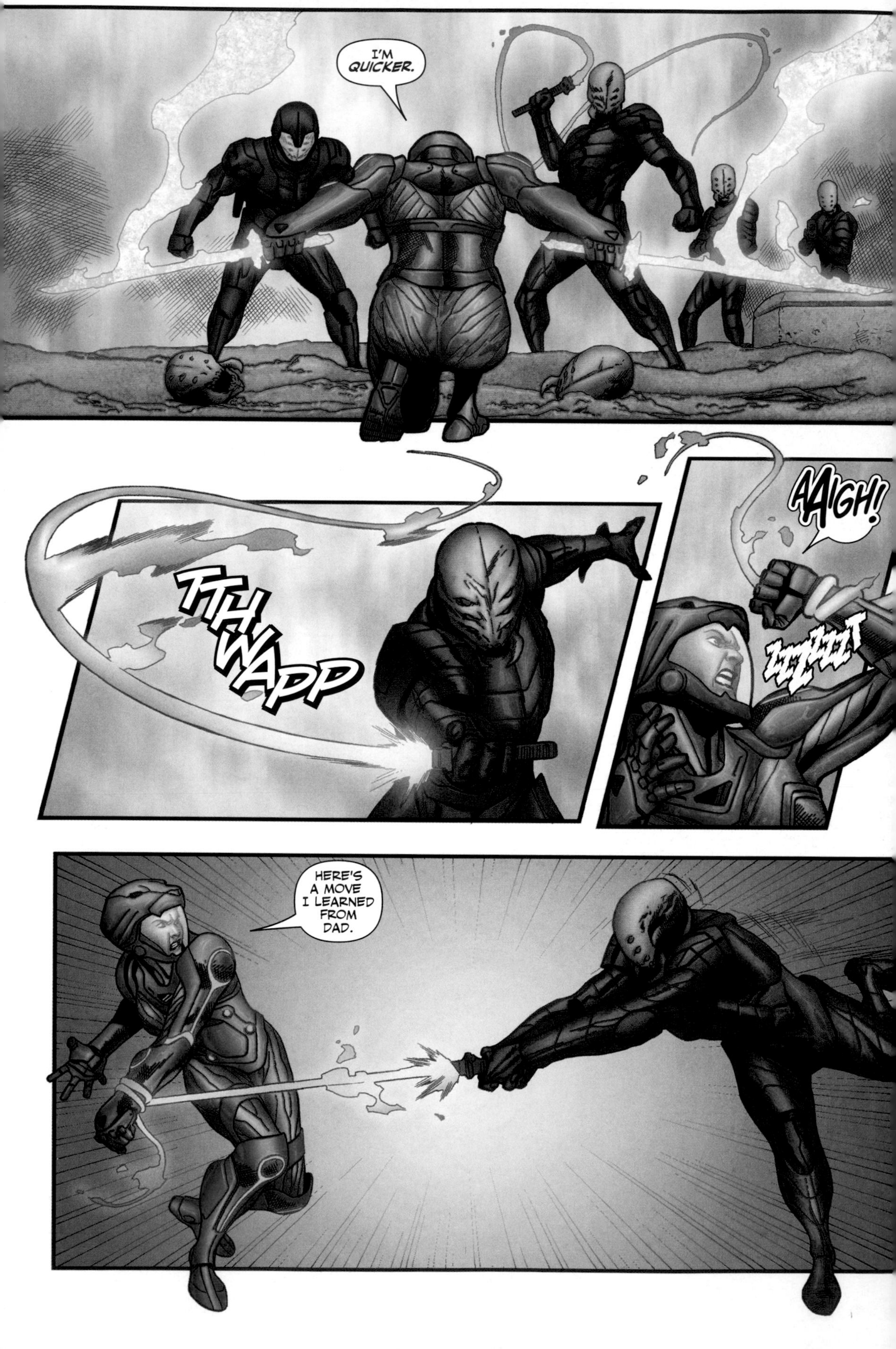
I'M QUICKER.
TTHWAPP
AAIGH!
ZZZZZZT
HERE'S A MOVE I LEARNED FROM DAD.

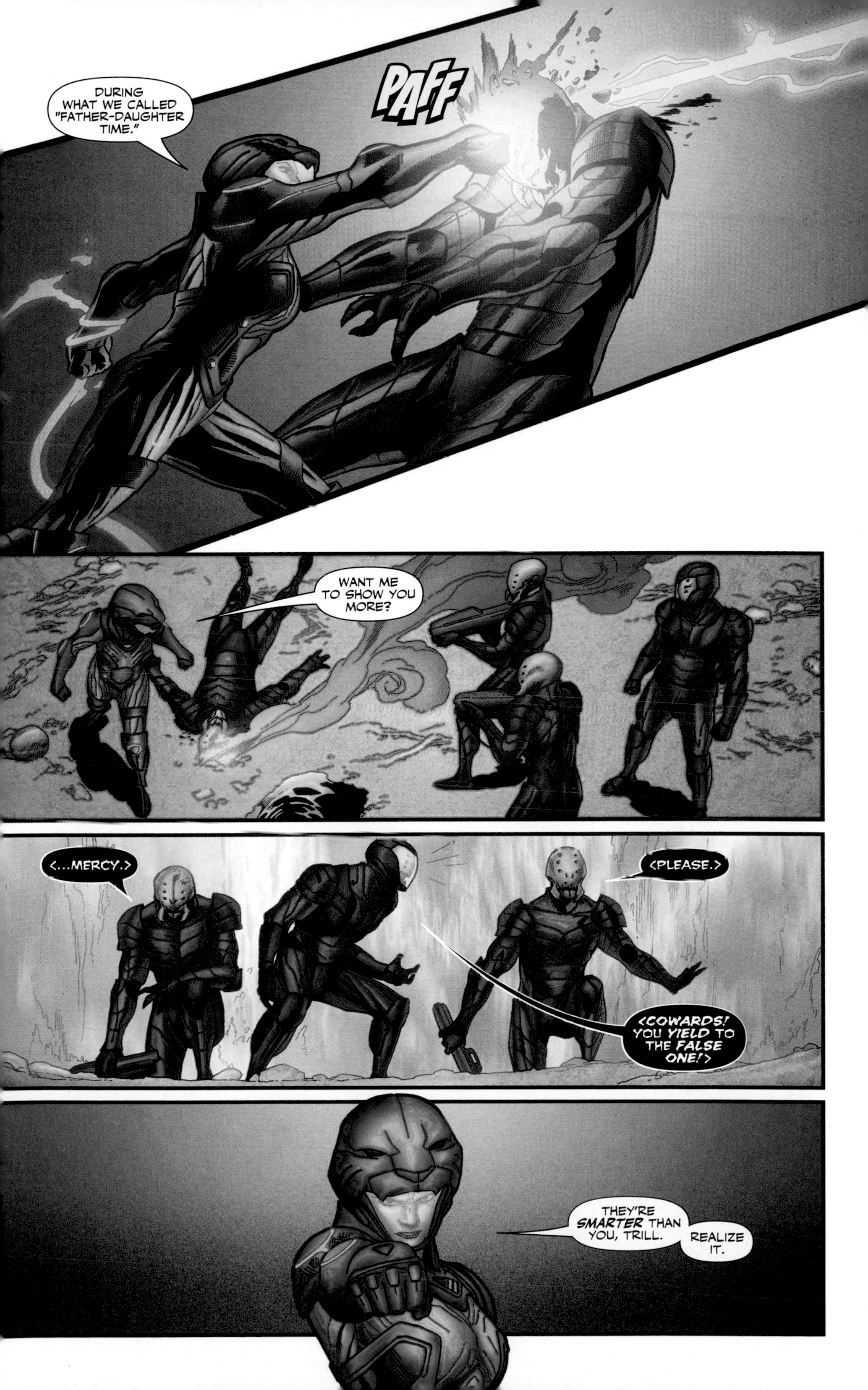
DURING WHAT WE CALLED "FATHER-DAUGHTER TIME."
PAFF
WANT ME TO SHOW YOU MORE?
<...MERCY.>
<PLEASE.>
<COWARDS! YOU *YIELD* TO THE *FALSE ONE!*>
THEY'RE *SMARTER* THAN YOU, TRILL.
REALIZE IT.

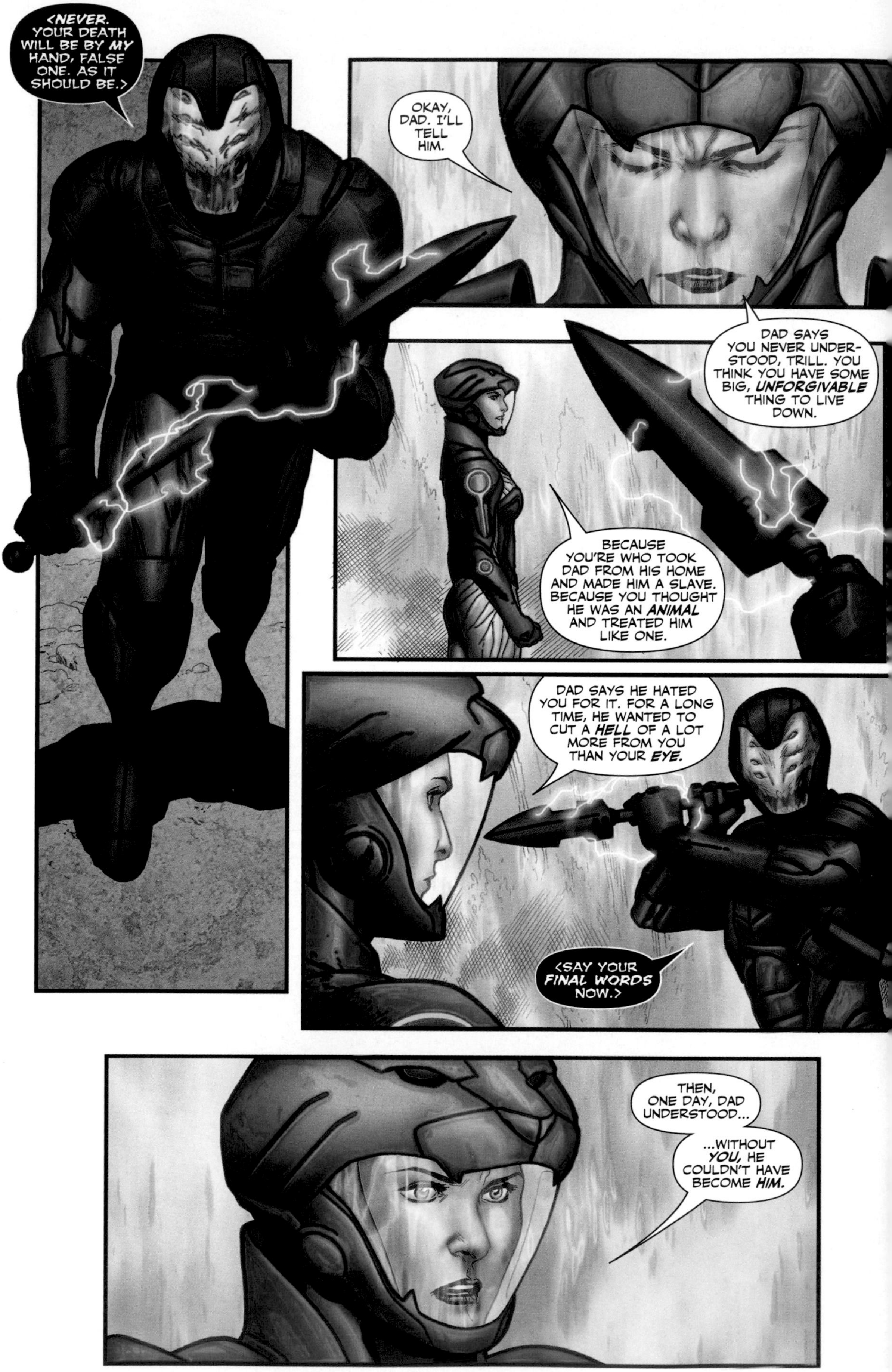
<*NEVER*. YOUR DEATH WILL BE BY *MY* HAND, FALSE ONE. AS IT SHOULD BE.>
OKAY, DAD. I'LL TELL HIM.
DAD SAYS YOU NEVER UNDER-STOOD, TRILL. YOU THINK YOU HAVE SOME BIG, *UNFORGIVABLE* THING TO LIVE DOWN.
BECAUSE YOU'RE WHO TOOK DAD FROM HIS HOME AND MADE HIM A SLAVE. BECAUSE YOU THOUGHT HE WAS AN *ANIMAL* AND TREATED HIM LIKE ONE.
DAD SAYS HE HATED YOU FOR IT. FOR A LONG TIME, HE WANTED TO CUT A *HELL* OF A LOT MORE FROM YOU THAN YOUR *EYE*.
<SAY YOUR *FINAL WORDS* NOW.>
THEN, ONE DAY, DAD UNDERSTOOD...
...WITHOUT *YOU*, HE COULDN'T HAVE BECOME *HIM*.

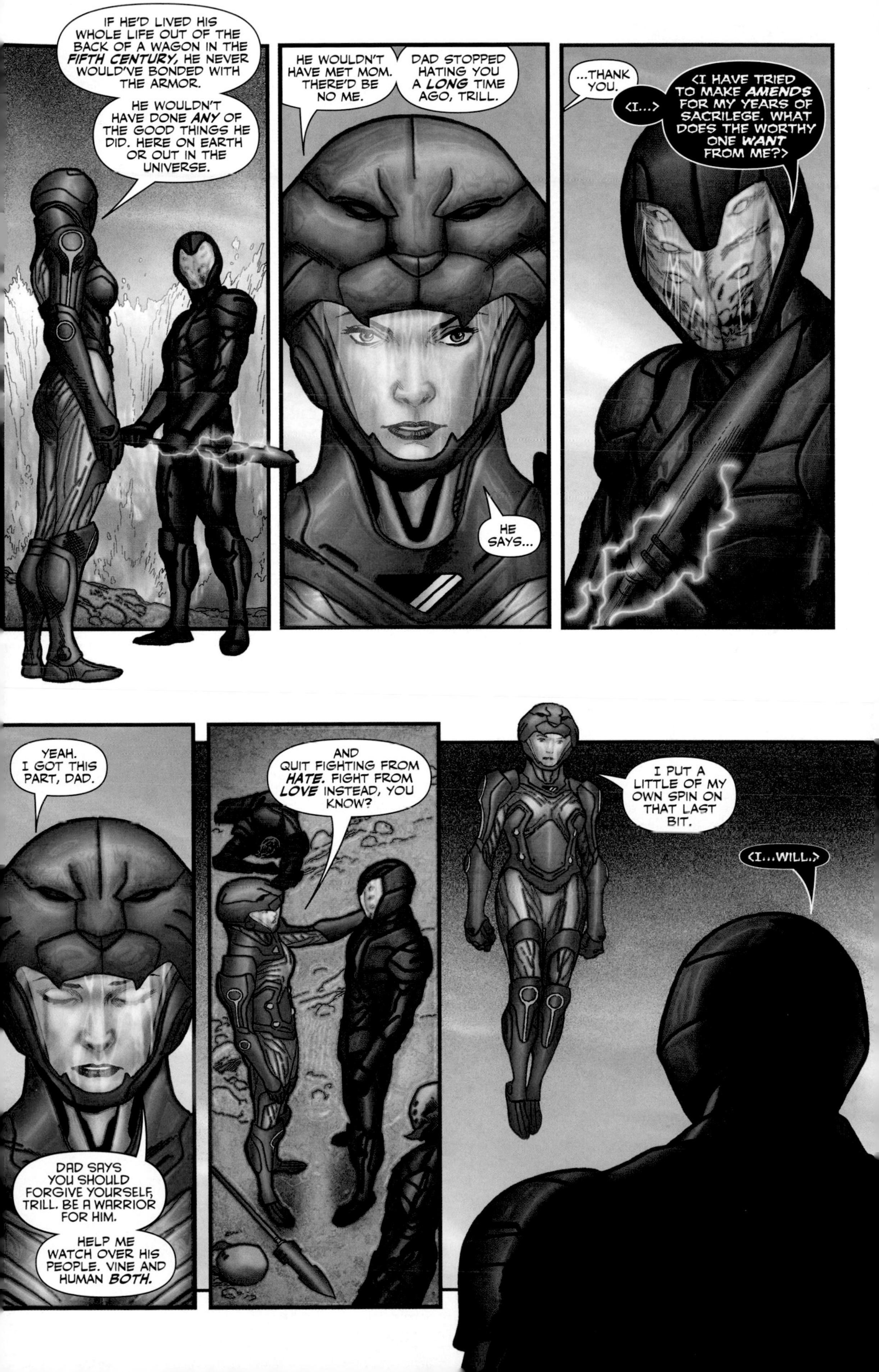
IF HE'D LIVED HIS WHOLE LIFE OUT OF THE BACK OF A WAGON IN THE FIFTH CENTURY, HE NEVER WOULD'VE BONDED WITH THE ARMOR.
HE WOULDN'T HAVE DONE ANY OF THE GOOD THINGS HE DID. HERE ON EARTH OR OUT IN THE UNIVERSE.
HE WOULDN'T HAVE MET MOM. THERE'D BE NO ME.
DAD STOPPED HATING YOU A LONG TIME AGO, TRILL.
HE SAYS...
...THANK YOU.
<I...>
<I HAVE TRIED TO MAKE AMENDS FOR MY YEARS OF SACRILEGE. WHAT DOES THE WORTHY ONE WANT FROM ME?>
YEAH. I GOT THIS PART, DAD.
DAD SAYS YOU SHOULD FORGIVE YOURSELF, TRILL. BE A WARRIOR FOR HIM.
HELP ME WATCH OVER HIS PEOPLE. VINE AND HUMAN BOTH.
AND QUIT FIGHTING FROM HATE. FIGHT FROM LOVE INSTEAD, YOU KNOW?
I PUT A LITTLE OF MY OWN SPIN ON THAT LAST BIT.
<I...WILL.>

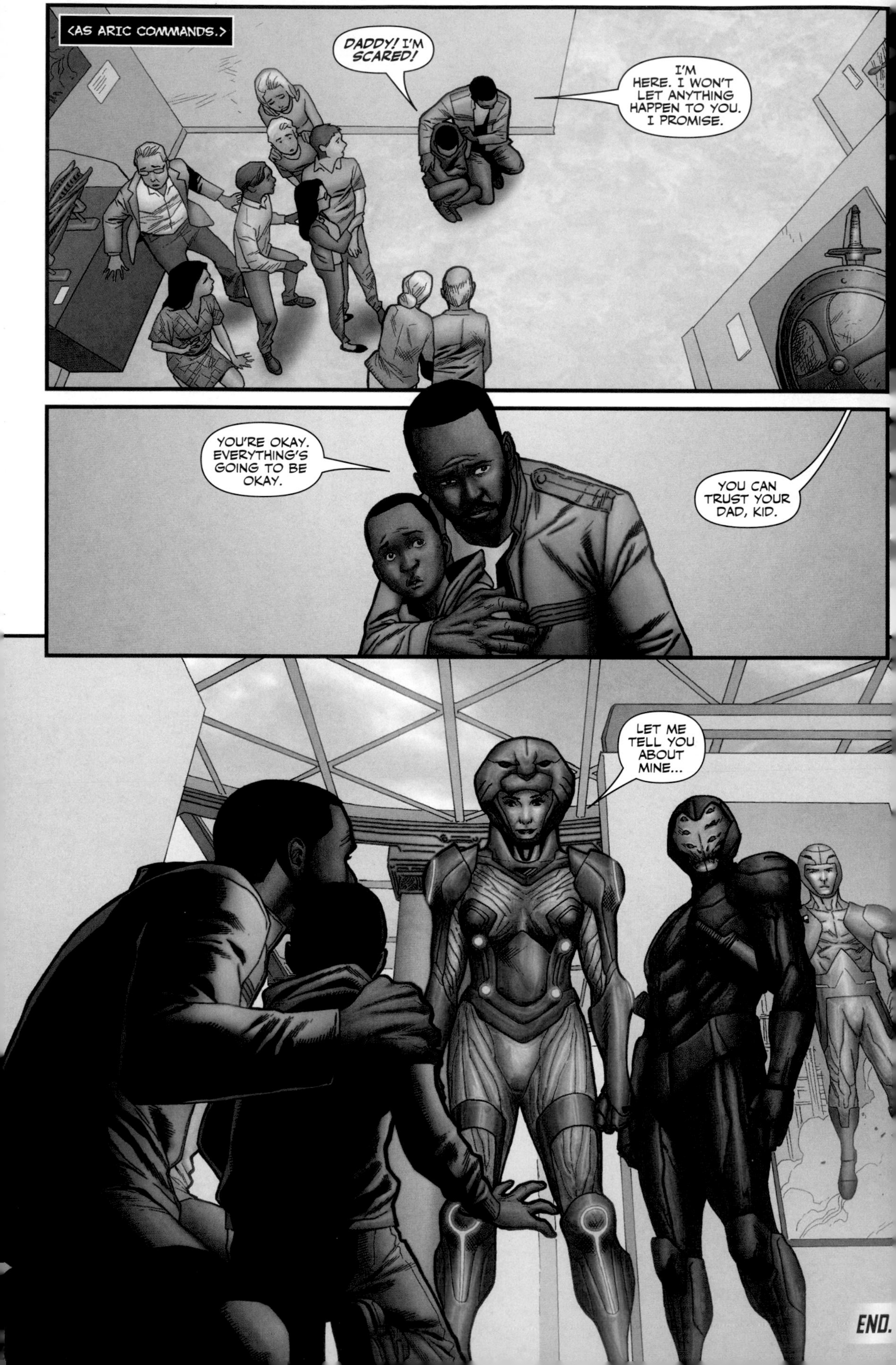

<AS ARIC COMMANDS.>
DADDY! I'M SCARED!
I'M HERE. I WON'T LET ANYTHING HAPPEN TO YOU. I PROMISE.
YOU'RE OKAY. EVERYTHING'S GOING TO BE OKAY.
YOU CAN TRUST YOUR DAD, KID.
LET ME TELL YOU ABOUT MINE...
END.

GALLERY

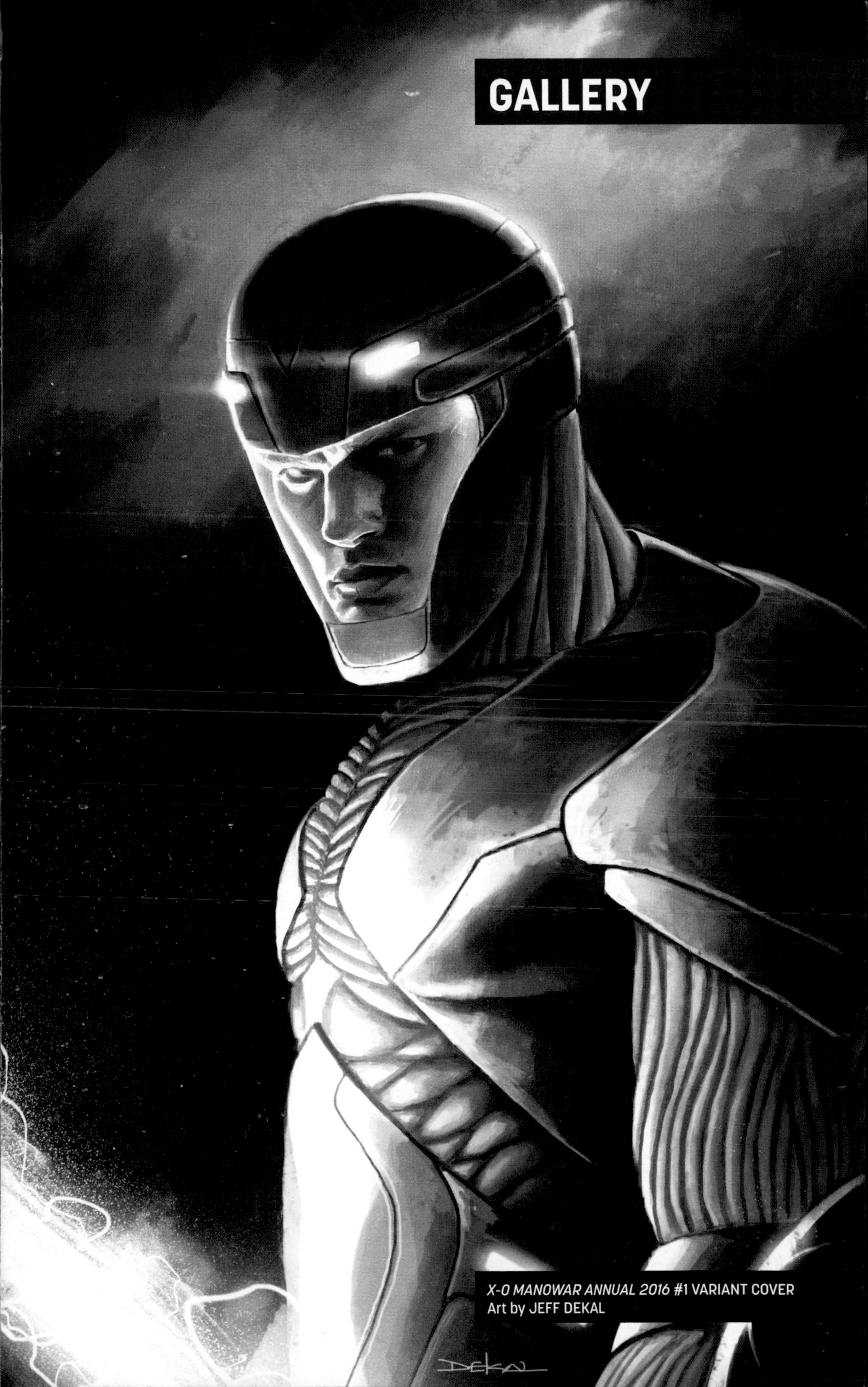
DEKAL

X-O MANOWAR ANNUAL 2016 #1 VARIANT COVER
Art by JEFF DEKAL

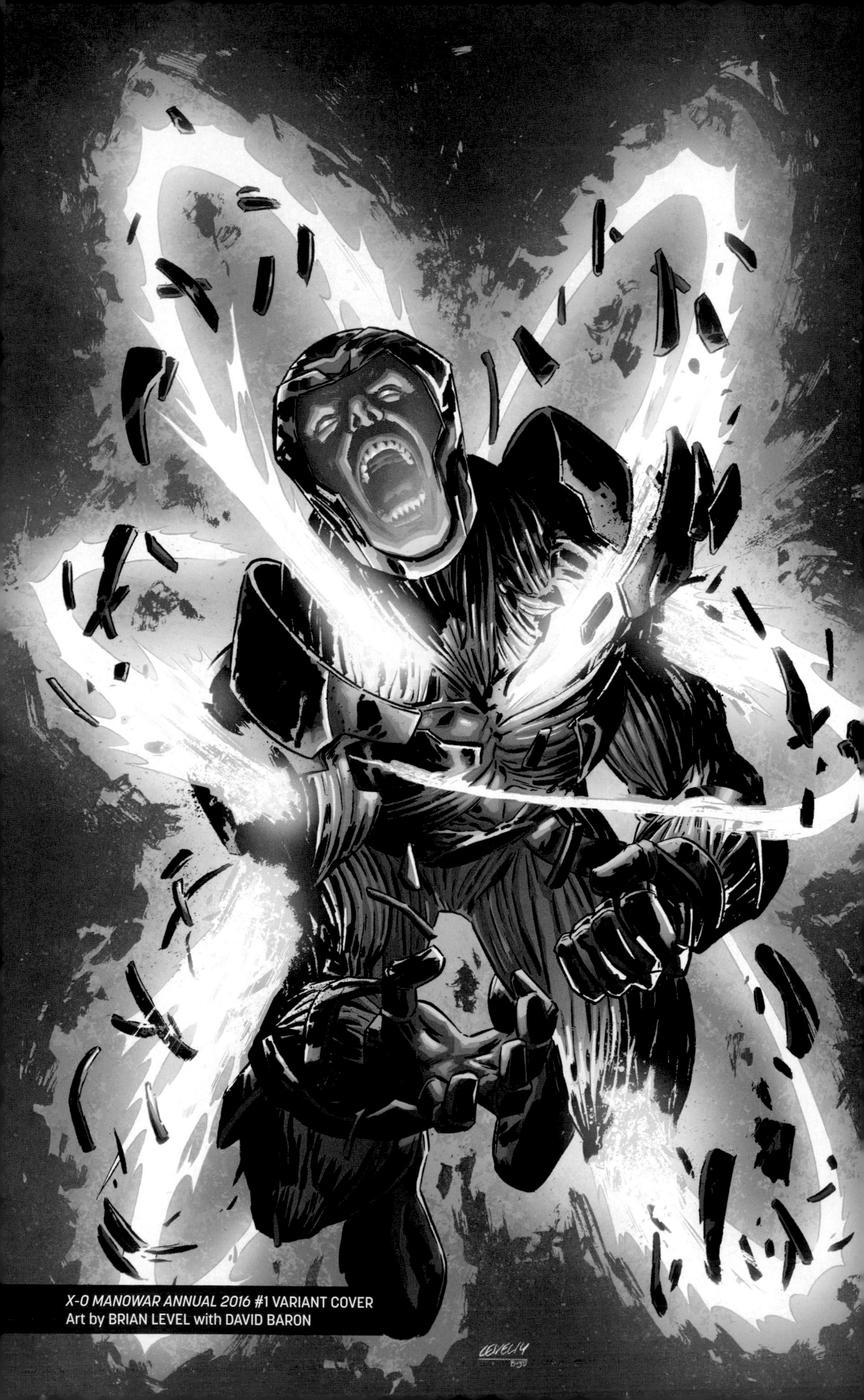

X-O MANOWAR ANNUAL 2016 #1 VARIANT COVER
Art by BRIAN LEVEL with DAVID BARON

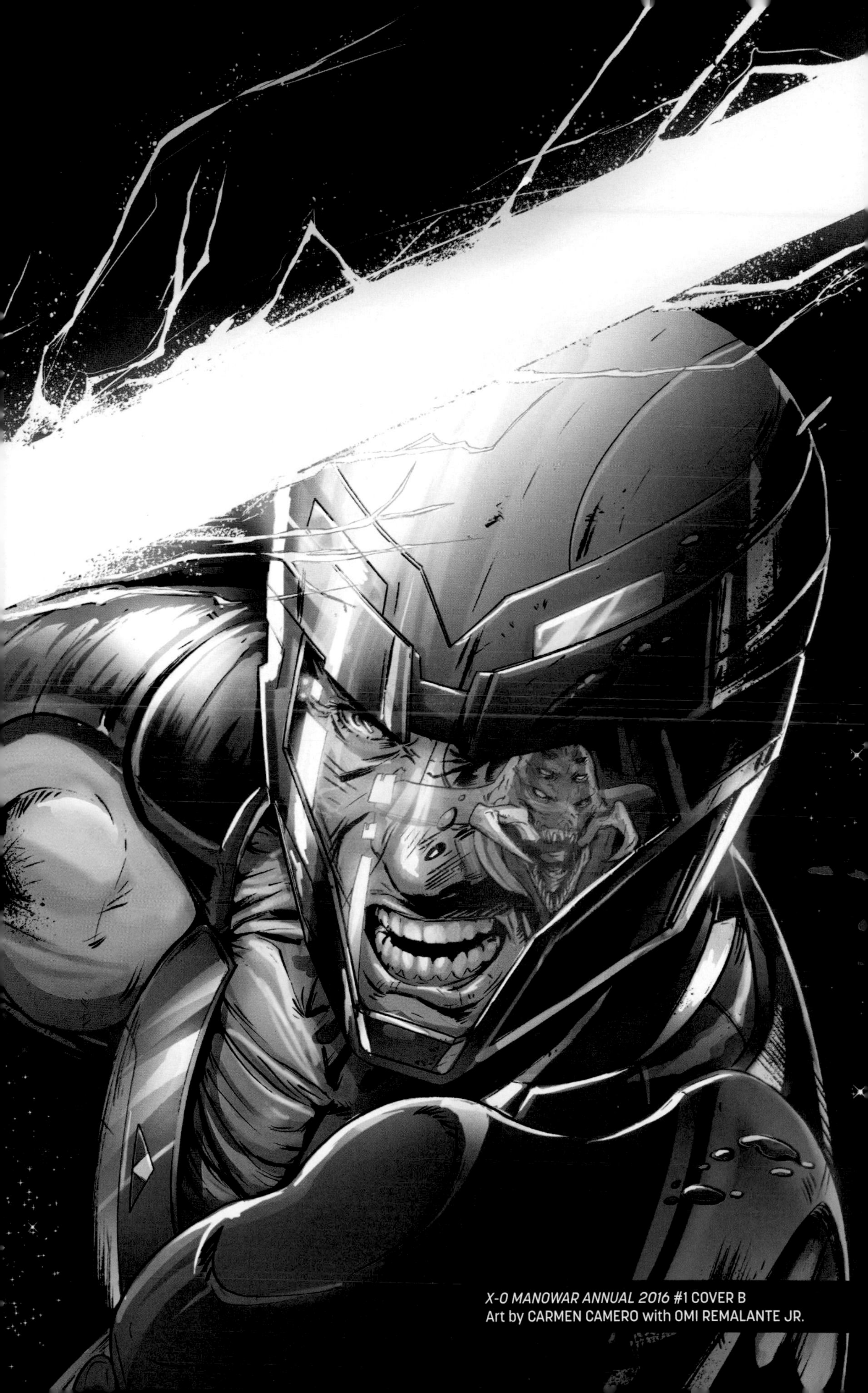

X-O MANOWAR ANNUAL 2016 #1 COVER B
Art by CARMEN CAMERO with OMI REMALANTE JR.

X-O MANOWAR ANNUAL 2016 #1, "HERITAGE," p.11
Art by PERE PÉREZ

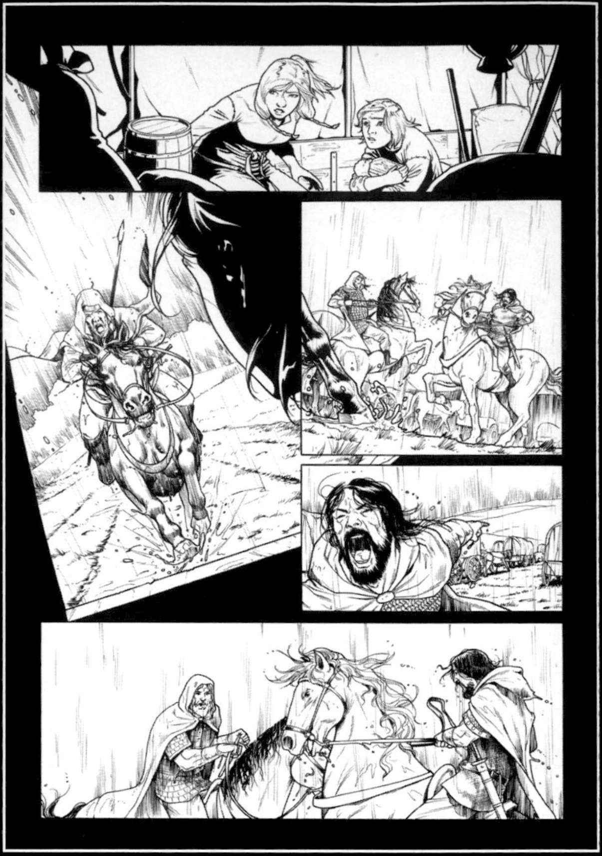

X-O MANOWAR ANNUAL 2016 #1, "HERITAGE," p.12
Art by PERE PÉREZ

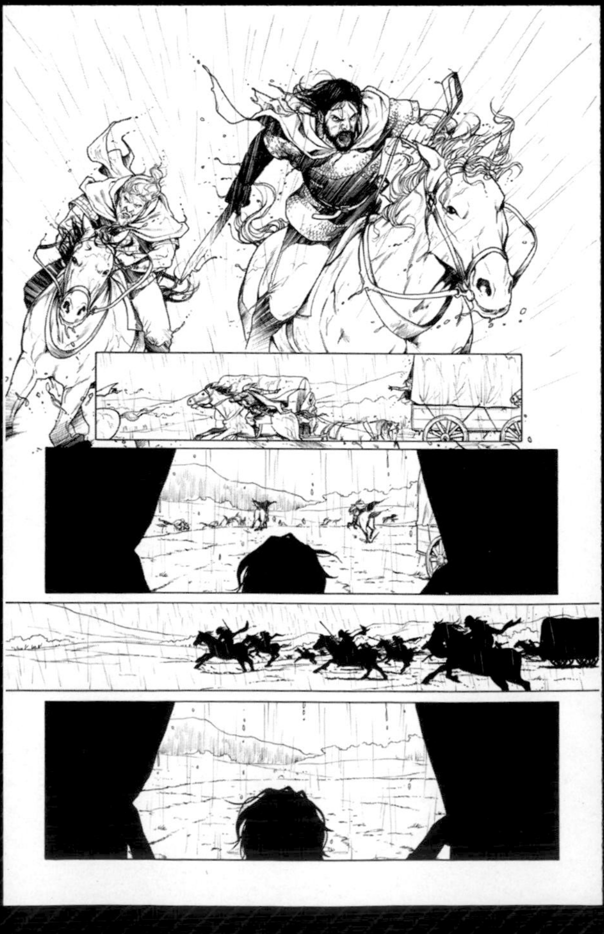

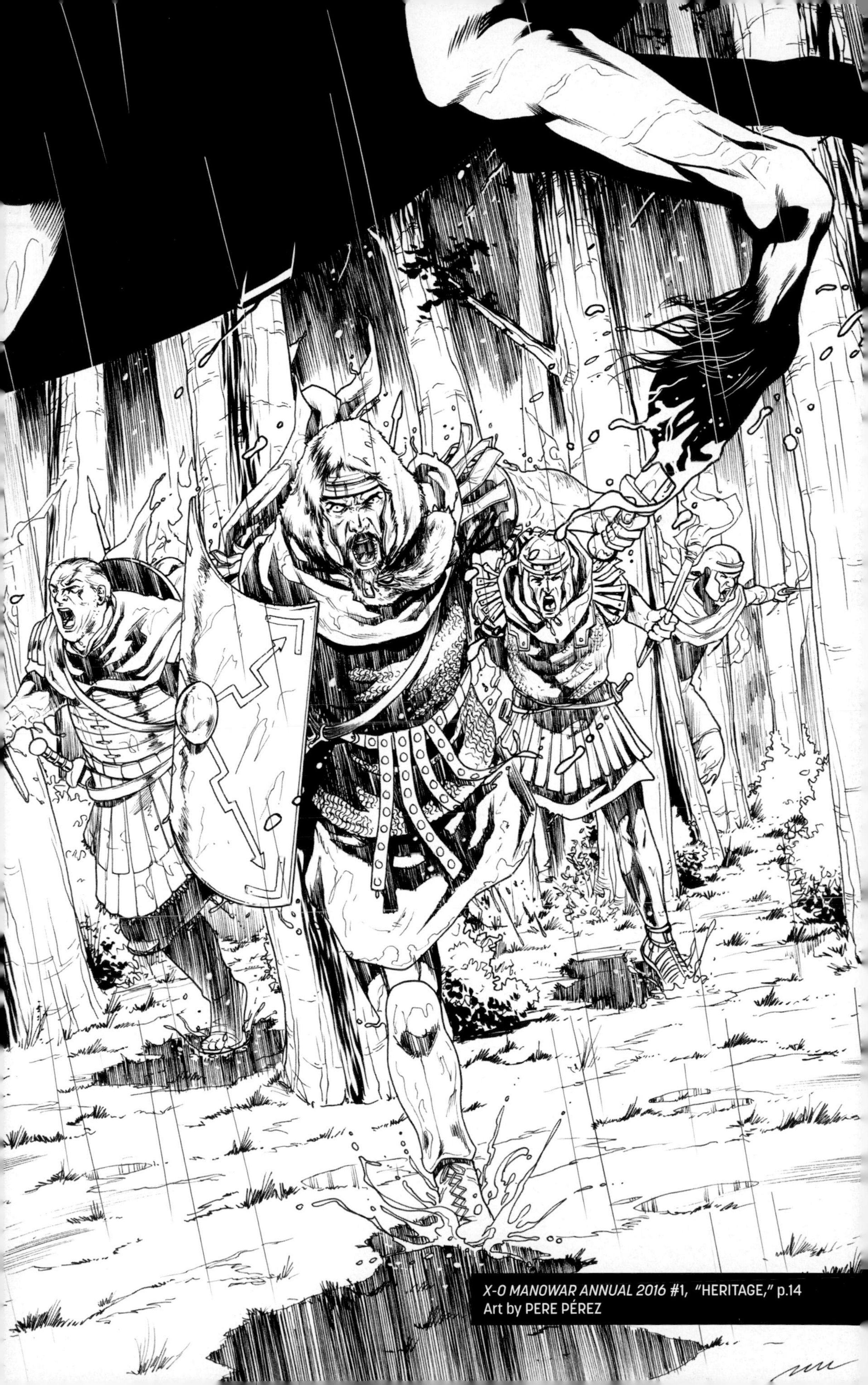

X-O MANOWAR ANNUAL 2016 #1, "HERITAGE," p.14
Art by PERE PÉREZ

X-O MANOWAR ANNUAL 2016 #1, "HERITAGE," p.15
Art by PERE PÉREZ

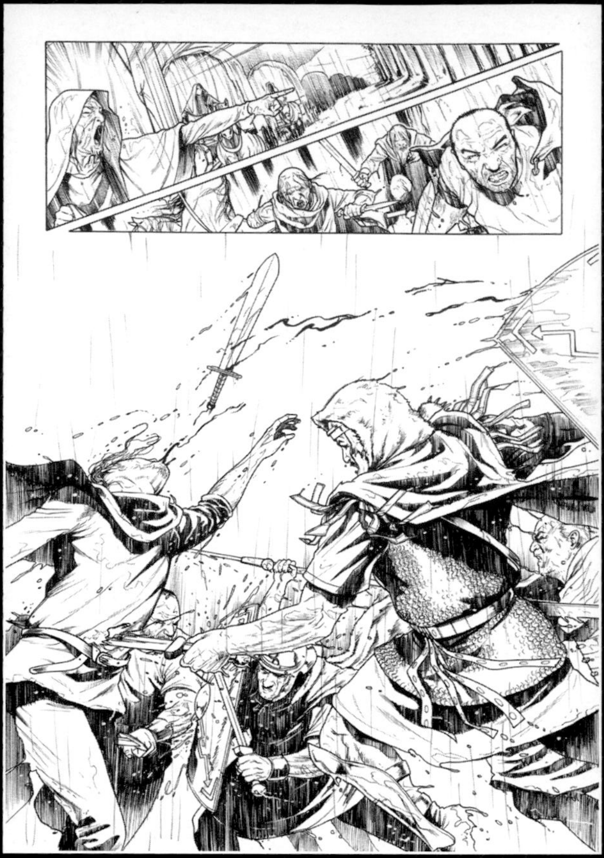

X-O MANOWAR ANNUAL 2016 #1, "HERITAGE," p.16
Art by PERE PÉREZ

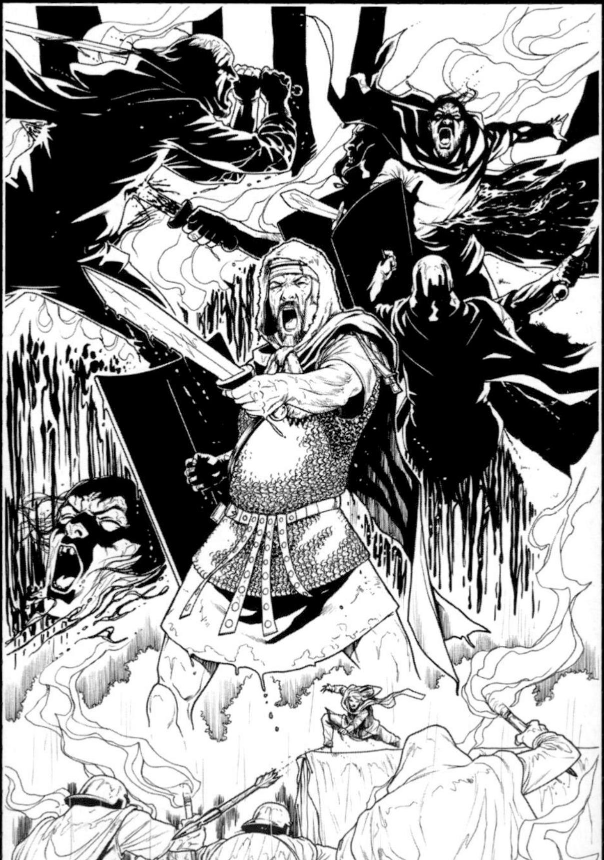

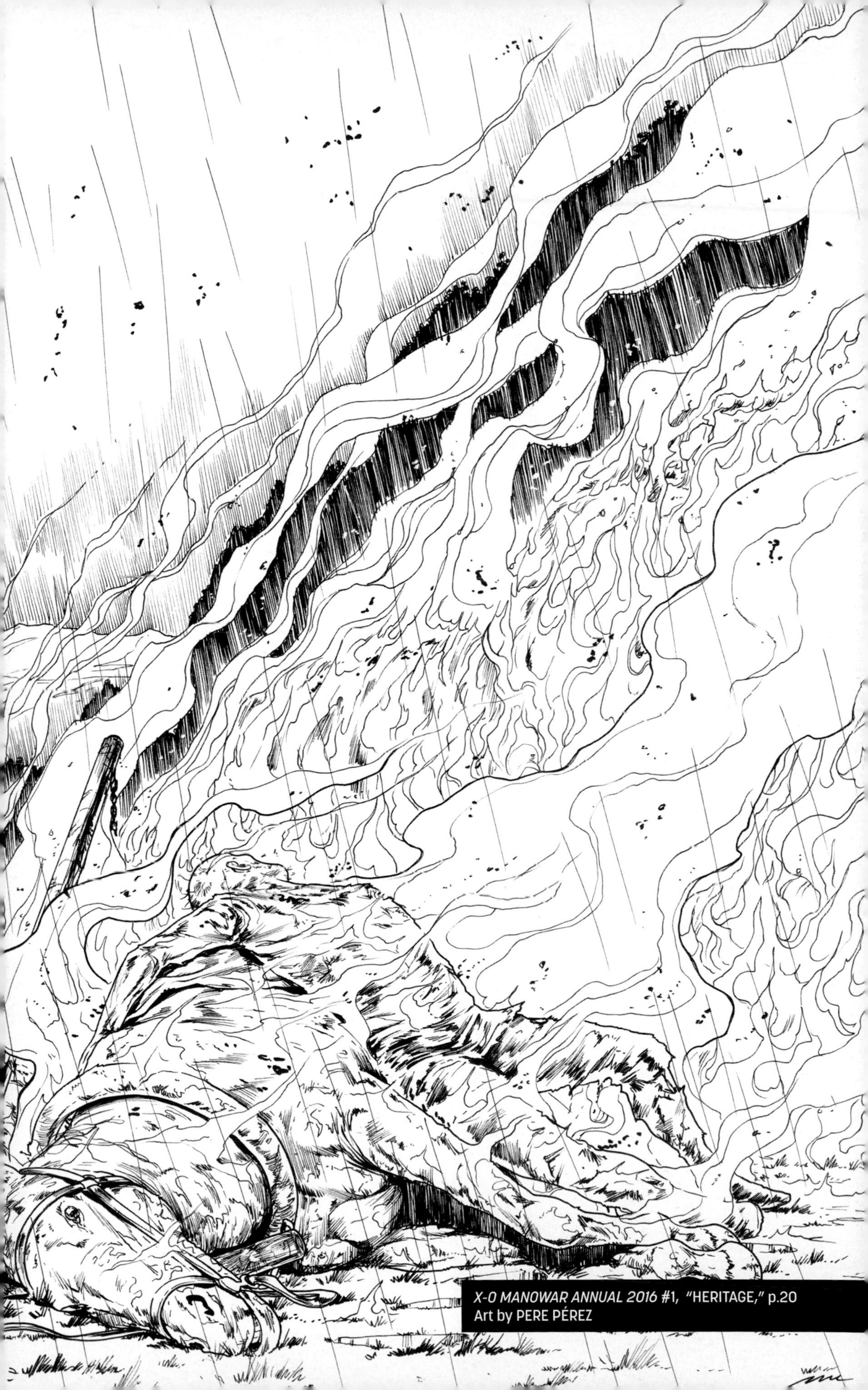

X-O MANOWAR ANNUAL 2016 #1, "HERITAGE," p.20
Art by PERE PÉREZ

BOOK OF DEATH: THE FALL OF X-O MANOWAR #1, p.2
Art by CLAYTON HENRY

BOOK OF DEATH: THE FALL OF X-O MANOWAR #1, p.17
Art by CLAYTON HENRY

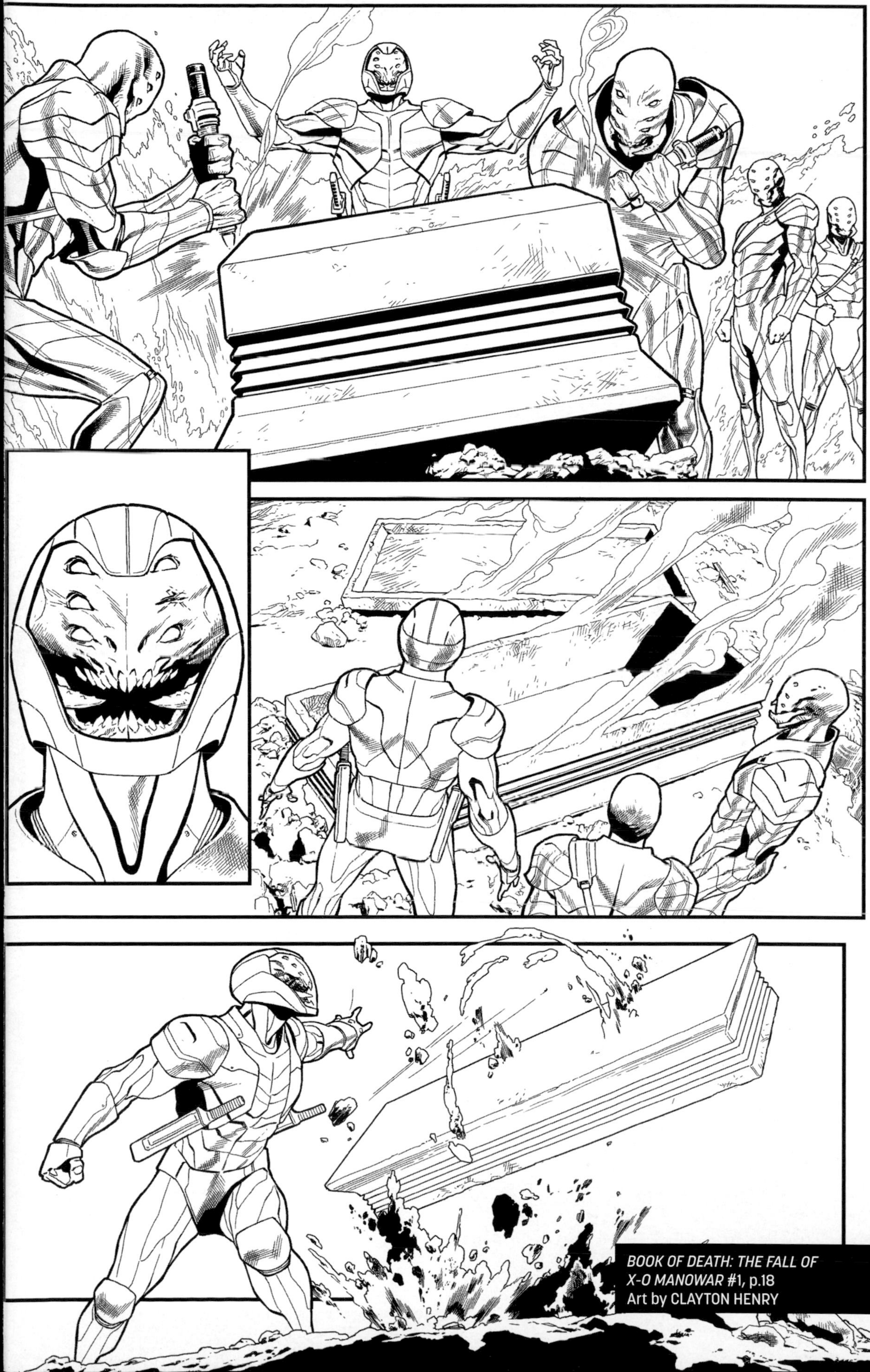

BOOK OF DEATH: THE FALL OF X-O MANOWAR #1, p.18
Art by CLAYTON HENRY

BOOK OF DEATH: THE FALL OF X-O MANOWAR #1, p.20
Art by CLAYTON HENRY

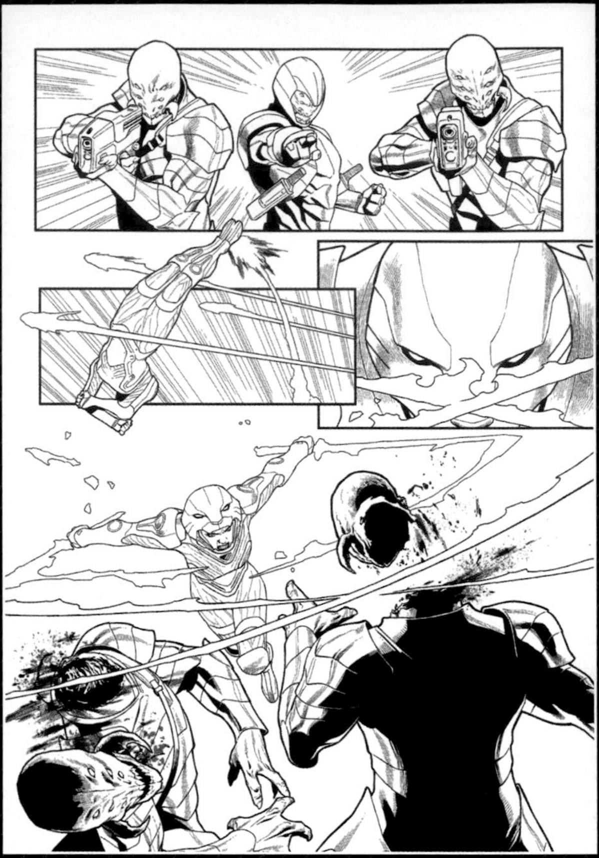

BOOK OF DEATH: THE FALL OF X-O MANOWAR #1, p.21
Art by CLAYTON HENRY

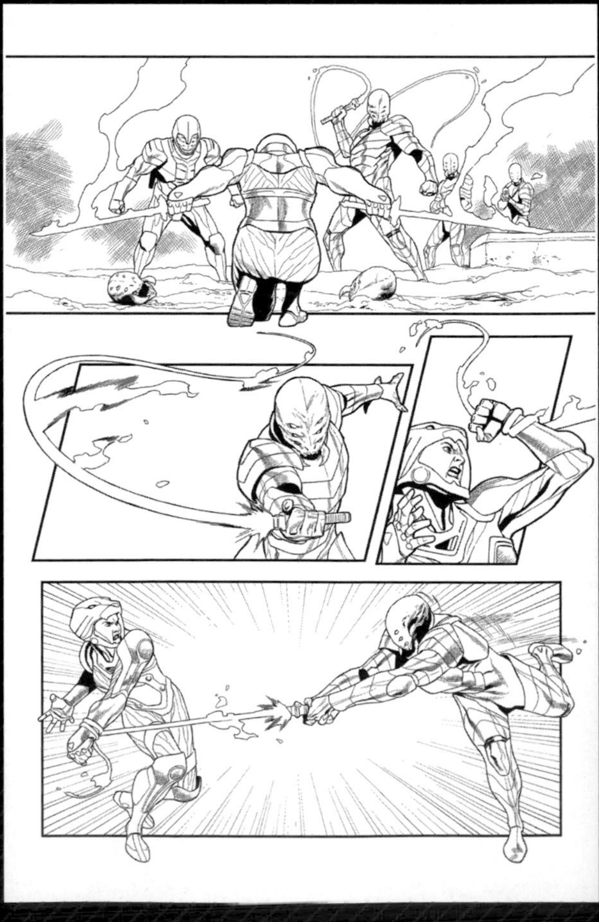

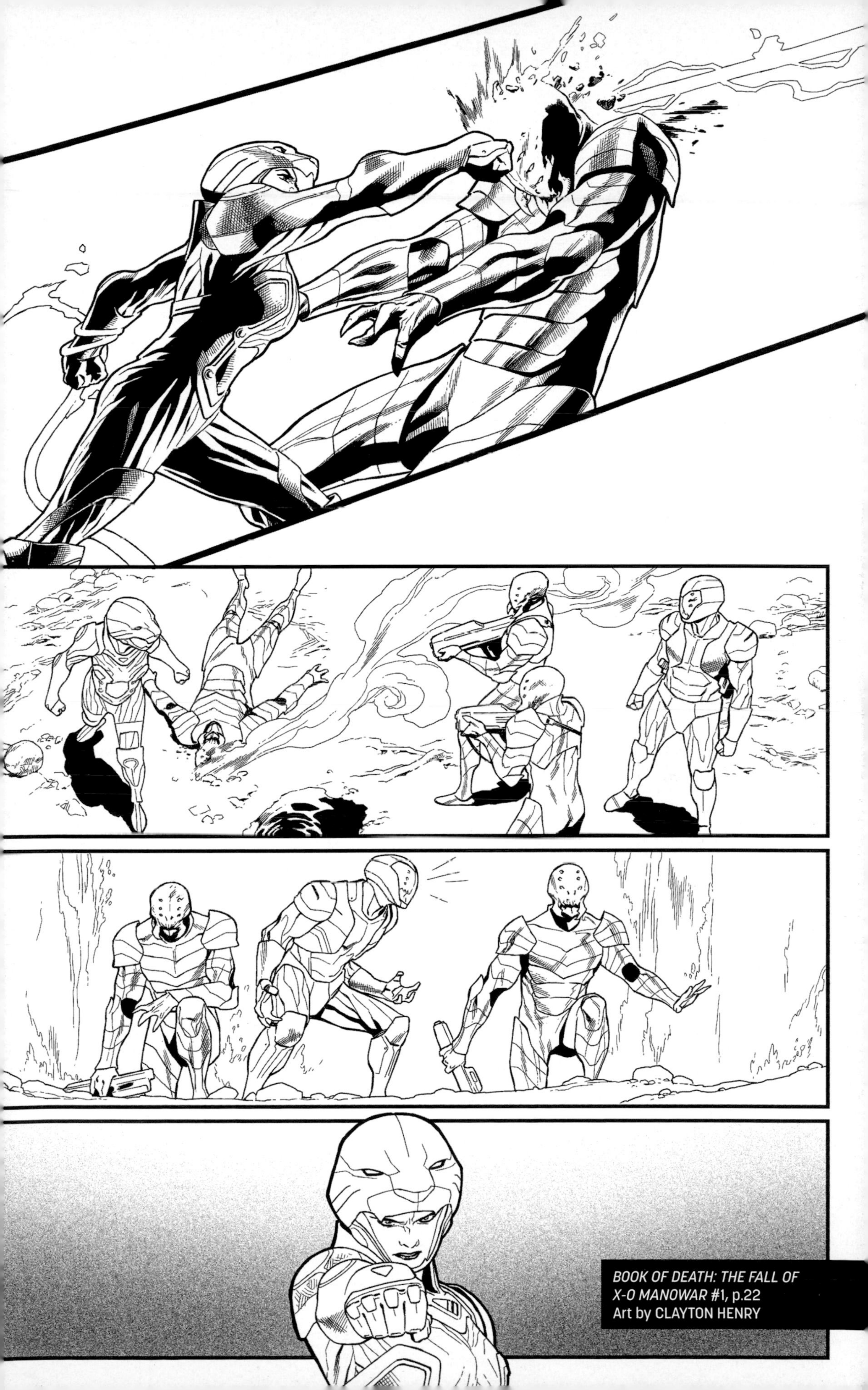

BOOK OF DEATH: THE FALL OF X-O MANOWAR #1, p.22
Art by CLAYTON HENRY

EXPLORE THE VALIANT UNIVERSE

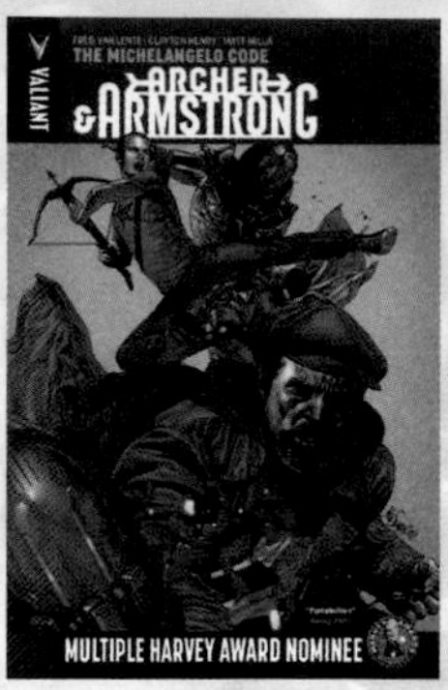
VALIANT
THE MICHELANGELO CODE
ARCHER & ARMSTRONG
MULTIPLE HARVEY AWARD NOMINEE
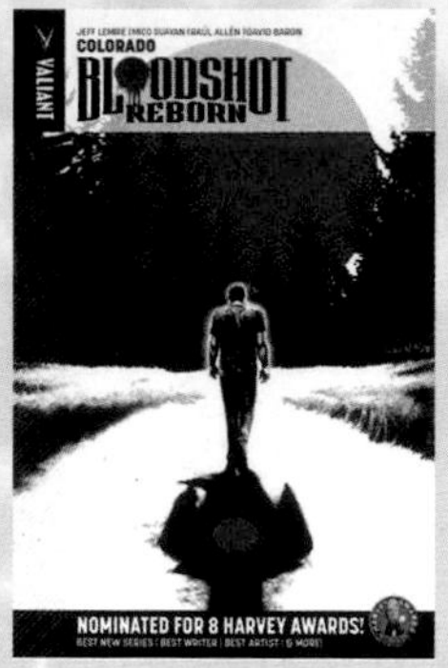
VALIANT
COLORADO
BLOODSHOT REBORN
NOMINATED FOR 8 HARVEY AWARDS!
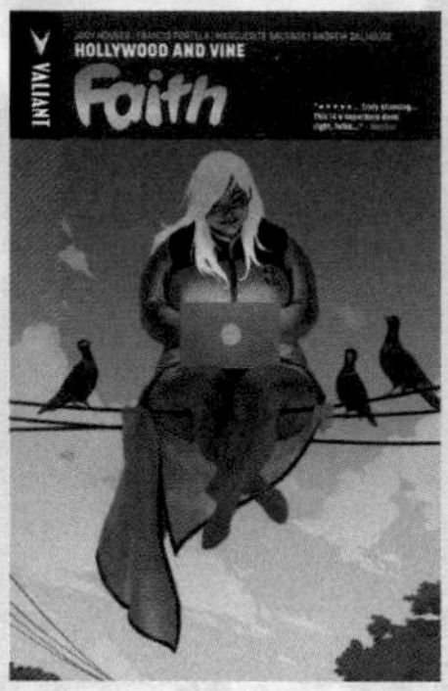
VALIANT
HOLLYWOOD AND VINE
Faith
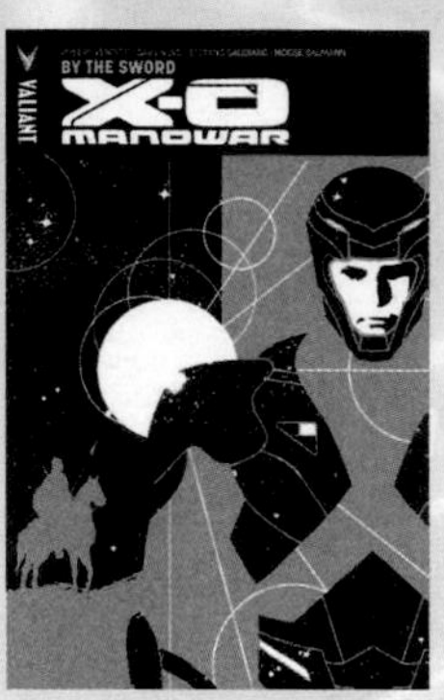
VALIANT
BY THE SWORD
X-O MANOWAR
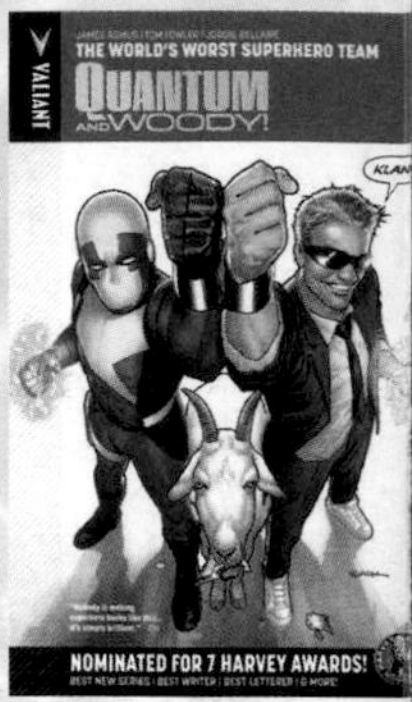
VALIANT
THE WORLD'S WORST SUPERHERO TEAM
QUANTUM AND WOODY!
NOMINATED FOR 7 HARVEY AWARDS!

4001 A.D.

4001 A.D.
ISBN: 9781682151433

4001 A.D.: Beyond New Japan
ISBN: 9781682151464

Rai Vol 4: 4001 A.D.
ISBN: 9781682151471

A&A: THE ADVENTURES OF ARCHER AND ARMSTRONG

Volume 1: In the Bag
ISBN: 9781682151495

Volume 2: Romance and Road Trips
ISBN: 9781682151716

ARCHER & ARMSTRONG

Volume 1: The Michelangelo Code
ISBN: 9780979640988

Volume 2: Wrath of the Eternal Warrior
ISBN: 9781939346049

Volume 3: Far Faraway
ISBN: 9781939346148

Volume 4: Sect Civil War
ISBN: 9781939346254

Volume 5: Mission: Improbable
ISBN: 9781939346353

Volume 6: American Wasteland
ISBN: 9781939346421

Volume 7: The One Percent and Other Tales
ISBN: 9781939346537

ARMOR HUNTERS

Armor Hunters
ISBN: 9781939346452

Armor Hunters: Bloodshot
ISBN: 9781939346469

Armor Hunters: Harbinger
ISBN: 9781939346506

Unity Vol. 3: Armor Hunters
ISBN: 9781939346445

X-O Manowar Vol. 7: Armor Hunters
ISBN: 9781939346476

BLOODSHOT

Volume 1: Setting the World on Fire
ISBN: 9780979640964

Volume 2: The Rise and the Fall
ISBN: 9781939346032

Volume 3: Harbinger Wars
ISBN: 9781939346124

Volume 4: H.A.R.D. Corps
ISBN: 9781939346193

Volume 5: Get Some!
ISBN: 9781939346315

Volume 6: The Glitch and Other Tales
ISBN: 9781939346711

BLOODSHOT REBORN

Volume 1: Colorado
ISBN: 9781939346674

Volume 2: The Hunt
ISBN: 9781939346827

Volume 3: The Analog Man
ISBN: 9781682151334

Volume 4: Bloodshot Island
ISBN: 9781682151952

BOOK OF DEATH

Book of Death
ISBN: 9781939346971

Book of Death: The Fall of the Valiant Universe
ISBN: 9781939346988

DEAD DROP

ISBN: 9781939346858

THE DEATH-DEFYING DOCTOR MIRAGE

Volume 1
ISBN: 9781939346490

Volume 2: Second Lives
ISBN: 9781682151297

THE DELINQUENTS

ISBN: 9781939346513

DIVINITY

Volume 1
ISBN: 9781939346766

Volume 2
ISBN: 9781682151518

ETERNAL WARRIOR

Volume 1: Sword of the Wild
ISBN: 9781939346209

Volume 2: Eternal Emperor
ISBN: 9781939346292

Volume 3: Days of Steel
ISBN: 9781939346742

WRATH OF THE ETERNAL WARRIOR

Volume 1: Risen
ISBN: 9781682151235

Volumel 2: Labyrinth
ISBN: 9781682151594

FAITH

Faith Vol 1: Hollywood and Vine
ISBN: 9781682151402

Faith Vol 2: California Scheming
ISBN: 9781682151631

HARBINGER

Volume 1: Omega Rising
ISBN: 9780979640957

Volume 2: Renegades
ISBN: 9781939346025

Volume 3: Harbinger Wars
ISBN: 9781939346117

Volume 4: Perfect Day
ISBN: 9781939346155

Volume 5: Death of a Renegade
ISBN: 9781939346339

Volume 6: Omegas
ISBN: 9781939346384

EXPLORE THE VALIANT UNIVERSE

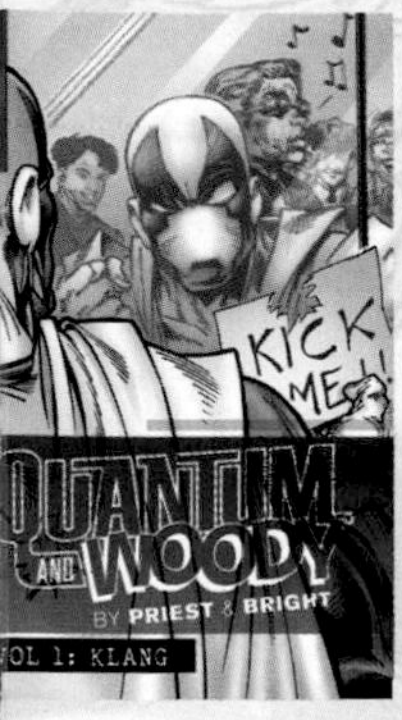
KICK ME
QUANTUM AND WOODY
BY PRIEST & BRIGHT
VOL 1: KLANG

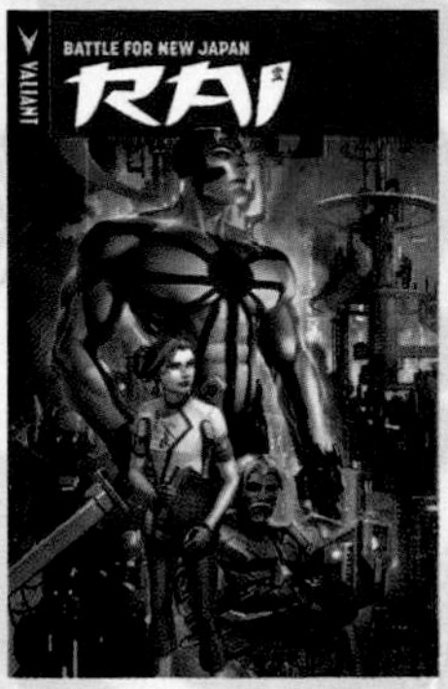
VALIANT
BATTLE FOR NEW JAPAN
RAI

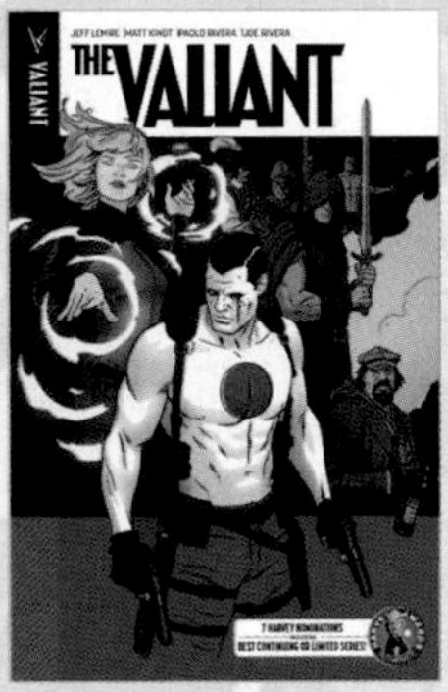
VALIANT
THE VALIANT

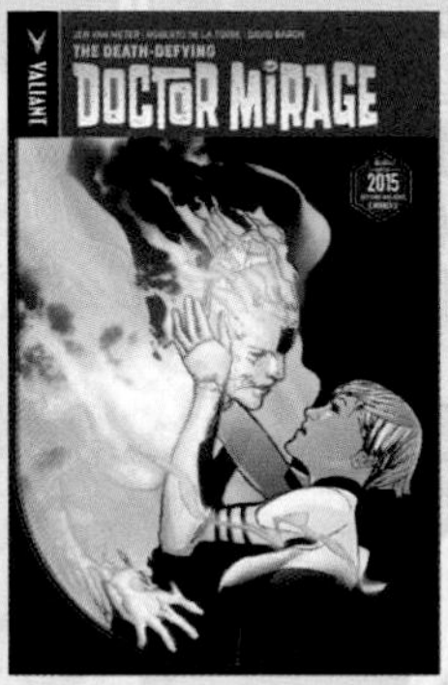
VALIANT
THE DEATH-DEFYING
DOCTOR MIRAGE

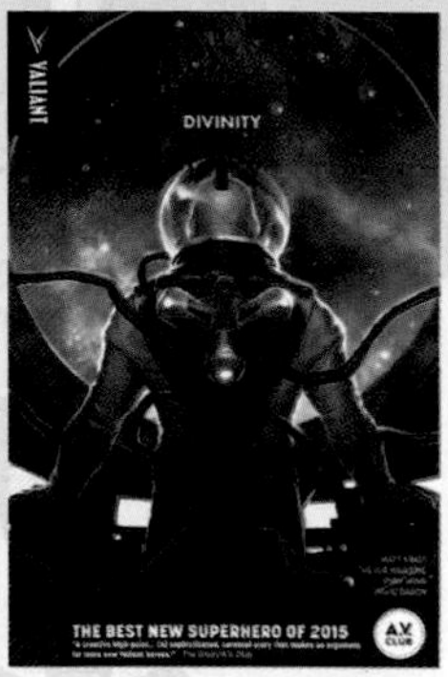
VALIANT
DIVINITY
THE BEST NEW SUPERHERO OF 2015

ARBINGER WARS

rbinger Wars
3N: 9781939346094

oodshot Vol. 3: Harbinger Wars
3N: 9781939346124

rbinger Vol. 3: Harbinger Wars
3N: 9781939346117

IPERIUM

lume 1: Collecting Monsters
3N: 9781939346759

lume 2: Broken Angels
3N: 9781939346896

lume 3: The Vine Imperative
3N: 9781682151112

lume 4: Stormbreak
3N: 9781682151372

INJAK

lume 1: Weaponeer
3N: 9781939346667

lume 2: The Shadow Wars
3N: 9781939346940

lume 3: Operation: Deadside
3N: 9781682151259

lume 4: The Siege of King's Castle
3N: 9781682151617

UANTUM AND WOODY

lume 1: The World's Worst Superhero Team
3N: 9781939346186

lume 2: In Security
3N: 9781939346230

lume 3: Crooked Pasts, Present Tense
3N: 9781939346391

lume 4: Quantum and Woody Must Die!
3N: 9781939346629

UANTUM AND WOODY BY RIEST & BRIGHT

lume 1: Klang
3N: 9781939346780

lume 2: Switch
3N: 9781939346803

lume 3: And So...
ISBN: 9781939346865

Volume 4: Q2 - The Return
ISBN: 9781682151099

RAI

Volume 1: Welcome to New Japan
ISBN: 9781939346414

Volume 2: Battle for New Japan
ISBN: 9781939346612

Volume 3: The Orphan
ISBN: 9781939346841

Rai Vol 4: 4001 A.D.
ISBN: 9781682151471

SHADOWMAN

Volume 1: Birth Rites
ISBN: 9781939346001

Volume 2: Darque Reckoning
ISBN: 9781939346056

Volume 3: Deadside Blues
ISBN: 9781939346162

Volume 4: Fear, Blood, And Shadows
ISBN: 9781939346278

Volume 5: End Times
ISBN: 9781939346377

SHADOWMAN BY ENNIS & WOOD

ISBN: 9781682151358

IVAR, TIMEWALKER

Volume 1: Making History
ISBN: 9781939346636

Volume 2: Breaking History
ISBN: 9781939346834

Volume 3: Ending History
ISBN: 9781939346995

UNITY

Volume 1: To Kill a King
ISBN: 9781939346261

Volume 2: Trapped by Webnet
ISBN: 9781939346346

Volume 3: Armor Hunters
ISBN: 9781939346445

Volume 4: The United
ISBN: 9781939346544

Volume 5: Homefront
ISBN: 9781939346797

Volume 6: The War-Monger
ISBN: 9781939346902

Volume 7: Revenge of the Armor Hunters
ISBN: 9781682151136

THE VALIANT

ISBN: 9781939346605

VALIANT ZEROES AND ORIGINS

ISBN: 9781939346582

X-O MANOWAR

Volume 1: By the Sword
ISBN: 9780979640940

Volume 2: Enter Ninjak
ISBN: 9780979640995

Volume 3: Planet Death
ISBN: 9781939346087

Volume 4: Homecoming
ISBN: 9781939346179

Volume 5: At War With Unity
ISBN: 9781939346247

Volume 6: Prelude to Armor Hunters
ISBN: 9781939346407

Volume 7: Armor Hunters
ISBN: 9781939346476

Volume 8: Enter: Armorines
ISBN: 9781939346551

Volume 9: Dead Hand
ISBN: 9781939346650

Volume 10: Exodus
ISBN: 9781939346933

Volume 11: The Kill List
ISBN: 9781682151273

Volume 12: Long Live the King
ISBN: 9781682151655

EXPLORE THE VALIANT UNIVERSE

VALIANT
HARBINGER
DELUXE EDITION 2

VALIANT
ARMOR HUNTERS
DELUXE EDITION

VALIANT
JIM SHOOTER | DAVID LAPHAM
CHILDREN OF THE EIGHTH DAY
HARBINGER
VALIANT MASTERS

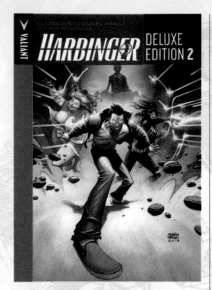

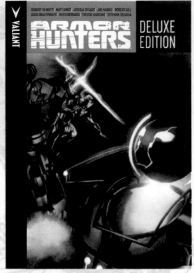

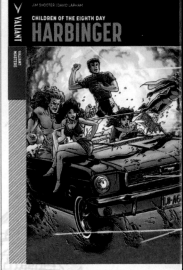

Omnibuses

Archer & Armstrong: The Complete Classic Omnibus
ISBN: 9781939346872
Collecting ARCHER & ARMSTRONG (1992) #0-26, ETERNAL WARRIOR (1992) #25 along with ARCHER & ARMSTRONG: THE FORMATION OF THE SECT.

Quantum and Woody: The Complete Classic Omnibus
ISBN: 9781939346360
Collecting QUANTUM AND WOODY (1997) #0, 1-21 and #32, THE GOAT: H.A.E.D.U.S. #1, and X-O MANOWAR (1996) #16

X-O Manowar Classic Omnibus Vol. 1
ISBN: 9781939346308
Collecting X-O MANOWAR (1992) #0-30, ARMORINES #0, X-O DATABASE #1, as well as material from SECRETS OF THE VALIANT UNIVERSE #1

Deluxe Editions

Archer & Armstrong Deluxe Edition Book 1
ISBN: 9781939346223
Collecting ARCHER & ARMSTRONG #0-13

Archer & Armstrong Deluxe Edition Book 2
ISBN: 9781939346957
Collecting ARCHER & ARMSTRONG #14-25, ARCHER & ARMSTRONG: ARCHER #0 and BLOODSHOT AND H.A.R.D. CORPS #20-21.

Armor Hunters Deluxe Edition
ISBN: 9781939346728
Collecting Armor Hunters #1-4, Armor Hunters: Aftermath #1, Armor Hunters: Bloodshot #1-3, Armor Hunters: Harbinger #1-3, Unity #8-11, and X-O MANOWAR #23-29

Bloodshot Deluxe Edition Book 1
ISBN: 9781939346216
Collecting BLOODSHOT #1-13

Bloodshot Deluxe Edition Book 2
ISBN: 9781939346810
Collecting BLOODSHOT AND H.A.R.D. CORPS #14-23, BLOODSHOT #24-25, BLOODSHOT #0, BLOODSHOT AND H.A.R.D. CORPS: H.A.R.D. CORPS #0, along with ARCHER & ARMSTRONG #18-19

Book of Death Deluxe Edition
ISBN: 9781682151150
Collecting BOOK OF DEATH #1-4, BOOK OF DEATH: THE FALL OF BLOODSHOT #1, BOOK OF DEATH: THE FALL OF NINJAK #1, BOOK OF DEATH: THE FALL OF HARBINGER #1, and BOOK OF DEATH: THE FALL OF X-O MANOWAR #1.

Divinity Deluxe Edition
ISBN: 97819393460993
Collecting DIVNITY #1-4

Harbinger Deluxe Edition Book 1
ISBN: 9781939346131
Collecting HARBINGER #0-14

Harbinger Deluxe Edition Book 2
ISBN: 9781939346773
Collecting HARBINGER #15-25, HARBINGER: OMEGAS #1-3, and HARBINGER: BLEEDING MONK #0

Harbinger Wars Deluxe Edition
ISBN: 9781939346322
Collecting HARBINGER WARS #1-4, HARBINGER #11-14, and BLOODSHOT #10-13

Ivar, Timewalker Deluxe Edition Book 1
ISBN: 9781682151198
Collecting IVAR, TIMEWALKER #1-12

Quantum and Woody Deluxe Edition Book 1
ISBN: 9781939346681
Collecting QUANTUM AND WOODY #1-12 and QUANTUM AND WOODY: THE GOAT #0

Q2: The Return of Quantum and Woody Deluxe Edition
ISBN: 9781939346568
Collecting Q2: THE RETURN OF QUANTUM AND WOODY #1-5

Rai Deluxe Edition Book 1
ISBN: 9781682151174
Collecting RAI #1-12, along with material from RAI #1 PLUS EDITION and RAI #5 PLUS EDITION

Shadowman Deluxe Edition Book 1
ISBN: 9781939346438
Collecting SHADOWMAN #0-10

Shadowman Deluxe Edition Book 2
ISBN: 9781682151075
Collecting SHADOWMAN #11-16, SHADOWMAN #13X, SHADOWMAN: END TIMES #1-3 and PUNK MAMBO #0

Unity Deluxe Edition Book 1
ISBN: 9781939346575
Collecting UNITY #0-14

The Valiant Deluxe Edition
ISBN: 97819393460986
Collecting THE VALIANT #1-4

X-O Manowar Deluxe Edition Book 1
ISBN: 9781939346100
Collecting X-O MANOWAR #1-14

X-O Manowar Deluxe Edition Book 2
ISBN: 9781939346520
Collecting X-O MANOWAR #15-22, and UNITY #1-

X-O Manowar Deluxe Edition Book 3
ISBN: 9781682151310
Collecting X-O MANOWAR #23-29 and ARMOR HUNTERS #1-4.

Valiant Masters

Bloodshot Vol. 1 - Blood of the Machine
ISBN: 9780979640933

H.A.R.D. Corps Vol. 1 - Search and Destroy
ISBN: 9781939346285

Harbinger Vol. 1 - Children of the Eighth Day
ISBN: 9781939346483

Ninjak Vol. 1 - Black Water
ISBN: 9780979640971

Rai Vol. 1 - From Honor to Strength
ISBN: 9781939346070

Shadowman Vol. 1 - Spirits Within
ISBN: 9781939346018

X-O MANOWAR READING ORDER

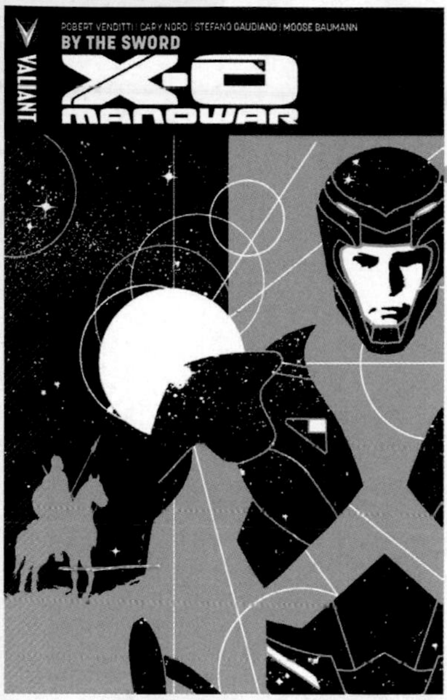
ROBERT VENDITTI | CARY NORD | STEFANO GAUDIANO | MOOSE BAUMANN
BY THE SWORD
X-O MANOWAR
VALIANT

X-O Manowar Vol. 1: By the Sword

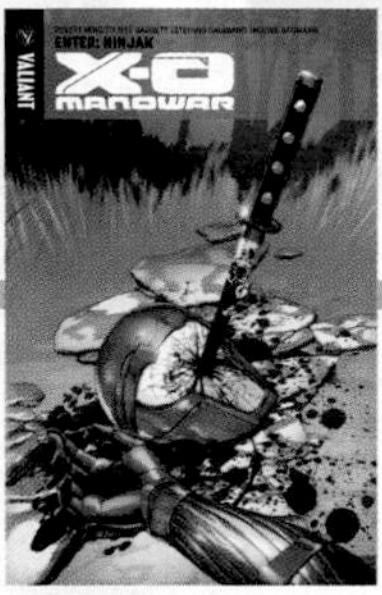
ENTER: NINJAK
X-O MANOWAR
VALIANT

X-O Manowar Vol. 2: Enter Ninjak

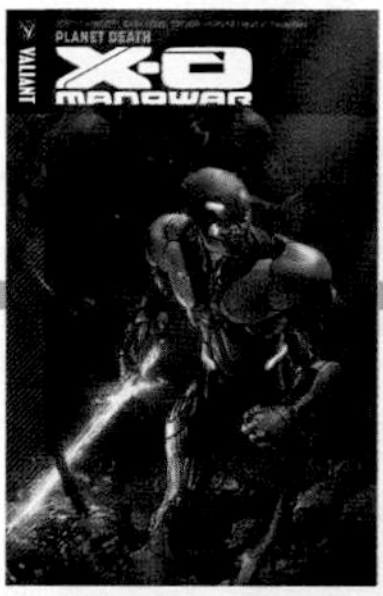
PLANET DEATH
X-O MANOWAR
VALIANT

X-O Manowar Vol. 3: Planet Death

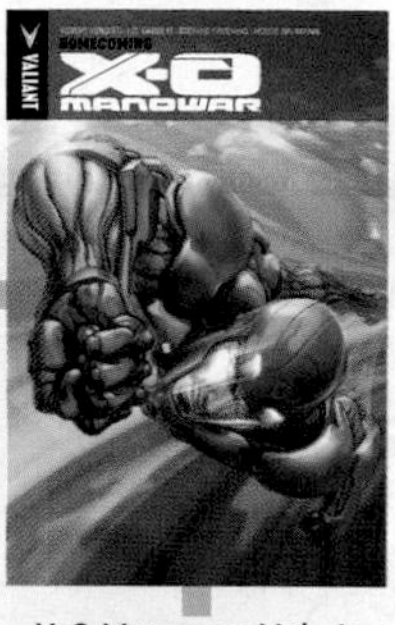
HOMECOMING
X-O MANOWAR
VALIANT

X-O Manowar Vol. 4: Homecoming

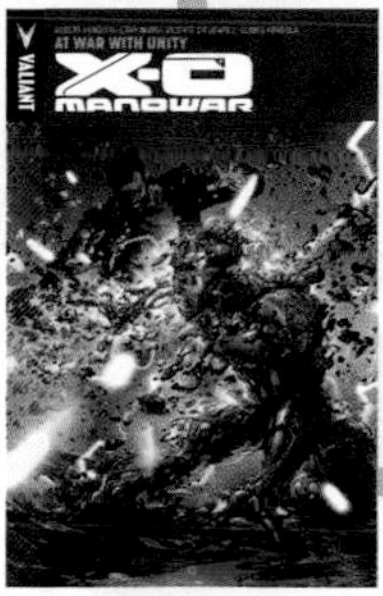
AT WAR WITH UNITY
X-O MANOWAR
VALIANT

X-O Manowar Vol. 5: At War With Unity

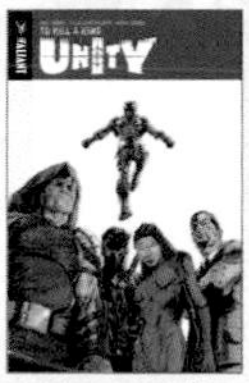
TO KILL A KING
UNITY
VALIANT

Unity Vol. 1: To Kill a King **(OPTIONAL)**

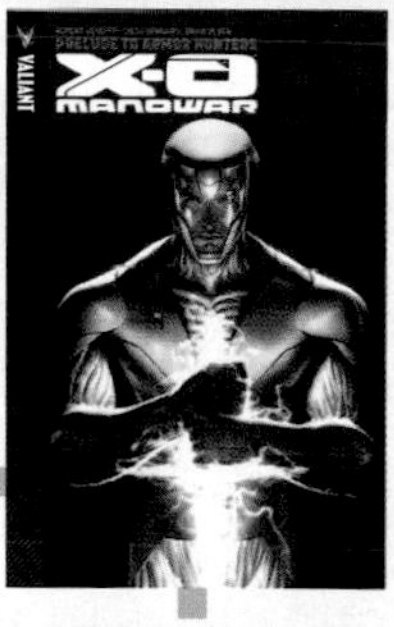
PRELUDE TO ARMOR HUNTERS
X-O MANOWAR
VALIANT

X-O Manowar Vol. 6: Prelude to Armor Hunters

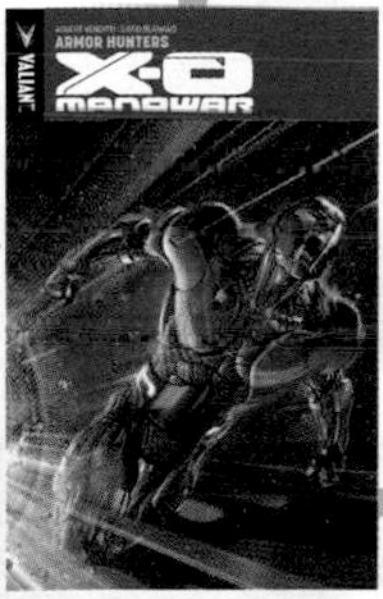
ARMOR HUNTERS
X-O MANOWAR
VALIANT

X-O Manowar Vol. 7: Armor Hunters

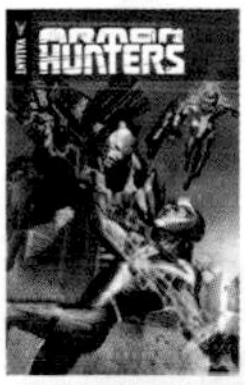
ARMOR HUNTERS
VALIANT

Armor Hunters **(OPTIONAL)**

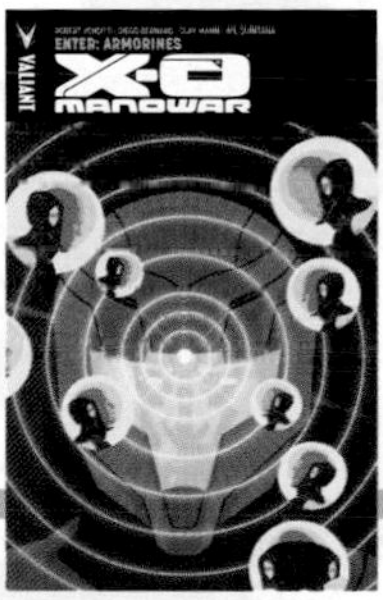
ENTER: ARMORINES
X-O MANOWAR
VALIANT

X-O Manowar Vol. 8: Enter: Armorines

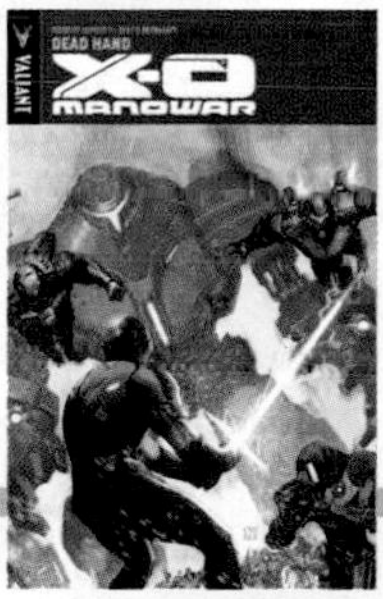
DEAD HAND
X-O MANOWAR
VALIANT

X-O Manowar Vol. 9: Dead Hand

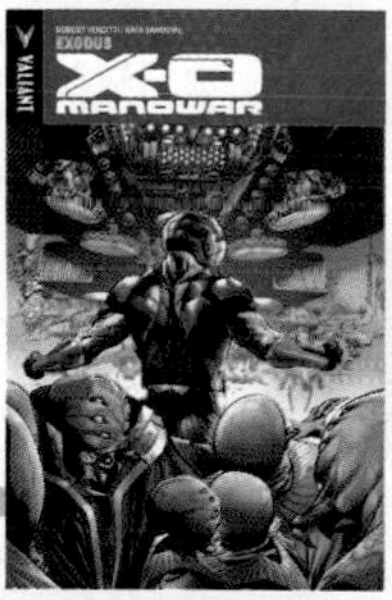
EXODUS
X-O MANOWAR
VALIANT

X-O Manowar Vol. 10: Exodus

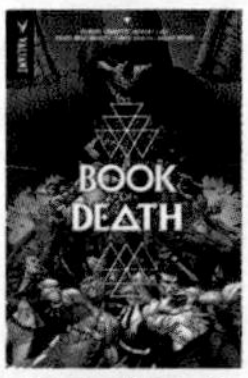
BOOK OF DEATH

Book of Death **(OPTIONAL)**

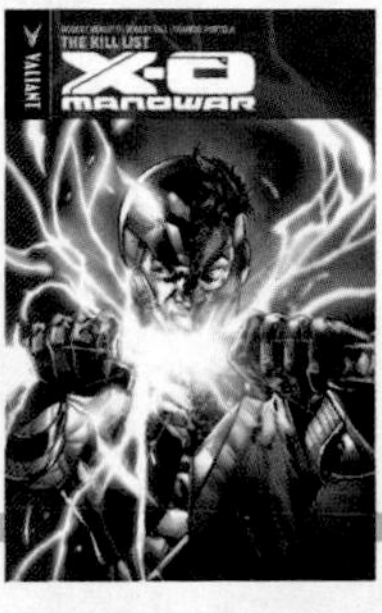
THE KILL LIST
X-O MANOWAR
VALIANT

X-O Manowar Vol. 11: The Kill List

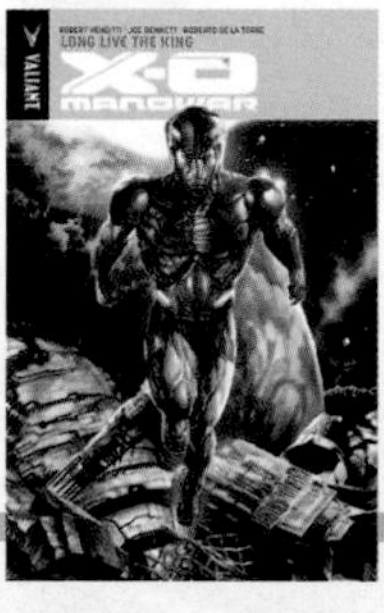
LONG LIVE THE KING
X-O MANOWAR
VALIANT

X-O Manowar Vol. 12: Long Live the King

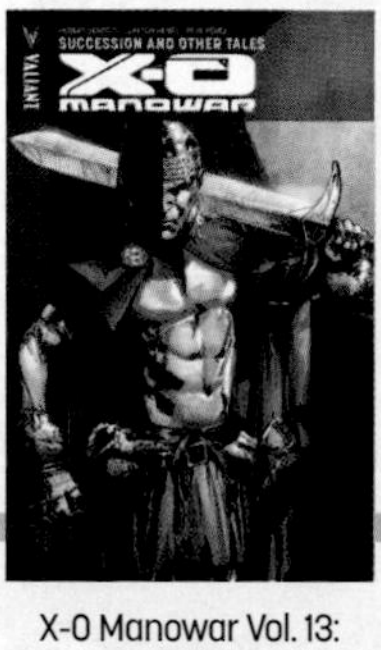
SUCCESSION AND OTHER TALES
X-O MANOWAR
VALIANT

X-O Manowar Vol. 13: Succession and Other Tales

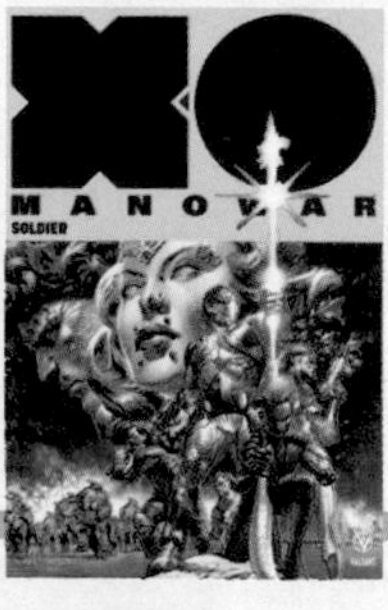
X-O
MANOWAR
SOLDIER

X-O Manowar (2017) Vol. 1: Soldier

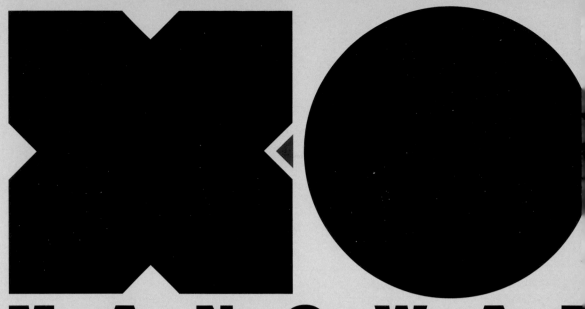

X O
MANOWAR

VOLUME ONE: SOLDIER

FROM VISIONARY WRITER AND BLOCKBUSTER ARTIST
MATT KINDT • TOMÁS GIORELLO

A STUNNING NEW BEGINNING FOR VALIANT'S MOST ENDURING ICON STARTS HERE,
TAKING ARIC OF DACIA BEYOND THE FARTHEST LIMITS OF OUR GALAXY...
AND INTO THE BRUTAL OPENING SALVO OF THE ULTIMATE X-O MANOWAR
TALE EVER TOLD!

COLLECTING X-O MANOWAR (2017) #1–3 • ISBN: 978-1-68215-205-8